CON TRICKS

MARTIN ASHFORD

CON

TRICKS

THE SHADOWY WORLD OF MANAGEMENT CONSULTANCY AND HOW TO MAKE IT WORK FOR YOU

SIMON & SCHUSTER

A VIACOM COMPANY

First published in Great Britain by Simon & Schuster Ltd, 1998
A Viacom Company

1 3 5 7 9 10 8 6 4 2

Simon & Schuster Ltd
West Garden Place
Kendal Street
London W2 2AQ

Simon & Schuster Australia
Sydney

Typeset by Palimpsest Book Production Limited
Polmont, Stirlingshire

Printed and bound in Great Britain by Butler & Tanner Ltd,
Frome and London

A CIP catalogue record for this book is available from the British Library

ISBN 0–684–82141–9

To Peter, without whose leadership I might still be a consultant.

And to a great team at the Columbia Centre:
I'd like to say it was a pleasure.

Acknowledgments

I am most grateful to the many members of the LBS (London Business School) Alumni Association who assisted me with my research, and to Sean, Martin and Nigel who piloted the questionnaire. Sincere thanks also to Tony for being so understanding and for his inputs to Chapter 4.

Data on the consulting industry has been taken from *Management Consultant International* with the permission of Lafferty Publications Ltd, The Tower, IDA Centre, Pearse Street, Dublin 2, Ireland.

Quotations from *Sloan Management Review*, 1993, vol. 34 no. 4 are by permission of the publisher. Copyright © 1993 by Sloan Management Review Association. All rights reserved.

A note on currencies

Where financial values appear in this book, I have given them either in US dollars or pounds sterling, whichever was more convenient or appropriate.

In many cases I have also shown equivalent figures in the other currency. Where this is done, I have used a rate of £1 = $1.50 without worrying too much about the niceties of exchange-rate movements. All such figures should be treated as indicative only.

Contents

INTRODUCTION: THE PROSTITUTES OF THE BUSINESS WORLD

CONSULTANCY IS BIG BUSINESS. FORGET THE COTTAGE INDUSTRY OF ONE-man-bands and part-timers, the retired troubleshooters and small specialist partnerships who eke out a living at the bottom of the pile. Let's talk about where the money is. The top thirty or so consultancy firms in the world were estimated to have a collective turnover of around $29 billion (£19 billion) in 1996[1]. They *averaged* 23% growth compared to the year before. Andersen Consulting, the world's largest, relieved its clients of over $5 billion and nine more firms were estimated to break the $1 billion barrier in fees. They do not just work for multinational giants: the big consultancies *are* global empires in their own right.

The phenomenon of consultancy on this scale is relatively recent. In the UK, the industry was virtually reborn in the 1980s and grew dramatically throughout the decade, fuelled by privatisation and other Government initiatives to introduce new thinking into the old public bureaucracies. Consultancies got used to double-digit growth and, even in the bad days of recession in the early 1990s, most of them managed to remain on the upward path. The Government has con-

---

[1] Source for this and the following data: *Management Consultant International*, June/July, 1997.

tinued to play the role of sugar daddy: between 1992 and 1996, the British Government spent £2.59 billion on consultants[2]. At the same time, however, consultants became almost omnipresent in industry and commerce: a survey in mid-1996 by the Management Consultancies Association found that 97% of *Times 200* companies were using MCA member firms at that time[3].

Even earlier, the use of consultants became a normal part of business life in the US where the scale of industrial corporations, combined with a hunger for dramatic change, offered a bonanza of opportunities for those quick enough to jump on the bandwagon. As advisers followed their clients from the New World back to the Old, the age of global consultancies was born.

By any account these are major service empires, especially when you take into account that consulting is often only part of a broad portfolio of services that they offer: from funding advice for the emerging business, through annual audits and tax planning to receivership and winding-up. From the cradle of business to its grave, the men and women in grey suits are never far away.

Paradoxically, this very greyness is the most conspicuous thing about the big consultancies. By and large, they prefer to be in the background, just out of camera shot when the company board lines up for its round of applause from the shareholders (and even less visible if those same shareholders are out for the directors' blood).

Consultancies which hail from an accounting background (Ernst & Young, Deloitte & Touche, Coopers & Lybrand, Price Waterhouse . . .[4]) are still hesitant about being in the limelight, never seen by the pin-stripe brigade as *quite the done thing*. The aggressiveness of their American leaders has tended to be moderated by the traditional reserve of their Old World partners. It is the big strategy houses (McKinsey, Boston Consulting Group (BCG), Bain and the rest) who defined the US style of consultancy and honed it to razor sharpness.

---

[2] *Financial Times*, 28 January, 1997.

[3] MCA Press Release, 16 October, 1996.

[4] At the time of writing, a new wave of mergers between these 'Big Six' firms is in prospect.

For them, client confidentiality is the first article of faith and they relish the secrecy of their boardroom access. Fundamentally, too, consultancies of all sizes have an interest in keeping clients to themselves and freezing others out: for this reason, if for no other, they are often reluctant for their activities to be in the public eye.

Many of the larger firms were, and often still are, constituted as partnerships and not as limited companies. While this (in theory, at least) can mean that the personal capital of the Partners is at stake in the event of a claim from a disgruntled client, it also has the effect of masking the true financial position of the consulting firm. Try asking a consultancy to show you their annual accounts. And if you can get them to produce a set, try finding any useful information in it. Early in 1996, KPMG was bold enough to publish its first annual report in the UK. As they put it: 'for the first time a leading accountancy firm is making public financial information that has hitherto been confidential to the firm's partners'. The fact that its Senior Partner earned £438,000 in the previous year attracted a good deal of press attention, but the rest makes dull reading for anyone who does not have a fetish about men in suits. Moreover, the report mixed consultancy in with auditing and only covered the UK – not much use in an increasingly international business.

Globalisation makes matters more complex in a number of ways. The major international firms are notoriously fond of describing themselves in terms like 'seamless practice' and 'global service lines'. A recent advertisement for a joint venture between two firms trumpeted that 'together, Bigcon and Lilcon will deliver seamless, total solutions – with unparalleled integration of people, processes and technology – on a global scale'[5]. This shows the consultancy bullshit generator at full output. In my experience, the so-called global firm may be little more than a coalition of national partnerships. How much its leaders know about their own colleagues' activities in other countries is often questionable, so it is little wonder that the outside world finds it hard to get to grips with what makes them tick as businesses.

---

[5] The names are changed, but nothing more.

Between them, these large firms employ an army of professional staff: over 150,000 consultants work for the top thirty consultancies[6], ranging from recent graduates through experienced managers, number crunchers and creative thinkers to well-seasoned greybeards and super-salesmen. Ubiquitous as they are, they seldom stand out from the crowd: merging into the ranks of business-class travellers on aircraft, gently pressing the flesh at conferences and exhibitions, swapping business cards with strangers met briefly in hotel bars. More often than not, though, they are shut away in some seedy back room where they do the business at hours when the client's own management has given up and gone to bed.

These are the prostitutes of the business world.

There is no shame in this description. After all, prostitution is said to be the oldest profession in the world. And there is a certain honesty about the trade: the prostitute sells you her (or his) body, for certain specified purposes and for a limited time. Which is exactly what consultants do: they hire out their bodies (or, perhaps, it would be more charitable to say their *minds*) on fee rates which go up to several thousand dollars a day. Which makes them pretty expensive as prostitutes go but, otherwise, what's the difference?

In truth, there is one quite important difference. The hooker's client is pretty sure of what he is getting: visual inspection tells him most of what he needs to know and there is no particular reason why his expectations should be too far from the reality of the experience. In consulting, this is not the case. Visual inspection tells you virtually nothing. Free sampling may give you more of an idea, and is sometimes on offer (whereas, as far as I know, prostitutes are not in the habit of offering the first five minutes for free). But for most buyers of consultancy services, the matter comes down to finding someone that they "feel happy" with and then taking a large leap of faith. Wham, bang, thank you, Arthur. Or thanks for nothing, as the case may be.

From the other side, meanwhile, the consultant is seldom able to rely simply on his or her natural charms to bring in the business.

---

[6] *Management Consultant International*, June, 1996.

Clients – ranging from naïve virgins to hardened old-timers – have to be convinced that they are about to have the mother of all good times, then continually stroked and reassured that they are indeed getting their money's worth. Up front, consultancy is all about trying to make yourself out to be the world's leading expert in whatever problem the client may have. Once the job has started, it is often about trying not to be found out. After all, if you cannot produce a real orgasm to order, you just have to get good at faking them.

So consultancy, at the limit, starts to look like a gigantic confidence trick. This should not be taken as a criticism solely of consultants: the street-corner conman succeeds by exploiting the greed and self-deception of passers by, not just their innocence. Nor does it mean that all consultancy is a fraud or a waste of money. But many consultancy jobs fail because clients are happy to buy an illusion and because consultants, as true professionals, will always try to make less appear as more. If you expect them to turn your dross into gold, you are putting them in a position where they are virtually obliged to spray a little gilt paint around in order to sustain the illusion.

Remember the story of the Emperor's new clothes? His tailors (actually, they were fashion industry consultants) told him that they had made the most perfect suit of clothes but that only clever people could see them. So he paraded through the town, stark naked, convinced that he was magnificently dressed. How many businesses have bought a strategic plan or process reengineering or a new organisational structure in the same way that the Emperor bought his suit?

Here is what Lord Weinstock, formerly Managing Director of GEC, had to say about consultants in a recent interview[7]: 'Consultants are invariably a waste of money. There has been the occasional instance where a useful idea has come up but the input we have received has usually been banal and unoriginal, wrapped in impressive-sounding but irrelevant rhetoric.

'Of course, consultants do vary. The best are those with highly specialist expertise in specific industrial or scientific fields. The worst are the generalists, mostly economists, who are ready – for a fee – to

---

[7] *Financial Times*, 31 December, 1996.

give advice on virtually anything and whose qualifications to do so are virtually nil.'

Not everyone has such a jaundiced view. As part of the development of this book I undertook a survey of views and experience of the consultancy business among alumni of the London Business School. Around 100 responses were analysed, divided almost equally into consultants and consultancy clients. The headlines from this study were as follows[8]:

- *Good news for consultants.* Over two thirds of clients agreed with the proposition that 'consultancy projects make a valuable contribution to most of their clients'. A slightly higher proportion agreed that 'consultants are good at catalysing change in their clients'. Best of all, 85% of this sample (who were, in the main, very experienced users of consultants) said that they were either 'quite likely' or 'very likely' to use consultants again.

- *Now for the bad news.* Only 24% of clients felt that consultants were good at coming up with original ideas (40% actively disagreed) and three-quarters agreed that 'consultants are better at fleshing out clients' ideas than at suggesting new ones'. Only 28% were prepared to say that consultants are good value for money. Almost a third of clients felt that business is now over-dependent on consultants. Turning the tables, consultants rated the management of projects by clients as showing 'room for improvement', or 'totally useless', in over a quarter of cases. Most remarkable of all, more than half of the consultants surveyed agreed with the suggestion that 'consultants are good at managing everyone's business except their own'.

- *You say tomatoes...* On a number of issues, the views of consultants and their clients were found to diverge significantly. Asked whether 'consultants' first loyalty is to themselves/their firm and not to their clients', only 29% of consultants but 56% of their clients

---

[8] More details are given at various places in this book. The full results, and the questionnaire used, will be found in the *Appendix*.

agreed. Consultants rated three-quarters of projects as completely or pretty successful, while clients gave this rating to just over half their work. When things went wrong with a job, consultants overwhelmingly identified 'unclear client objectives' as the main reason while clients were about as likely to blame the proposal, a weak plan or simply poor work by the consultants.

The research cannot answer the most fundamental question of all: what value are consultants really adding to businesses and other organisations? What the survey does is highlight issues and suggest some answers in three more limited areas.

Firstly, the results show that consultants are not (just) in the business of selling snake oil. Despite Weinstock's pronouncements, and the public perception of consultants, the great majority of clients in the sample gave an overall thumbs-up to their advisers, particularly in the acid test of whether or not they anticipated using their services again. Now, all sorts of caveats may need to be made at this point: for a start, the sample of clients was highly educated and experienced and therefore may be dealing with consultants better than others might. More fundamentally, clients were rating projects in which they themselves were implicated and this may well have made them disinclined to judge the jobs to have failed. Nonetheless, despite these warnings, the inescapable message of the survey is that most clients are favourably impressed by their experience of dealing with consultants.

Secondly, despite this, the research shows that there is still plenty of room for further improvement. Many clients are concerned that consultants are pushing standardised solutions rather than really listening to the issues and being guided accordingly. Substantial minorities of projects are judged by clients to have failed and substantial minorities of clients are judged to manage consultants poorly. There is evidence in the results, in my view, to suggest that clients are focusing too much on technical skills in selecting their consultants and not paying enough attention to human and process skills. Consultants themselves, in many cases, are unhappy with the way their own firms are run.

Thirdly, the message comes out loud and clear from the questionnaire responses that consulting can be very bad, or very good, dependent upon how it is done. This applies both to clients and to consultants. Getting the right consultants on your project is tremendously important if you are a client. Dissuading the client from moving the goalposts halfway through the project is equally vital if you are a consultant. A lot of the advice offered by respondents, from their experience, may not be particularly original but it bears repeating: get senior level commitment to the project, be clear what you are trying to achieve, put client and consultant staff together on the project and so on. All of these ideas will be discussed further in later chapters.

I have written this book with several types of reader in mind:

- The experienced consultant will, I hope, be prompted to reflect on exactly what it is that consultants should be doing for their clients, how this is best delivered and how they should organise themselves to achieve it.

- Those (and there are many) who wish to get into consulting as a career may find in this book something of the flavour of the business. If it helps a few business students decide that, perhaps, there are other job options that they might like to consider then it will have achieved something useful.

- Most of all, I have written for clients and for would-be clients. So many managers are having to come to terms with consultants, to work with them, to have them imposed from above or indeed to commission projects themselves. What should managers do to ensure that consultancy projects deliver real results? What pitfalls should they watch out for and what tricks of the trade may the consultants try to pull on them? I hope my book will go at least some way to answering these questions.

This book could have been called *pros and cons*. Consultants (or *cons*, for short) are also professionals (or *pros*). As George Bernard Shaw wrote: 'Every profession is a conspiracy against the laity', so consultants' clients need to be no less professional in dealing with them.

Knowing how to handle cons, and being aware of the sorts of tactics that pros may use, may be vital to a manager's career. Knowing how to manage clients is certainly an indispensable skill for any con.

Love it or hate it, consulting is here to stay. The key thing is to make it work, for you.

CHAPTER 1: A LONGLIST OF BAD REASONS FOR USING CONSULTANTS

JUST WHY DO ORGANISATIONS USE CONSULTANTS? THE QUESTION MAY SEEM naïve but it should perhaps be asked more often than it is, both by cons themselves and by their prospective clients. My father-in-law, a single-company man all his life, used to raise the issue from time to time in a way which I interpreted as indicating his lack of faith in my ability to earn a steady income from such an apparently marginal business. The gist of his questioning was: 'Why should a big company come to you when they could do the job themselves?' Why indeed. It seems a good place to start this book.

There are many possible answers to the question; a variety of reasons why not only businesses but also public-sector organisations use consultants either on an occasional basis or almost routinely. There are exceptions, of course: big companies with a reputation for doing it themselves rather than bringing in consultants – GEC to name but one. But they are heavily outnumbered by the roll call of multinationals, large national enterprises, Government departments, quangos and agencies of all kinds, local authorities and even small businesses who consider it worth their while bringing in an outsider to assist them. Most startling of all, perhaps, are those who have *always* got consultants working for them on some project or other – tasks which succeed each other and roll on for years on end. They all have their reasons. But just as some animals are more equal than others, some reasons are more reasonable than others.

Consultancy clients, in my experience, can be divided into three categories:

- **Type 1:** those who need help with a particular issue and who bring consultants in with a well-focused remit to deliver it.

- **Type 2:** those who need help but are not getting it from their cons, because the job which they asked them to do, although in the right general area, is not the job that they really needed.

- **Type 3:** those for whom the consultancy project is completely irrelevant to their real problems (a fact of which individual managers within the client organisation may be either cynically aware or blissfully ignorant).

I would also contend, based on long and painful experience, that far too many clients fall into the second or third categories. It may well be, in fact, that more organisations are buying consultancy for the *wrong* reasons than for the *right* ones[1]. The former are the topic of this chapter, while the good reasons for using consultants are discussed in the next.

First, though, two examples of the sort of misguided projects which are all too common.

A public-sector bureaucracy had a substantial store, full of office equipment, stationery and furniture. They asked us to make recommendations for its modernisation. What the client *wanted* was a fancy new storage operation using automated equipment, which they could show off to visitors. What they *needed* was a more commercial

---

[1]Although a majority of projects was deemed to be 'successful' by the clients taking part in the research, this is certainly not the same thing as saying that those projects were properly focused or delivered real value. Clients are not impartial judges of a project's worth.

approach to purchasing and inventory management, to eliminate the waste of money which the cons found wherever they looked. This was a Type 2 client who had bought a consultancy project for a number of wrong reasons but mainly because it flattered the prestige of the functionary responsible for it.

A multinational supplier of consumer goods, with a strong track record in product innovation, brought us in as consultants to look at centralising advertising and promotional activities across all their European subsidiaries. Given that the company was releasing different products, at different times, to different target markets in the various countries, the centralisation of advertising was pretty irrelevant. The cons eventually discovered that it was a bright idea suggested by the Chief Executive on a day when he had nothing better to do. This was a Type 3 case. The manager who had commissioned the study had very little real interest in it and was confident of moving on to higher things before anyone even got around to thinking of implementing the consultants' report.

This raises an interesting point. Consultants are not infrequently blamed for writing fancy reports that are never implemented. In plenty of cases, no doubt, the fault lies squarely with the cons, for being too vague in their conclusions or for putting forward recommendations which, however theoretically sound they may be, are simply not practical. How many projects, though, fail in the implementation stage because they were wrongly set up from the start? The problem may originate in the fact that the client is using consultants for the wrong reasons. The Type 2 client may well implement the results of the consultancy project but, since the project was not addressing the right questions, it is unlikely that the implementation will be of much use. The Type 3 client will probably not implement the cons' recommendations because everyone will have lost interest in the project, even assuming that they were ever committed to it in the first place.

I discuss below some of the bad reasons for calling in consultants, a longlist of the ways in which projects are often seriously compromised before they even begin. Would-be buyers of consultancy could do worse than to check their motives against the list. To expect your consultants to tell you, on the day that the work begins, that you are doing the wrong project (or even the right project, but for the wrong reasons) is frankly unrealistic. No consultant will refuse to relieve you of your spare cash if you are really determined to spend it, and if you insist on employing a con to prove that black is white you can doubtless find one who will do so. But, in my experience, no consultant really **wants** to be used to rubber stamp someone else's strategy or to pander to the Chairman's vanity. In the longer term, it is in everyone's interest that consultants are used for the right reasons and not these wrong ones.

'We don't have a clue what to do'

This one sounds reasonable enough. After all the role of consultants is, presumably, to tell their clients what they should be doing, which supposes that they do not know it already. Doing the converse, telling the client what he or she already knows (but dressed up in a fancy package) is a criticism often levied against cons. So how can needing help be a 'bad' reason for bringing in the advisers?

Part of the trouble is that, when a client is so completely at a loss, he will probably also be unable to specify properly what is expected of the consultant. One of the most critical factors in the success of a project is getting the terms of reference right: setting out exactly what the cons are expected to do and, more impor- tantly, what they are going to deliver. Different organisations may approach this in different ways. For some it is treated as an exercise for the lawyers, who draw up a contract of complexity worthy of an international treaty. Others go to the opposite extreme, giving the green light to the cons after no more than a brief conversation and a handshake. I take the view that the form of the terms of reference is unimportant but they must be clearly defined (which means, almost always, putting them in writing, although this does not mean they have to be long or complex). Imagine what they might look like in the case of that well-known British manufacturer, Clueless plc:

The consultants are required to:

- *Work out how we got into this mess.*

- *Think of some way out of it.*

- *Tell us how to do in the future all the things that we have been so unsuccessful at doing in the recent past.*

This may be a parody, but I have seen terms of reference that are not much more concrete than these. Some of the best come from governments who have decided to fund projects in places like the former Soviet Union: the briefs for these usually combine vast ambition with extreme vagueness, requiring the consultants to 'modernise the industry of Central Asia' or 'introduce Western techniques into the Russian Civil Service'. No wonder that, when the cons have all packed up and gone home, the locals still have no clue what to do.

The other problem with cluelessness is what it tells you about the management of the business. Consultancy should add to the expertise and vision that is to be found within an organisation, but cannot be seen as a substitute for it. It is perfectly respectable for managers to seek help when they do not have the resources or experience to tackle an issue themselves, for example to introduce innovative practices or to respond to radical change in their market. But when a management cannot even define the framework for the cons, or come up with at least some options for them to work on, it has lost its ability (not to say its right) to manage. The cons will not respect the client, nor believe in the client organisation's ability to implement whatever changes the project suggests. Cluelessness on the one hand will breed cynicism on the other.

Fortunately, the totally clueless client is probably a rarity. But I have seen many projects born in indecision and staggering from review meeting to review meeting. Because the brief was so vague, no one knows how to finish the job. Because the situation was so complex, the options proliferate. And because the client was so weak from the start, getting any kind of decision is virtually impossible.

One of the more recent vogues in consulting (an industry which latches onto new '-isms' with the ferocity of a bull terrier getting hold of a postman's ankles) was Business Process Re-engineering, or BPR to its disciples. This promised such unspecific results as *complete overhaul of the organisation*, the introduction of *radical change in the way you do business* and even a *quantum leap in performance.* At first sight, such a programme seems to have been conceived specifically to serve the clueless client. How can you write the terms of reference for a quantum leap?

This view of BPR, although it might be shared by many (with the result that the whole concept of re-engineering has fallen into some disrepute), is a corruption of what it was really intended to be. The notion of a complete rethinking of how a business works actually implies a very clear view of where it is trying to go. Clients who call in a re-engineering consultant for the *right* reasons may have no idea what the shape of their organisation will be at the end of the job, but there is a world of difference between that and not knowing what they want to achieve.

If you don't have a clue, don't get a con. Or, to put it another way, pros help those who help themselves.

'It saves us having to do anything in the meantime'
Calling in the cons can be a wonderful cover for inaction. The bigger the study and the longer it will take, the more scope there is for those who commissioned it to avoid making any hard decisions.

After all, we don't want to change anything now, only to find that the consultants recommend something different. With a bit of luck the cons will file a report two inches thick, and then another six months can decently elapse while everyone reads it and tries to work out what it all means. Then we'll have to get a working party together to decide how we're going to imple-ment it. A summary paper will have to go before the Board, and they won't be able to look at it until after the end of the financial year. And by that time the report will be out of date so we'll have to get some more consultants to come and review the conclusions of the first lot . . .

The beauty of this is that not only does the consultancy assignment hold things up for a period of months or even years but, in the meantime, the client's managers appear to be busily engaged on furthering an important project. First, there is the whole business of recruiting the consultants, which can involve lengthy drafting of the invitation to tender, days of meetings to finalise the terms of reference and agree a longlist of bidders, endless presentation sessions and yet more meetings to choose a firm to work with. After that, there are data to be provided, interviews to be arranged for the cons, review meetings to attend, workshops and discussion papers and brainstorming and visioning and option generation and first-cut scenarios and interim reports and validation and all the paraphernalia of the project.

There is nothing wrong with any of this if it is aimed at real objectives and stands a chance of achieving real results. But for some clients it is enough that they should be seen to be doing something. Working with consultants can provide a perfect front concealing more or less total inaction.

Why should this happen? In some cases, the cause may be defence of a vested interest. A particular individual may cynically set up a consultancy project in order to stave off the loss of his own position, a reduction in her authority or cuts in his staff or budget. By playing for time he or she may hope either that the impetus for change will be lost (notably, in cases where the original idea stems from very senior management, who may lose interest or no longer be around by the time the job is completed) or that they will be able to manoeuvre themselves into a better position before the consultants have finished.

I did a job for a paper manufacturer who was considering merging two recently acquired subsidiaries. Consultants were brought in for good reasons, namely to show the real benefits of merger and to build consensus between the two organisations. Unfortunately, the senior manager with overall responsibility fell seriously ill and was absent for some months, giving the general manager of one of the subsidiaries the chance to subvert the project and do everything he could to avoid it coming to conclusions which would reduce his own power. Not surprisingly, the whole project got badly delayed and finally ended in tears.

In other cases, probably more common, it is not so much that client managers set out cynically to defend their vested interests as that they are scared, lazy or just downright incompetent. Companies with labour problems may call in consultants rather than bite the bullet and confront their unions. Managers who do not really understand information technology may feel that, by commissioning an IT strategy from a whizzkid consultant, they have done enough and can go away and forget about it for another twelve months. Governments have always set a fine example in their use of Royal Commissions, Congressional Hearings and other forms of enquiry to bury politically damaging issues for as long as possible. Not surprisingly, using consultants in order to avoid taking a decision is a particularly popular device in the public sector.

It is to the discredit of cons that they will go along with clients who are playing this particular game. Ultimately, it is bad for both parties. Working on jobs of this kind makes cons as sloppy as their clients. Slipped deadlines? *No worries.* Vague recommendations? *Just the ticket, old boy.* Reports with many pages and few actions? *Excellent piece of work, excellent . . .*

'I already know the answer, but . . .'

If the clueless client can be a nightmare, the one who knows the answer before you even start work poses real problems, too.

It may seem pretty bizarre that anyone should pay good money to a consultant to tell him what he already knows. In fact, there are several reasons that can lead to this and they are not all bad ones. Take for example the case of the paper manufacturer cited in the previous section, who was merging two subsidiaries and asked consultants to look at the implications. The cons were probably not going to come up with anything that the senior management had not thought of by themselves but, by working through the issues step by step with the managers of the two businesses, and by being seen as independent outsiders, they could aim to build consensus in a way that those on the inside found hard to do.

'I know the answer, but . . .' In the case of the paper company, the sentence might have continued '. . . but I want my managers to see it, too.' Unfortunately, in many cases, the explanation is nothing like as convincing. That 'but' can conceal all manner of hidden agendas, and this is where the problem begins. The hidden thought may be:

- '. . . but I'm not sure that I like it and I'm hoping not to have to face up to it,' or:

- '. . . but I think I'll look really big in front of the Board with consultants behind me,' or:

- '. . . but I can't get those silly buggers in marketing to agree.'

In all of these cases, the cons are probably on a hiding to nothing. At best, they will do a pile of analysis simply in order to come up with the predicted answer, which (frankly speaking) is a pretty boring thing to have to do. At worst, they will come up with a contrary result, which may annoy the client intensely. In many cases, since the client is playing politics of one kind or another, the study will turn out to be pretty irrelevant: the guy who cannot get Marketing to agree with him may not do any better in that respect however many consultants he wheels in to take his side.

A colleague of mine once carried out a market study for a property developer, who wished to put together a financial justification of his latest venture in order to attract investors. Unfortunately, the con concluded that there was insufficient demand to warrant going ahead. The client decided that the many pages of supporting evidence looked serious enough to give the desired credibility but rewrote the conclusion in order to turn it from a 'no' into a 'yes', before passing the research on to the investors.

A producer of confectionery was selling mainly to large retailers who used to give the manufacturer a tough time. No matter how hard the supplier tried to meet its customers' needs, whenever its sales manager called on the large retailers they would find something to complain about: phone calls that took too long to answer, deliveries that were ten minutes late, invoices that had the wrong price on them, or whatever. The supplier 'knew' that these were isolated incidents and called in consultants to prove that its service was as good as, if not better than, its competitors. The cons found, however, that there were indeed real deficiencies in the way that the company was serving its customers. The weight of evidence was such that the client had no choice but to accept it . . . but he showed no readiness to act upon it. This was a classic 'Type 2' client: they needed help, but the job that they asked for was not the one that they needed.

Cons should not be expected just to act as rubber stamps. A pro has to know when to say no. And the client who, for reasons of vainglory or politics, wants the consultant simply to agree with him is playing a dangerous game.

'Someone has to take responsibility'

This reason is a subset of the last one. Some clients know what the answer is but cannot or will not face up to the facts. Perhaps they do not dare to tell the Board the true picture. They may be unwilling to grasp the nettle of declaring redundancies, even though they know these are required. Or they have made a commitment, whether to staff, suppliers or customers, that they feel unable to break.

I was asked once to review a contract for the purchase of railway equipment. The equipment was both very expensive and technologically advanced, and only one supplier had existing products that fitted the bill. The railway company, however, was keen to see more competition and ended up placing the order with a small and untried supplier. The contract went badly wrong. The first prototypes were delivered late and failed to perform to specification, while the supplier was on the brink of bankruptcy. By the time I got involved, there was only one sensible course of action: cancel the contract and go back on bended knee to the only supplier who was known to have a tried and tested product.

When I put this to senior management, it became clear that they had known all along that this would be the outcome. So why had they needed me to tell them? Presumably because they could not, of their own volition, accept the loss of face involved in cancelling a contract that they should never have signed in the first place. But if a consultant told them to do so? Well, that was different.

There is little to be said in favour of using consultants to force you to do what you know you should be doing anyway. Cons should certainly be expected to take responsibility for their recommendations.

But using them to relieve you of **your** responsibilities is another matter. 'It's not my fault, he made me do it' is the language of the playground, not the Boardroom.

'The Chairman's had this idea . . .'
Calling in cons to take a fresh look at a familiar problem is certainly not a bad reason for using them. And the instigator of such a project is likely to be one of the senior executives in the business: one who is close enough to it to be aware of the issues which it needs to address, but sufficiently removed from the day-to-day intricacies to be able to come up with – or at least see the scope for – some new ideas. So there is nothing wrong with the Chairman having ideas (by and large, it is probably a pity that it does not happen more often).

Difficulties arise, however, when the motivation for using consultants turns out to be little more than a whim. At the end of this book I shall discuss how, as a client, you should manage a consultancy assignment – how to 'get it right'. To anticipate, I believe that three of the most critical factors in using consultants, from the perspective of the client, are:

- Clear definition of the objectives and terms of reference for the project.

- Real commitment to act on the outcome of the consultants' work and, where appropriate, to implement their recommendations.

- Ownership or championing of the project by a manager with sufficient standing in the organisation to clear the obstacles which may be placed in the way both of the cons doing the job and of the subsequent implementation plan.

We have already seen that the first of these three is a problem when the client has no clue what to do. The other two, and particularly the third, can be stumbling blocks in cases where the top man or woman in the organisation has simply thrown out a bright idea but has probably not stuck around long enough for anyone to be sure what they are supposed to do about it. If the Chairman or Chief Executive is seeking to challenge perceived wisdom in the organisation, but then leaves the project to be run by a manager who is part and parcel of that prevailing culture, there is likely to be a very distinct lack of commitment. In other situations, no one may be prepared really to take ownership of the project at all, leaving the cons to grope in the dark, without proper input or feedback from the client. If the top person loses interest halfway through the job, things are likely to grind to a halt, leaving everyone embarrassed and unsure even whether to bother finishing the project.

In multinational companies, this kind of thing takes another twist. I did a project for a US-based diversified corporation with substantial operations in Europe. The idea had come from senior management *in the US* that there should be far more cooperation between the various business units in shipping their goods to Europe and distributing them here. After working for some time on the possible benefits of this approach, I became concerned at the lack of interest being shown by most of the European management. Raising the issue with them, I was told that they were frequently informed of new initiatives coming from the States, but that they generally ignored them since the American senior management seldom lasted long enough in the job for anything actually to happen.

In that particular case, all was not lost and it was possible to make a success of the project by taking time to get buy-in from the European management. Generally, though, projects will fail if they do not have the right champion, fully committed to making them a success. This means that they must be based on something more than a passing fancy of the Chairman.

'The Board can't agree'

Consultants do not generally make good politicians. Perhaps that is why they ended up as consultants, on the basis that they lacked either the ability or the taste for politics which would have enabled them to climb the corporate ladder. So, expecting consultants to sort out your internal political wranglings is foolishly optimistic.

Now, there is nothing wrong with a good honest disagreement. On the face of it, if the board is split between two possible routes, consultants should be able to look at the potential benefits and pitfalls of each and come up with a balanced recommendation. In the real world, though, things are seldom that simple. Inevitably, when the sales director wants to launch a new product and the production director wants to rationalise the range, there is more at stake than simply the number of pages in the company's catalogue. Bringing in a con is likely to have a somewhat unpredictable effect, with the following alternative scenarios:

- The con attempts to solve the dispute though rational argument and factual analysis, in which case the argument will almost certainly continue since political disputes are not solved in that way. Indeed, the con's intervention may simply inflame the situation.

- The con plumps for one of the warring sides, for possibly irrational reasons of his or her own (which may be as crude as the fact that one side was friendlier to the con, or got to her first). In that situation, you could have achieved an equally good result simply by tossing a coin.

- The con shies away from taking sides and tries to find some consensus way forward, in which case everyone will regard him as a complete prat.

The worst thing about this situation is that the client is unlikely to tell the con up-front that what he is expected to do is cut the Gordian knot in some long-running dispute. In consequence, the consultancy team may not have the right people on it to cope with the situation that they will find themselves drawn into as the work progresses. What you need is someone capable of staring down the warring factions and either whipping them into line or pushing one of them into quitting. That is not a description of the average con.

In most cases, political issues need political – not consultancy – solutions. Be honest and recognise such disputes for what they are. And if, at the end of the day, you decide that a consultant *is* what you need to resolve the situation, do everyone a favour and be honest with the cons in setting their objectives. Otherwise you could end up pouring petrol on the flames.

'This'll be one in the eye for Smith'

It would be tempting to condemn all 'political' motives for using consultants. Certainly, as already noted, most consultants make poor politicians. A persuasive case can nonetheless be made to support the view that politics is the lifeblood of many organisations, and it would be naïve of consultants to imagine that they can somehow operate outside its influence.

Politics is the use of (mainly) interpersonal skills to enhance your own power and have it recognised by others. Within an organisation, managers may start from more or less powerful positions: for example, in some corporate cultures marketing is 'king', while elsewhere it may be production or accounting that rules the roost. But all managers need to have and to use some degree of power if they are to be capable of achieving the objectives of their role. On top of this, many also see power games as a way of enhancing their own personal position and advancing their own agenda and career. This is not only natural but may well be a positive force. After all, nothing much would get done in business if we all adopted an 'after you' approach. Where things go wrong is when the playing of political games becomes an end in itself, disconnected from the real business of the organisation.

John Hunt, Plowden Professor of Human Relations at the London Business School, puts it this way[2]: 'We should remember that these games generate conflicts, which in turn energize the system and make it very productive. Without conflict, organizations may well die, just as families and marriages without conflict collapse. However, the conflict can become destructive, and much destructive conflict arises from power games.'

The use of outside 'experts', such as consultants, is one of the recognised techniques used by managers to expand their own power. There can be nothing intrinsically wrong with this: it generates a very

---

[2] *Managing People at Work* – McGraw-Hill, 2nd Edition 1986.

necessary championing of the consultancy project by those within the organisation who feel that they stand to gain from it, and may be one of the best guarantees that there will be continuing drive and commitment to implement the consultants' results.

I have worked on a number of projects involving the integration of operations on a pan-European scale. The key objective was always to reduce costs and/or improve customer service, and as such there were real benefits which the business was striving to gain. At the same time, since the projects tended to lead to the downgrading of national management positions (or even their wholesale abolition) in favour of a small number of key European roles, they were inherently political in nature and there were almost bound to be winners and losers among the individuals concerned. In this kind of situation, Smith – whoever he or she is – may well get one in the eye. That is the way the Euro-cookie crumbles.

So what is the problem? The problem, as John Hunt says, is when the politics become destructive. Unfortunately, there is no rigid dividing line between 'constructive' and 'destructive' politics but it relates to the balance between the organisation's objectives and those of the individual.

At this point, like the good con that I am, I feel a matrix coming on to show how this applies to consultancy projects and their sponsors:

Figure 1.1: Impact of politics on consultancy projects

Potential benefit of the project to the organisation

	Low	**High**
High	*Destructive conflict: abusive pursuit of self-interest*	*Best chance of successful championing*
Low	*Perceived irrelevance of project*	*Destructive conflict: cynical defence of self-interest*

Potential benefit of the project to the individual

Where an individual attempts to pursue personal ambitions that are out of sync with those of the organisation, unless he is already in an extremely powerful position, the result will be to unleash opposition from all his rivals and others who stand to lose out. Where, by contrast, the manager responsible for a project feels that it is contrary to her own interests, there is a real risk that she will do everything in her power to sabotage or stifle the work of the cons.

The best chance of a successful outcome is where there is not only a perceived benefit to the organisation but, at the same time, the manager or sponsor of the consultancy work feels that he or she stands to gain personally from it *and already holds sufficient power in the organisation to be able to fight successfully for it*. The con who takes on a job knowing that its sponsor is solely motivated by doing others down is playing with fire. The con who is also aware that the sponsor does not have sufficient power within the organisation to get away with his devious intents is guilty of serious misjudgment. Apart from anything else, he stands a high chance of not being paid for his work since it is most unlikely to end in success.

What, then, of the project which starts out well, with an apparent congruence between the aims of the manager and those of the organisation, but then leads the cons to quite different conclusions? What if, for example, they judge that the sponsor's preferred strategy is a complete turkey? What if they find that the interests of the company are to close down the manager's own department?

These are the kinds of problems – by no means unknown in consulting – that separate the pros from the boys. They may call for great diplomacy or just great balls. About the only useful generalisation that can be given is the old war-cry of the cons: 'No Surprises.' In other words, the cons have to prepare the client for the outcome, whether it is one that she is going to like, or not.

But this is a subject for a later chapter: the fact that a project gets sticky does not mean that it should never have been started. The ones that should have been consigned to the dustbin before they ever began are those directed solely towards the political advancement of the sponsor.

If your only interest is playing politics, kindly play with yourself.

'We've heard that it's the latest thing'

We live in an age whose time horizons grow shorter every day. The song that fails to reach the top of the charts in its first week is binned and forgotten. Our food has to be *fast*, our photos *instant*, credit *immediate*. The software that this book is written on will be superseded in a year's time and in two the hardware will be obsolete. Long term, for many people, means waiting until next week's lottery draw. Long term, in business, means anything beyond the next set of annual results and is, by definition, too long to wait.

In this kind of environment, there can be little surprise that business leaders (or more commonly, perhaps, those who aspire to be the business leaders of tomorrow) will grasp at any promising new trend or idea in the hope that it may turn out to be a winner. If it worked for Fastlane Inc in the US then surely it will work for Slowcoach plc in the UK. No matter that Fastlane is a hundred times larger, sells to a totally different market segment, has suppliers who will do things unheard of in Europe or was in such a complete mess to begin with that almost anything would have worked some kind of improvement. As long as it's the latest thing, has a classy name to it and will look good in our annual report, we'll take some of it.

So what do you expect cons to do in response? Come on now, get real. The market is screaming out for new remedies to new problems (which may, in fact, be old problems – but as sure as heck no-one is going to thank you for offering old solutions). Do you really think cons are going to sit around waiting for everyone to calm down a bit? Forget it. Remember, cons are pros and if there is a demand in the market you can be sure that there will be cons rushing in to meet it.

The change which has crept in gradually in recent years is that cons are now also leading this process and carefully nurturing and launching each 'latest thing' in turn. Consultancies have been vying with each other to come up with new *products* where previously they sold simply on the basis of their experience and the quality of their personnel. This is partly a result of the market's hunger for new ideas and partly driven by a recognition that it is very expensive to devise an approach individually for each client's pet project. Far simpler to devise a standard methodology which can be branded, packaged, sold off the shelf and delivered from the consulting equivalent of a production line.

The one thing that is not easy, however, is patenting the idea. Where one leads, others follow immediately. Who cares where the idea for re-engineering came from? As soon as it started to take off, everyone had their own version of it. Being an imitator rather than an inventor may, in any case, be the better strategy. What counts is capturing the mood and imagination of clients: if you can do this by popularising the 'latest thing' without having to put the work into developing the original idea, then so much the better.

Does it really matter that the top consultants are the ones who can think up the sexiest-sounding names for the latest business fad? All consumer markets are driven by fashion and product innovation and we generally regard this as healthy, even if the pace of obsolescence of the things we buy is starting to outstrip our ability to keep up. Why should consultancy be any different? Don't clients have a right to the latest thing, if that is what they want?

The difference, as I have touched upon before, is that when you buy consultancy you buy sight unseen. If a sports shoemaker persuades you that you need a gas-filled sole, you know what you are getting and you have at least some chance to try it out first. When a consultant tells you that you need to re-engineer your business processes and that this will deliver a quantum leap in performance, you probably have little idea of what is involved and no guarantee of success of any kind. Now, if the project is right for your situation and the cons are the right ones for the project, it may indeed be exactly what you need. But if you buy just because it is the *latest thing*, because you read about it in a magazine or you heard of some other company that used it, you are running a major risk of failure and disappointment.

For a consultancy project really to deliver, there has to be more to it than just fashion.

'We had a report done before'
One reason for writing this book is that, for many managers, working with consultants can be a once-in-a-career experience. The

popular image of the consultant remains that of the 'troubleshooter', called in to deal with a particular issue and come up with a life-saving plan to get the client out of the mire, then riding off into the night. Despite this, there are some organisations which seem to turn into consultancy junkies, with one project leading to another and successive waves of cons following each other around.

There are two underlying factors that can contribute to this situation, neither of them particularly commendable:

- For a con, the best way to develop business is to win a job – almost any job – which gives him or her access to a new client and then, once inside, to look for opportunities either to extend the project or to sell other work for colleagues with different skills. I will discuss this further in Chapter 5: ('Tricks of the Trade') but suffice it to say that finding a new client is infinitely harder and more expensive than selling on to an existing one.

- For some clients, having consultants about can be a comforting experience. Some of the reasons have already been discussed: the cons can be used as an excuse for inaction, they save management facing up to its responsibilities, and so on. They also flatter the vanity of those responsible for their work. Weak managers, allowed to commission consultancy work, can all too easily become hooked on what is the management equivalent of smoking cannabis.

As elsewhere in this chapter, I have to caution that there is nothing absolutely wrong with consultants selling on or with clients finding consultancy a pleasant experience. Both are quite legitimate. In the research conducted for this book, as shown in Figure 1.2, both clients and cons recognised that consultants like to leave clients wanting more. It is a matter of balance, though, and at the limit a cynical con can exploit a weak client in order to keep the job rolling almost indefinitely.

Figure 1.2: 'Consultants like to leave their clients wanting more'

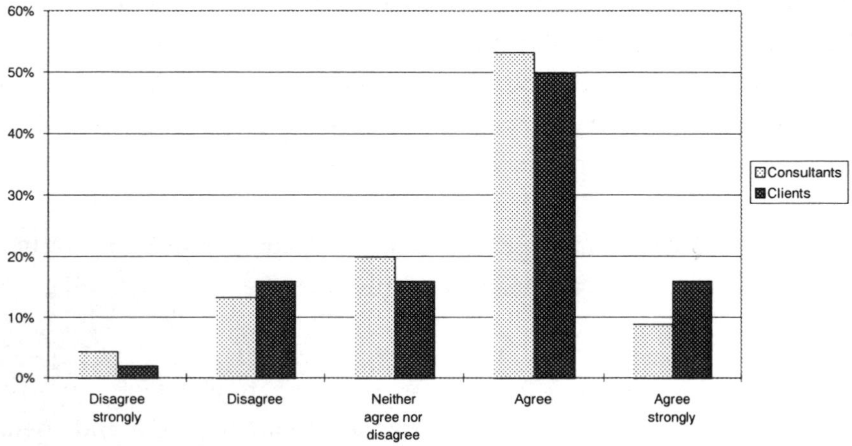

'We had a report done before which identified the need for further work' can mean that genuine new areas of concern have been opened up and need to be explored. It is equally possible that it means the cons made quite sure that they left a lot of loose ends hanging from their previous work, in the expectation of being able to sell the follow-on. They will have done this quite legitimately if the first study was set up to 'define a strategy . . .' or 'recommend an overall approach . . .' But this kind of strategic first stage is used systematically by consultants to get their teeth into an organisation, and the buyer needs to be aware that this is the way pros do business.

The classic case, at least in the 1980s, was Information Technology (IT) consulting. Faced with a need for a new system to handle (say) the processing of customer orders, clients were encouraged first to buy a review of their 'Systems Strategy'. This typically took several months of consultancy effort and delivered nothing implementable at all. What it did lead to was the highlighting of a series of issues that had to be addressed: for example, it would identify the weakness of the central corporate database (which would need a more detailed study) as well as suggesting that, in the specific area of sales order processing, the client's business was sufficiently unique to make standard off-the-shelf packages inappropriate.

This then led to a detailed 'Systems Specification' study, which would take several more months to draw up a list of things that the computer needed to be able to do, followed by the production of tender documentation (another project), management of the bidding process and the evaluation of the responses (several more months of work). Only at the end of this lot would the client have a specific recommendation as to how he should source his sales order system. Meanwhile, all sorts of other avenues would have been opened up: a taxation specialist would have been introduced to review the VAT implications of overseas sales, an organisational study would have been needed to consider the interface to manufacturing, and so on.

Happily, the sheer pace of technological change in Information Technology has made this kind of laborious step-by-step approach rather a thing of the past. Few clients are now prepared to spend two years and a minimum of perhaps £100,000 ($150,000) getting to a purchasing decision. Most exceptions are probably in the public sector. This remains one of the most fertile territories for cons in the UK and each successive wave of Government initiatives (privatisation, competitive tendering, market testing, Private Finance Initiative . . .) seems only to have increased the number of cons required to devise strategies, review plans, resolve issues and – which is really what it comes down to – provide reassurance and comfort to functionaries who are often completely out of their depth. There is *always* potential for another project just around the corner and the thought of it can be much more reassuring than the idea of having to face up to things on your own.

'We have a budget . . .'

My own work as a consultant spanned both the private and public sectors. I have no doubt that there are many, including former colleagues of mine, who might feel that I am too negative about the latter: to be sure, private-sector organisations have their share of poor managers and weak leaders, both of whom are easy prey for a good con. But there are some vices that do seem to be the speciality of the public sector, and I am not talking about the ones you learn at boarding school.

In Government and its related agencies, budgets are power. As I have discovered to my cost, it can be unbelievably hard to persuade a public-sector administrator that it is a good thing to reduce costs and save everyone money. In my early days as a con I was working for a large department when I stumbled across the fact that they were paying way over the odds for one of the buildings that they rented. Potentially, they could have saved around $1 million annually by renegotiating the deal or moving out. I bounded into the next meeting to deliver this astonishing piece of news, only to be greeted with a resounding shrug of the shoulders. Were they spending too much? So what, it was in the budget. And the prospect of underspending their budgetary allocation, far from being a feather in the department's cap, was a source of concern. It would lead to a reduction in their budget next year. And lower budgets meant reduced power and credibility in their own Alice-in-Wonderland world.

The same principle extends to consultancy. Have budget, will buy. What can I say?

This chapter called itself a longlist and I could extend it almost indefinitely. For now, I have given ten reasons – ranging from the dispiriting to the downright scandalous – why hundreds of millions of pounds are wasted every year on unnecessary, unhelpful or irrelevant consultancy projects.

There are two words which sum up most of this: weakness and cynicism. Both characteristics can be found in any organisation: cons themselves may be either or both and the same goes for clients. Cynical cons will exploit a weak client. But a cynical client may exploit well-meaning cons, just as he exploits his own people, to manoeuvre for political advantage. The reason why this matters can be summed up in a single word: waste. I have a low tolerance of people wasting my time, but that is relatively trivial in the great scheme of things. Much more troubling is the 'wasting' of people: careers can be ruined, people sacked, on the back of work performed by the weak for the cynical (or vice versa). And, ultimately, the organisation which plays around with irrelevant consultancy projects when it should be investing in new products or taking urgent steps to improve customer service may not survive. Consultancy for the wrong reasons is a luxury that only the really successful can afford, and they are the least likely to indulge in it.

If I sound negative, it is deliberate. Without understanding what can go wrong, you are unlikely to get things right. Without appreciating how easy it is to call in the cons for the wrong reasons, you will stand much less chance of identifying and responding to the right reasons. Because there *are* (wonderful to relate) good reasons for summoning external support and – at best – consultants can help you turn round an ailing business or take a successful one to new heights. It would be kind of nice, though, if more people had that experience rather than the depressing one of feeling that the smart suits had been and gone without leaving any lasting contribution.

CHAPTER 2: A SHORTER LIST OF GOOD REASONS

JOEL BARKER IS AN AMERICAN BUSINESS GURU WHO HAS MADE A NICE LIVING from the word *paradigm*. At the conference where I heard him speak, he deployed it more often than I have ever heard it used in the whole of my life before or since. I do not exaggerate.

Despite a touch of overkill, the gist of his message struck me as useful. Businesses, or other organisations, develop a kind of prevailing orthodoxy concerning their markets, products, competitors, people, image and everything else, which gives them a model to guide what they do from day to day. This model, or *paradigm*, is refined over time. The companies that find the best paradigm, or get closest to the ideal structure or operation for the prevailing environment, are the ones that are the most successful.

Until something else comes along. A paradigm which starts out as a strength may, in time, become fossilised and inappropriate to new conditions. Businesses sometimes brag about the strength of their paradigm: their annual reports or corporate advertising may tell you about the 'Bigco approach' or the 'Biggercorp way of doing business' or even the 'Biggestbyfar Inc philosophy'. Some of the very largest and most successful, however, have found that what succeeded in one market or one decade can come hopelessly unstuck in another. The fall from grace of the once-omnipotent IBM has been perhaps the biggest example but only one among many. For those with memories of even a few years standing, the cry 'Where are they now?' comes easily.

This collapse of many once-great empires can be attributed to their inability to update the paradigm on which they have based their success. There is nothing startling about this insight; nonetheless, a focus on the need for continual reinvention of the paradigm does raise interesting questions. How should companies set about searching for the next new paradigm? Is it better in this to be a leader or a follower? How do you know whether a bright star on the distant horizon is going to grow into tomorrow's paradigm or simply fade away into oblivion? I could go on but I will leave it to Mr Barker, who does this stuff far better than I can.

This idea of successive, and continuously updated, paradigms provides a useful framework for understanding consultancy. Almost all consultancy is about *change* but not all change is of the same nature. Consultants can work to introduce or develop change in any of three different ways:

- As **paradigm-polishers**, helping organisations to improve the 'way they do things' so as to be able to compete with the best of their peers. This is the basis for most efficiency programmes, cost-reduction studies, productivity reviews and the like.

- As **paradigm-spotters**, scanning the horizon for the next big wave that may come along and wash over the business just as it thought it had got the hang of things, or (preferably) the new one that the client can ride in order to outflank the competition. This is the blue-sky role of the strategic consultant.

- As **paradigm-shifters**, working to move the client organisation from where it is now to where it perceives that it needs to be in the future (and sooner if possible). This is the most complex form of consultancy intervention and may range from helping the client copy the success of a pioneering rival, through implementing the recommendations of an earlier strategic study to developing the skills of the people in the organisation and helping them adapt to what will be required in the future.

There is no value judgment implied by this separation of consulting work into three categories. Each has its place. I suspect that consultancy fashion will tend to bring different categories into vogue on a periodic basis. The trend in recent years has been away from the nitty-gritty work of paradigm-polishing (or perhaps it would be more correct to say that the big consultancies have tended increasingly to leave this to smaller firms) while, at the same time, disillusion has set in with the purer forms of paradigm-spotting. This has left paradigm-shifting as the in-thing of the 1990s, exemplified by the rise of both re-engineering and change management as key consultancy products. However, each of the three forms of intervention is equally valid and any of the three may – or may not – be just what the client needs. If, that is, they have a good reason.

A consultancy study needs to be justified, and defined, in two stages. Firstly, what is it that the business is trying to change? Is it setting out to polish an existing paradigm or search for a new one? This is the *goal* which has to be the ultimate guide for the change process and those involved in it. Secondly, what is it that consultants are expected to bring to the party? This will largely define the *objectives* for the work of the cons.

It is not enough just to feel that the business 'needs to change'. As we saw in Chapter 1, not having a clue what to do is a poor basis for bringing in consultants. The first thing that any prospective consultancy client needs to do is define the goal that they are aiming at. Implicit in this will be whether it involves polishing, spotting or shifting a paradigm or two. The second question is then to ask what the organisation can do for itself and what it needs help with. Asking *why* it is that they do not have the required expertise or resource in-house, and whether it might be sensible to acquire these for future occasions, is optional but on occasion might not come amiss. The essential thing, however, is to instil clarity into the definition both of the change goals and of the consultancy objectives.

I can give no absolute definition of what constitutes a 'good' reason for buying consultancy but the reason is unlikely to be a good one unless the client can show:

- A perception of why the business or organisation needs to change.

- Clear goals for this change imperative.

- An understanding of what the organisation currently lacks and which impedes its ability to make the necessary changes.

- Specific objectives for the external support which is consequently sought.

I have deliberately separated the 'perception' and 'understanding' of the situation from the definition of goals and objectives. This is because the process of understanding is not always easily communicated: it may remain with a small group or even a single individual among the client's team (such as a visionary chief executive – provided, as shown in the previous chapter, that this is more than a whim). The definition of goals and objectives, by comparison, should be shared more widely among both client staff and consultants. It is also capable of being set down in writing, which is a worthwhile exercise.

So what is it that the client may lack and which the cons may be expected to provide? Figure 2.1 summarises the answers given by respondents to my questionnaire:

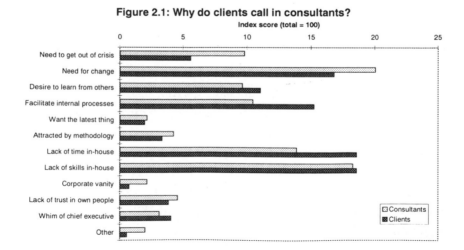

Figure 2.1: Why do clients call in consultants?

According to clients, the most important things that they want from consultants are time – simple man-hours to fill a gap in the client's own resource – and additional skills. These are followed by a general need for support in introducing change and by facilitation of the client's internal processes.

Consultants themselves tend to see their role more in terms of introducing change, or even getting the client out of a crisis, and less as a simple matter of providing extra pairs of hands.

In the pages which follow I discuss these and some of the other inputs that cons can sensibly be expected to contribute.

Additional resources

Any consultant likes to think that the client is buying his services because of the brilliance of his analysis, the depth of his knowledge, the business acumen that he keeps up his sleeve and the wide-ranging experience on which he bases it. Often, though, the truth is far less glamorous. As seen in Figure 2.1, many clients bring in cons when they simply need an extra pair of hands or two. The job concerned may not involve anything that the client could not do for herself, given the time to address it. But *time* is a precious resource and there are plenty of managers who simply cannot step outside their day-to-day roles for long enough to research a new market or to carry through a major development programme.

Time is not the only resource that clients may need to bring in for a defined purpose or period. Other forms of resource include data, computer software of various kinds (cost models, statistical packages, presentational tools and so on) and the analytical brainpower to make the best use of them. All of these *can* be bought, employed or developed as part of the permanent staff or resources of the client. Consultancy, however, offers a number of advantages:

- It allows the client to hire in the resource just for a short period: this is the classic 'project' situation with consultants briefed to do a given piece of work in a defined timescale of weeks or months.

- It gives greater flexibility in the deployment of the resource: should

the project prove to be more difficult than expected, additional cons
can be wheeled in or alternative software brought to bear.

- With suitable terms of reference, the client may have more control
over what the cons do and what they deliver than might be the case
with an in-house team. If you lift a manager from her usual role and
ask her to develop a new strategy, she can only do her best (in what
may be very unfamiliar circumstances to her) and there is no
guarantee of results. If you bring in cons to do the job, you should
be able to hold them to delivering what you require and you *may*
have a greater guarantee of success. Before you get overconfident
about this, however, you could do worse than read Chapter 5.

- Consultants, through their training and experience, can be
expected to hit the ground running and to deliver results faster
than may be the case with new hirings. If they are using a particular model or technique, the time required to train in-house staff
may be avoided completely or at least substantially reduced.

This last point, speed of work, is often fundamental. One of the best
roles for consultants is as accelerators of a project. A senior manager
who had just been on the receiving end of a McKinsey study made
this comment to me: 'I'll say this for them, they got through an
enormous amount of data analysis in a few weeks. There's no way we
could have done that without them.' Whether this is sufficient justification for the very substantial fee that he had paid could be open to
dispute. But if you need a team to work through the night in order to
meet impossible deadlines, you may have to call in the cons. Figure
2.2 confirms from the research that both clients and cons themselves
share this belief in consultancy as a fast track approach.

There are two health warnings that must be added. The first is this. If
you need short-term additional resource, fine. Just be careful that you
do not find yourself slipping into treating it as *long-term* additional
resource. Every consultant worth his salt will try to get his foot in
your organisational door and then keep it there. If you need number-
crunchers for two years, is it sensible to be paying £650 ($1000) a day

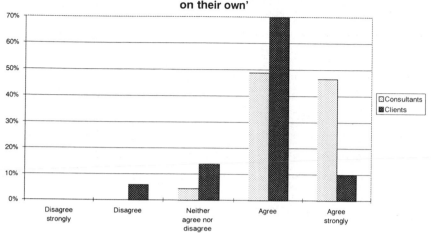

Figure 2.2: 'Consultants achieve results faster than clients could on their own'

for them? Get yourself a quick fix, by all means, but beware of becoming a consultancy junkie. I have several times come across information technology and other projects where the same cons had been working for the same client for at least two years, where they had 'gone native' with a vengeance, and where they had made themselves so indispensable to the client that they were ultimately recruited by him. This can be a very expensive way of finding the resources that you need for the long term.

The second warning is even more fundamental. If you need a particular kind of resource, make sure that this is what you buy. It sounds obvious but consultancies are always eager to sell you the whole package, to offer a 'one stop shop' and to broaden the scope of the work, and it is easy to lose sight of what it was that you really needed. If what you want is a bright accountancy junior to crunch the business case numbers, do not end up employing a senior organisational consultant to interview all your sales team. If you need data, buy data; if you already have the data, make sure you do not pay someone to get it all over again. Be clear, be honest and be sure to get what *you* need. Chapters 8 and 12 will return to this theme.

Technical inputs and skills
I have already touched on the acquisition of outside skills in general,

as one reason why you may look to consultancy for extra resources. A specific case is the hiring of technical inputs that you are most unlikely to need on a long-term basis but which you may require for a specific purpose.

Consultants are often thought of as smart suits with MBAs and portable computers who will turn their hand to anything. There are plenty of these clones about but there are also many cons whose work is essentially technical and specialist in nature. You would not expect your office manager to design an extension and get planning permission for it. By the same token, your warehouse manager probably does not have the skills to draw up a new racking layout and get permission from the Fire Officer. Your factory manager may need specialist inputs if she wants to analyse labour productivity in detail. Your IT Director may simply never have had in-depth experience of migrating to a new operating system. And even the Director of Strategy may find it useful to buy specialist expertise to identify and value prospective take-over targets.

I am not sure that corporate financiers and strategic consultants will really welcome being lumped alongside materials-handling engineers and time-and-motion experts. However, they can all be seen as providing technical inputs which clients probably do not need to own for the long term.

The same comment applies to the buying of technical inputs as to all acquisition of resources: be sure that what you buy is what you need. In the case of technical inputs, be particularly careful to focus on the *skills* of the cons and not on the *methodology* in which they may be wrapped up. Impressively-named methodologies are not hard to devise; real knowledge, however, is worth paying for.

A good example is benchmarking, where some element of a client's business (for example, the speed with which orders are fulfilled or the number of redesigns needed to get a product right) is compared to best practice elsewhere. To do this properly implies having full access to some very detailed operational statistics for other companies: data which it is by no means easy to acquire. This in itself is a good reason for bringing in consultants but on one condition: *if and only if* they have or can obtain that data.

I plead guilty to having used the term benchmarking, as a consultant, very loosely. But at least I had some scruples about promising more than I could deliver. The problem is that the term can mean as much – or as little – as you want it to mean. A less scrupulous con might promise to *benchmark* a client's operations to comparable businesses, knowing that all he could actually do was make some very general comparisons using whatever data he could cobble together from previous clients' reports. While this might be sufficient in some cases, it will certainly not satisfy the needs of a client who wants the job doing properly. The buyer of this particular sort of technical input needs to be absolutely certain where the numbers are coming from. General assurances and fine-looking methodologies should not be taken at face value.

Transfer of experience
Another good reason for bringing in consultants, and a further variation on using them to add resource, is the transfer of expertise and experience from other businesses. This can apply both within and beyond the client's own industry.

The transfer of experience is particularly important where the client needs to shift its paradigm in order to catch up, or overtake, what competitors are doing. One of the first jobs that I got involved in as a consultant was for a major UK food retailer. During the 1980s, its rivals had built up their own networks for buying goods and supplying them to their stores. They had found these networks to be a major source of competitive advantage through better product availability and increased margins. Our client badly needed to catch up and – if possible – leapfrog what had been done elsewhere. An interesting issue for the student of paradigm shifts is whether it is better to be the first to make a major leap forward or whether you actually benefit from being just slightly slower to jump. Certainly, the true pioneer may have to learn by mistakes which followers can avoid. That, at least, was the notion which we had sold to our client.

Consultants have a somewhat delicate balance to maintain when expected to transfer skills between businesses. What they are doing, after all, is lifting the results of work done for one client and selling them, suitably modified, to another. Where the clients are in completely different industries or continents this is unlikely to cause trouble. Where it is almost literally a matter of walking out of one company's back door and walking in through the front door of their main competitor, there is clearly a real conflict of interest and no consultancy worth its salt will wish to be seen abusing client confidence. The interesting part is the grey area between these two extremes. What if the new client is a *potential* rather than actual competitor of the old? What if a different team of cons, even though from the same firm, is deployed for the second client? How long has to elapse before the slate is wiped clean? The answers are not straightforward which means that there can be quite a lot of room for manoeuvre if what you are after is a transfer of expertise through your chosen consultants.

Conversely, if you are worried that your cons may take too much away with them when they leave, make sure that you get their signature to whatever confidentiality agreement you may feel necessary. Do not kid yourself, though, that this can be watertight. As a general rule, data can be safeguarded but experience cannot.

Strategy consultants may make a big play out of the fact that they do not work for competitors in the same industry. This is precisely to avoid the accusation that they are betraying confidential work carried out for their last client. Client-specific experience of all types may, though, be absorbed into a more generic framework or model which can then be sold on elsewhere. The problem for the client is the risk of buying a pig in a poke. It is all too easy to buy a model which has become detached from the specific knowledge on which it was once based. That knowledge probably remains with a few individuals and, unless you are very careful to get the right cons on your project, you may get a whole lot less than you bargained for.

Bringing out hidden knowledge

What might be termed the classic role of consultants is their use as external experts. As has already been seen, this can embrace bringing to the client their time, skills, brainpower and experience of other businesses. All of these elements are externally focused; that is, they are aimed at adding something to the client from outside.

There is another very important use of consultants which is perhaps less well understood. This is their contribution to the *internal* workings of the client. As with the external role, it can take a number of forms:

- The externally-focused project brings in outside skills and knowledge. The internally-focused project seeks to unlock skills already inside the company.

- There *may* be a need to add resources from outside the organisation, or simply a need to make more effective use of those which it already has.

- Transfer of outside expertise can enable the client to make a paradigm shift, but so can better communication and the development of new ideas within the business.

It is a common criticism of consultants that they simply feed back to clients what they know already – 'A consultant is a man who borrows your watch to tell you the time.' If this is the case, what is going on? There are at least three possibilities:

- Perhaps the client is totally dumb. Well, what else do you call someone who lends you his watch and then asks the time?

- Perhaps *someone* in the company knows what the time is, but he isn't telling the Chief Executive. The obvious question is, 'Why not?' The easy thing to do if you are the Chief Exec, however, is not to ask the obvious question but to find someone else who *will* tell you the time.

- Perhaps the client *sort* of knows what the time is, but needs someone to help her define it a bit more precisely and maybe ask a few awkward questions about what time it might be in other countries. With the benefit of hindsight, it will seem obvious. In advance, possibly not.

Consultants do a lot of obvious things, like going round the company talking to people. In my experience they are better at this than at rocket science. They are good at picking up information, whether quantified or anecdotal. They are good at processing this information into something that tells a story (which is not quite the same as something that tells the *true* story). They are, some of them, good listeners – which is one reason why senior management may like having them around. And, by doing all of these things, they can stimulate debate and argument which may be at least as useful as any input of external expertise. In short, as Figure 2.3 confirms, they can make good catalysts.

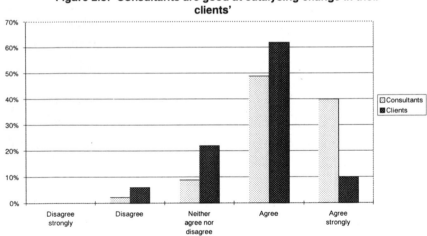

Figure 2.3: 'Consultants are good at catalysing change in their clients'

A term which was in vogue a few years ago, although less is heard of it now, is *process* consulting. The idea was that consultants should not attempt to tell the client what to do, but should work with the client's own people to bring out the ideas latent within them. It is not a role that I ever felt particularly happy with and I would be very cautious about any project that amounted *solely* to this. One reason for my hesitation is that it is all too easy for process consulting to become vanity consulting. The con will persuade the Chief Executive that his ideas contain the seed of the next industry-sweeping paradigm. She will teach the Board how important it is to develop their mutual interaction and team roles. She will take them all off on awaydays, think-tanks, team-building sessions and expensive weekends in luxury hotels. It will not take long for this sort of ego-massage to become an end in itself and lose contact with the corporate goals, if not with all reality.

Having said that, within *any* project there tends to be an element of 'process' consulting and it is a valid one. The client has to be led either to come up with the answer for himself or at least to feel a real engagement with your answers. The best technical results are useless unless the client can and will implement them. Conversely, if your results go in the bin because you have managed to get the Board to think of a far better strategy than your own, the project has surely been a success. It's just a pity that you won't get paid.

Clearing internal obstacles and resistance

Another aspect of the internal role is clearing blockages, both to the flow of information and to the carrying of decisions into action.

Organisations are networks of people and people are both brilliant and appalling communicators. Invariably, the informal network is far more effective than the formal hierarchy at disseminating information. People can be filters: they let certain things through but stop other elements from being passed on. Just what they filter out may be determined consciously or unconsciously, for political reasons, selfish reasons, altruistic reasons or no reason at all. Whatever the reasoning, the upshot is that the information reaching senior management may bear as little resemblance to the true message as in a game of Chinese Whispers.

What can the cons do? I think it would be an exaggeration to suggest that they can fix this problem or circumvent it entirely. They can help, though, by:

- Having the time to talk to people in the organisation.

- Being seen as – relatively – neutral.

- Having the courage to ask awkward questions.

- Having no particular motive to keep what they uncover from senior management.

At the same time, it would be no bad thing if some organisations tried to free up their own channels of communication rather than relying on outsiders to do it for them. If senior management does not get to hear what is going on below, may not some of the blame lie with them for not taking the trouble to listen?

I was working on a project for a software developer which had staked a lot of future hopes on moving from commercial to consumer applications. For no particular reason, I dropped in on a few shops selling the new products and discovered that they were perceived as complete 'no-hopers' by the retailers. Returning to the client's office, I started asking awkward questions of the Sales Manager and found that he was well aware of the true position but had been keeping it from the senior management in order to build up his own empire. In half a morning I learned more about the client's sales and marketing strategy than the Managing Director had ever managed to uncover.

It can also help (although it was not the case in my work for this software firm) if the cons have some experience of the client's industry. This may, to be blunt, be rather more than the top man or woman has. It can be difficult to call the bluff of those lower down the hierarchy when they are able to run rings round you technically.

If consultants can help get information moving upwards in an organisation, they can also have an important role in freeing up the blockages and inertia that impede change. Sometimes they do this just by the process of asking questions and challenging assumptions. At other times it may be a formal process of workshops and presentations to staff. Or it can be a matter of laying out choices more starkly than the client has been used to, challenging managers either to put up or shut up.

At the limit, cons can and do identify individuals who are blocking change and (directly or indirectly) have them removed. The Sales Manager in the software company lost his job. I have more than once seen IT directors shown the door when they failed to deliver the systems to implement a project for which cons were responsible. On the other hand, I fought very hard (and successfully) to save a Divisional Director in another company who was being portrayed by some as an obstacle to change simply because he was given to asking awkward questions. Being independent is not the same as sitting on the fence.

Communicating and persuading

Most cons are great wordsmiths. They sell their services through written and verbal presentations. They deliver their results in reports and meetings. At worst, they can seem lost without an overhead projector and a set of slides (or, increasingly, without the presentation package on their Tosh). They are experienced communicators and it is a skill which can be put to good use for their clients.

Meetings, workshops, brainstorming . . . The terms vary, but the business of getting a small group around a table to receive and review information is basic to the way most organisations work. It can be fundamental at various stages of a project: to collect data, to review options and initial findings, to hear results. When a decision has been taken and needs to be communicated as widely as possible to the organisation, the cons may still be there; talking through their results, explaining, selling, persuading.

One of the best experiences of my consulting career was presenting a strategy to a so-called 'workshop' at which the client had assembled forty or fifty managers, including handfuls of Vice-Presidents most of whom had flown the Atlantic for the occasion. Our case was reasonably sound, although it had been put together in a great hurry, and I went out on the floor to sell it to an audience who were both accustomed and encouraged to interrupt and challenge. They bought the strategy, a decision which led to the investment of well over $100 million. But the feeling of satisfaction that it gave me had less to do with the amount at stake than with the sheer hands-on thrill of knowing that I was leading a major business to think deeply and choose a path for the future.

At the other end of the satisfaction scale, I went to discuss my final recommendations with another client, a major Hungarian utility. I had become used to working through interpreters and expected the usual group of perhaps twenty of the client's people. Instead, I found myself sitting in a hall the size of a theatre, trying to understand over headphones, via the interpreter, questions raised by some two hundred representatives of the shopfloor unions and others. Again I felt that we had a good, if sketchy, case. The problem (both for myself and, I do not doubt, for the client) was how to get real communication going in an environment which was more sterile than hostile. I will not pretend that the result was a complete success.

Managing the project

The final good reason for using consultants spans the boundary between internal and external roles. Whatever the scope of a change programme, however internally- or externally-focused the work may be, it is always essential to manage the project. Far too often clients fail to give this element the attention it deserves.

Managing a project includes:

- Setting, and then keeping up to date, a plan of the key elements and how they interrelate.

- Agreeing timescales and deadlines for tasks, reviewing their completion and taking action where necessary to bring them back into line.

- Ensuring that all the individuals, departments or organisations involved in the project understand their tasks and how they relate to those of everyone else.

- Monitoring their progress towards completing what they have to do.

- Matching resources of all kinds to the work which has to be done.

This is a very simple overview of what can be a complex job. I am not suggesting that the cons should be left to manage themselves (although I have known this to happen). What cons can do is provide project management for the overall change programme, within which their own work may be only a small part. Indeed, they may have no involvement at all other than as project managers. At this level, project management skills become another form of external resource brought in for a defined purpose.

I personally believe that project management is one of the most
valuable of all forms of consultancy. We used to tell our clients that
there is a big difference between the day-to-day management of a
company or an operation and the management of a programme
designed to change the way things are done. Major projects or
programmes, by their nature, are finite and exceptional. Professional
project managers can make a substantial contribution to their success.
I have known cons manage projects of all sizes, including the digging
of a new coal mine. The consultants involved knew little about
mining (when they started, at any rate) but a great deal about running
a project. Which is the point.

It also returns me to where I started this discussion of the good
reasons for using consultants. One of the first reasons I suggested was
that adding appropriate resource can accelerate a client's project or
ensure that a tight schedule is met. Likewise, one of the goals of
project management is always to manage the programme to time
deadlines, often tight ones.

There are plenty of poor projects that dribble on indefinitely and
never seem to deliver. If your consultancy project is like that it may be
because you are doing it for the wrong reason, because you are
managing it poorly or because you have the wrong team on the job.
Choosing the team is the topic of the next chapter.

External and internal roles
I opened this chapter with some discussion of that high-sounding
term, *paradigm*. Let me summarise by using another grand word,
contingency. This one I picked up on an MBA programme where it was
about the only thing I can remember from many an hour spent study-
ing theories of leadership. There is even an entire contingency theory
of organisational design which, to my mind, has a lot going for it. It
states that there is no 'right' structure for an organisation, no absolute
model (or, dare I say, paradigm), but that it all depends on circumstances. Which is what contingency means.

Applied to consultancy, the same logic would lead us simply to
conclude that there is no 'right' reason for bringing in cons and that it
all depends on the situation. While undoubtedly true, this is not a

very interesting analysis. More useful is to say that different types of consulting input are appropriate to differing situations.

Figure 2.4 summarises at least some of the alternatives:

Figure 2.4: The nature of consultancy input

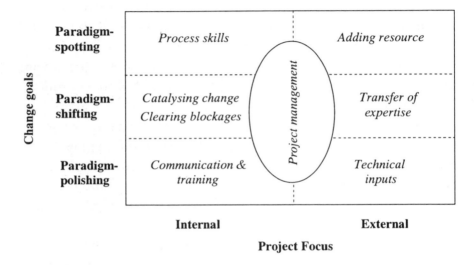

Organisations searching for a *new* paradigm may well already know much of the answer: their need is to face up to what they know, listen to the ideas already within the business and analyse them creatively. In this situation, the process skills which cons may bring with them can help the client develop its own *internal* vision for the future. At the same time, additional *external* resource may be needed to gather data from outside sources, analyse the market or the competition and focus the whole creative process.

When the emphasis lies on paradigm-shifting, the *external* input of experience and expertise from other organisations or industries becomes valuable. Equally or more significant, however, may be an *internal* focus on clearing away the blockages which prevent effective communication or stifle initiatives. All textbooks refer to the importance of top-level commitment; where the cons may contribute is in helping to bridge the gap between this commitment and its translation into action throughout the organisation.

At the level of paradigm-polishing, technical inputs may dominate as the cons are called in to sweat the last fractions of a per cent from manufacturing efficiency or to fine tune the sales strategy. Alongside this injection of *external* expertise, *internal* communication and training come to the fore especially where new methods or new technology will be deployed to improve the day to day running of the client.

Finally, across all of these types of consultancy input lies the coordinating role of project management. This binds together both internal and external elements of the change process.

The role of the cons will *always* be contingent, which means that there are bound to be many grey areas in the simple categorisation depicted above. There are times when technical inputs are needed to assist the search for a new paradigm and occasions when every kind of process facilitation may be needed to build the internal team charged with polishing the existing paradigm. The model depicted in Figure 2.4 will, however, be useful if it leads prospective clients to ask themselves three basic questions:

- What sort of change am I trying to achieve in my organisation?

- What do I need to happen if the knowledge, expertise and skills of my own people are to be used to best effect in this process of change?

- What do I need from outside because I cannot find it inside my organisation?

If you can answer these questions, you are well on the way to having a good reason for using – or for deciding *not* to use – consultants.

CHAPTER 3: CONSULTANCY TYPES AND HOW TO RECOGNISE THEM

I SAID IN THE *INTRODUCTION* THAT BUYING CONSULTANCY IS MADE DIFFICULT by the fact that there is little to be learned from visual inspection of the product. One consultancy's re-engineering methodology looks much like the next. Every con has a CV stuffed with impressive-sounding references. All those bidding for your project will probably put forward a superficially similar approach depicted on a presentation slide as a series of little boxes joined by arrows. So how *do* you choose? At the end of the day, many clients do little more than select a team or individual that they feel happy with and then simply hope for the best.

Fortunately, this is a more sensible approach than it may sound. Consultancy is, to an almost unique degree, a 'people' business. If you are buying a car, you may be influenced favourably or otherwise by the salesman but you are not, thankfully, buying *him*. Even in most service businesses, although the quality of the people is an important consideration, it is only one element in a broader package. Your bank manager may be the friendliest on earth and have a string of impressive qualifications to her name, but if the cash machine keeps breaking down you are likely to take your business elsewhere.

In consultancy, however, at least 90% of the quality of the product that you get depends purely and simply on the quality of the consultants themselves.

The previous chapter discussed what clients may hope to gain from a consultancy project and the issues which, if you are in this position, you should consider before going any further. Having sorted out the answers in your own mind it is as well to commit to paper the requirements that will govern your discussions with potential consultants and, subject to any final amendments, the proposals that they will then make. Once this is done you can start on the round of meetings and presentations which will lead you to decide which cons to work with. This is the point at which you will start to get a feel for them as individuals.

If the job is a technical one, you can almost take it for granted that by the time you get to proposal stage the consultancy presenting to you will have the technical tools (computer packages, simulation tools, modelling software or whatever) required to undertake it. Were this not the case, they would probably not have been bidding in the first place or you would have disqualified them already.

For projects of a less technical and more strategic nature, you can probably assume that all of the bidders will have done their homework on your industry and your company, as well as demonstrating a deep mastery of bullshit in all its forms. They will all have near-identical MBAs from Harvard or other top schools and familiarity with the process of advising the Boards of blue-chip companies, none of whom they can mention as their experience is far too confidential to divulge.

In both of these cases the difference between competing proposals will often have little to do with technical merit and a great deal to do with the personalities involved. If the consultancy brief is primarily a 'process' role (that is, the consultants are to spend a lot of time holding your hand and trying to make intelligent contributions to other people's conversations) then personality and chemistry are even more fundamental. Achieving a good fit between the cons and your organisation's culture becomes vital to success. This is one reason, incidentally, why it is hard for cons to work effectively in countries where they have not grown up or at least spent many years. For instance, American consultants and French business culture tend to be incompatible.

So, by the time you reach a shortlist of cons, the choice should be simple: go for the people who seem to fit with your organisation and in whom you have the most confidence. Easy, right?

Unfortunately not. What you see is not always what you get. Clients often fail to assess correctly the personal characteristics of consultants or may be persuaded by the lure of a glitzy product to ignore the importance of the human factor. Three reasons why clients may find it hard to pick out the good guys from the injuns are:

• Consultants – thinking, rightly or wrongly, that this is what clients want – have a dreadful habit of dressing up their services in terms of methodologies, programmes, approaches, critical paths, milestones, solutions, models, databases . . . In short, everything under the sun rather than simply saying, 'Look, what you are getting is twenty days of *me*. How about it?'

• The cons that you meet may not be the ones who are going to do the work. This is probably one of the commonest complaints that one hears about consultants. It is hard to see why it should be such a stumbling block. For starters, have a bit of common sense: if the guy's card says he's a Partner (or, even better, a Senior Partner) then it's not very likely that he'll be the one interviewing your plant foremen, is it? Secondly, if you want to meet the people who will be doing the job then why not *ask* to do just that before you take your decision? I can never remember such a request being refused. But then I can hardly remember such a request being made.

• Clients often fail to see through or beyond the mask worn by any con who is a real pro. One of our project managers was once asked by a client whether the 10% fee proposed by a contractor was reasonable or whether they should try to get him down to – say – 5%. The consultant (who had no more idea than if you had asked him for the molecular composition of DNA) looked the client straight in the eye, pursed his lips, and said simply: 'In my experience, you could be looking for something around seven and a half per cent.' And the client team lapped it up. Why? Because they had fallen for the consultant's image as an expert in all things and had failed to look beyond it at the real person or question his experience.

There are various types of con and, in the sections which follow, I describe (if not entirely seriously) at least some of the commoner ones. If you know the characters that consultancy attracts, you will be better prepared when you meet them and that gives you at least a fighting chance of seeing through the bullshit that they may throw at you. So here is a brief ornithology of that queer bird, the management consultant.

Type 1: The Suit

Habitat. Frequently seen at initial meetings, proposal presentations and kick-off sessions. Seldom spotted during the thick of the consultancy work. Some sub-species pop up at final presentations and workshop sessions, in the hope of spotting some more fat worms to gobble up (known as 'extension work').

Key characteristics. Smart appearance, loud voice, good eye contact. Many male specimens in their middle years like to sport boyish haircuts to prop up their self-impression as youthful go-getters. The female of the species has helped to define the concept of power dressing. Whatever the sex, the briefcase is always thin and may contain little more than a mobile phone (strangely, never switched on if you try to call it). That is one thing more than their heads may hold.

Social behaviour. The species dislikes hunting alone, and is usually seen accompanied by other types such as the Guru, the Slave or the Controller, all of whom will be introduced shortly. Two or more Suits together is a frightening sight and likely to end in violence since they seldom cooperate with each other. Clients faced with a brace of the species are therefore advised to stand back and wait for the dust to settle before taking further action.

Treatment. On the whole, the Suit is best just ignored but this advice can be hard to follow. They have a way of imposing themselves on the conversation and can be aggressive: the worst cases are those whose early years were spent with IBM, as they may refuse to leave your office until you have signed something. The best strategy for dealing with troublesome Suits is to ask direct questions about the technical aspects of the proposed job and then, as they turn to pass the question to their bag-carrier, to insist 'Excuse me, I didn't ask him: I want *you* to answer.' Repeat treatment is seldom necessary.

Type 2: The Thought-Leader

Identification. This can be tricky, as the Thought-Leader is easily confused at first sight with the Suit. Appearance can be similar, and Thought-Leaders also prefer the sunny regions of sales meetings and initial presentations to the cooler climes of real work. However, this species is most likely to appear on conference platforms as it is very inclined to public display. It seems little bothered whether it is alone or in a group, as in all situations it continues to sing almost without pausing for breath. Their methods of reproduction are uncertain, since they do not appear to need a mate in order to reach orgasm.

Call. As mentioned, the species is best known for its singing. It gets its name from the characteristic refrain: 'We are the thought-leaders in . . .' The precise subject is unimportant, as Thought-Leaders are infinitely wise in all matters. Given the opportunity, they will tell you everything about your business, your mission statement and your wife. They know everything that there is to be known, and they are absolutely hellbent on telling you. They punctuate their song with TLAs (three-letter abbreviations) and consultancy-speak of all kinds, often accompanied by much waving of arms or the use of many pages of flipchart.

Defensive measures. Patience is no defence against this type: they can keep up their ritual display indefinitely and will wear down the stoutest listener. Nor is challenging them advisable, as it is liable to prolong the agony. Feigning death has been known, eventually, to encourage them to leave. In the shorter term, flight may be the only option: if you suspect that you may have let a Thought-Leader into your office, arrange for your secretary to call you at a predetermined time to 'remind' you that you are due on Concorde or that the Prime Minister of Luxembourg is expecting you. A more subtle technique may be deployed if the Thought-Leader is accompanied by his own colleagues: you can bet that they will be even more sick of hearing his voice than you are, and with some negotiation you may be able to persuade them to remove the battery from his pacemaker.

Type 3: The Guru

Population. Far less numerous than is often assumed. In common parlance, 'guru' is sometimes treated as a synonym for consultant. However, relatively few cons have the real in-depth knowledge that distinguishes the true Guru. It is argued by some watchers that the Guru is an endangered species, since the bird's habitat has often been taken over by flashier species. Moreover, its expertise is seldom matched with the communication and selling skills needed to survive in the consultancy jungle, and for this reason the life expectancy of the Guru in larger firms can be limited. Most eke out a precarious existence on the fringes of the business. For some reason, the female form is virtually unknown.

Plumage. Not a pretty sight. In the information technology area, Gurus are often seen in beards and sandals. Elsewhere their plumage is disfigured by moulting (dandruff on the collar is an immediate sign of the true Guru) and by ties in the worst possible taste. Some have been reported in Hush Puppies.

Behaviour. Gurus should never be confused with Thought-Leaders, as their interactions with clients are totally opposite. Unlike the Thought-Leader, who is keen to display his knowledge but has little, the Guru has a wealth of knowledge but it will have to be teased out of him. They seldom make a good presentation, having a tendency to ramble incoherently, and rarely put forward clear recommendations in reports, being much too ready to see all possible sides of every argument. A common problem is analysis-paralysis, in which vast amounts of data are requested from the client and then appear to sink into a black hole.

Control. For all his faults, the Guru may just have the knowledge or ideas that you need. What you must *never* do is allow him to run the project, as this is a recipe for hazy objectives, slipped deadlines and – at worst – failure to produce any results at all. Having spotted a Guru it is worth keeping him on the project team, but try to ensure that his role is stated to be that of quality controller or technical reviewer, rather than one where success or failure of the job is down to him. And never, never allow him to talk to your Chief Exec or your Board, where his failure to put across his ideas may embarrass you far more than it will worry him.

Type 4: The Controller

Origin of the Species. The subject of considerable scientific debate. Most consultancy types can be traced back to proto-ancestral fossils of the Small Firm era. Thus, the Suit is an adaptation of the Founder-Owner to the new ecology of the big consulting practices, in which entrepreneurial skills have ceased to be valued as highly as bright plumage. Similarly, the Old Hand (see Type 9) is a clear hang-over from this earlier age. No known ancestor of the Controller has yet been discovered, however, in Small Firm strata. The most likely suggestion is that the species migrated in from the jungles of industry, at a relatively late date. This would appear to be confirmed by the irregular dispersion of the type: in some large firms it has scarcely been sighted, while others appear to have been overrun by Controllers. For more details on what happens in large firms with no or very few Controllers, see Chapter 10 for an explanation of why so many management consultancies cannot manage their own business.

Domestication. When domesticated, the Controller is highly valued. Often, he or she may be the only con on the team who actually tries to organise the work and who retains any recollection of the original terms of reference. The best of them will certainly prove very useful in ensuring that the rest of the team keeps moving in the direction of the defined objectives. Key features which enable you to recognise Controllers include their readiness to agree the dates of meetings more than two days in advance, their frequent use of Gantt charts, checklists, formal minutes and other documentation, and their impatience with most other members of their own team (including Suits, Thought-Leaders and Gurus). *Warning*: do not assume that the consulting team includes a Controller unless you have specific evidence to this effect. As mentioned, they are sometimes in very short supply.

Pest Control. Given the value of this species, readers may be surprised to know that they may also be pests. Some firms appear to have suffered from a population explosion of Controllers, and any con who appears brandishing a thick methodology (particularly one in several volumes) should be treated with suspicion as this may be evidence of a widespread outbreak of standardisation. At a more local level, individual Controllers can become aggressive and turn on their clients. A useful diagnostic tool is to review one of their lists of action points: if the client has been tasked with more actions than the consultant, proceed with care.

Overall Assessment. Every project should have one. I stress, *one.*

Type 5: The Slave

Habitat. There are relatively few species of cons that regularly inhabit clients' premises (other exceptions being Team Players and Grunts, but even for them it is not necessarily their preferred habitat). The Slave feels lost when not on-site. Moreover, it is not sufficient to the Slave simply to be in the client's building: he or she prefers to be in the client's own office, and is never happier than when sitting within touching distance at the client's own desk. Unconfirmed reports suggest that they may attempt to stow away in the client's car, but earlier scare stories of them being found in the back of wardrobes at the client's home are probably the result of media overreaction.

Call. The call of, 'Oh, you're *so* right' is one of the easiest ways of spotting a Slave, even at the first encounter.

Behaviour. Slaves have a number of characteristics which can make them useful:

- They never say no. This can be handy if you wish to pass responsibility for something difficult onto the cons. On the other hand, it is most unlikely that the Slave will actually deliver what has been promised.

- They produce the 'right' answer. As long as you take sufficient care to supply them with the answer that you require, they are thoroughly reliable in delivering it back to you (or to the Chairman).

- They pass the time nicely. If you have an empty diary, a Slave is a godsend since they have an inexhaustible appetite for meetings, reviews, workshops, brainstormings, briefing sessions or plain conversation. Just don't expect them to go away or add any discernible value.

Treatment. Slaves do not need treatment, but their clients may. If the species did not exist, someone would have to invent it since there are clients who need Slaves like an aging rock star needs groupies. Despite rumours to the contrary, such clients are not limited to the public sector, although it is certainly a favoured environment for them. Clients and their Slaves live in happy symbiosis: the client cannot understand how he or she ever managed without the help of the con, while the Slave's boss is ecstatic as the fees roll steadily into the firm. Watching it happen will probably make you feel distinctly queasy. But who asked your opinion?

Type 6: The Team Player

Population Distribution. The distribution of Team Players in the consultancy business is known to be irregular, but the unshowy nature of this species means that few detailed studies have been carried out. What can be said with confidence is that they are seldom found at senior levels in the pecking order, and it appears that many young individuals are either driven from the flock or voluntarily move to other habitats more congenial to them. Most big consultancies are dog-eat-dog environments where Team Players struggle to survive.

Behaviour. The Team Player's lack of success may at first seem surprising, given that cons habitually work in teams. However, Team Players exhibit behavioural characteristics which are very useful to clients but are seldom highly valued within their own firms:

The Team Player:	*The successful con:*
☺ helps his colleagues, even without charging his time to their client, and shares his knowledge freely with them;	☻ zealously guards his own expertise and makes damn sure he gets the credit for any input he gives to a project;
☺ passes on sales leads to his colleagues or juniors, when they are better qualified for the job than he or she is;	☻ grabs any and every opportunity for him or herself, regardless of the fact that someone else could do it better;
☺ makes sure that everyone is kept briefed, that the project administration is done and the papers get filed.	☻ is far too busy to waste time on mundane tasks like communication, and leaves everyone else to clear up the mess he or she leaves behind.

In short, *rara avis*.

How to catch one. This is a problem. The Team Player's behaviour may be rather handy for clients but, as mentioned, there are not always a lot of them about in the consulting game. You might just strike lucky with the old 'keep 'em dangling' routine, which goes like this. You call in some cons for a preliminary meeting and ask them to write a proposal. When you have got it, you ignore their follow-up calls for at least three weeks, after which you phone them, say that the project is now really urgent, and get them to come in the next day. At the meeting you ask for a revised proposal and start the process all over again. By the time you have been through the loop three times, the Suits and the Thought-Leaders will have lost interest and looked around for someone else in their organisation prepared to put up with the hassle. **That** could be the Team Player.

On the other hand, it might just be some dumb Grunt who happened to be standing around the office that day.

Type 7: The Grunt

Identification. Old reports speak of this species being identifiable by the ink-stains on their fingers or their frayed cuffs. Evolution of the species has meant that now they are best spotted by the portable computer that they carry around with them. Not one of those trendy notebooks, nor even a slimline Tosh, as these are all likely to have been snapped up by higher forms of life. The Grunt hauls around a portable the size of a suitcase, which is all that was left.

Domestication. Fortunately, the Grunt is a docile and predictable creature and no further domestication is necessary. In 'Big Six' firms, many of the Grunts have migrated into consulting from the audit department, and they are usually so pathetically grateful for being allowed out that they will do anything to please. Stand on street corners conducting market research? No problem. Add up a ten thousand record database by hand? Yes, please. Proofread a *Quality Manual*? OK, even Grunts have their limits.

Treatment. If treated reasonably, Grunts will last for years. They do not like to be exposed to high ambient noise levels, being happiest when they are parked in a quiet corner to get on with a spreadsheet. Nor do they respond well to fellow cons or clients moving the goalposts just when they have got everything nicely formatted. The safest bet is just to ignore them. Everyone else does.

Type 8: The Clone

Key characteristics. The larger consultancies have developed the technology to produce Clones of standardised appearance and behaviour. Their characteristics are well documented in the *House-Style Manual* which each firm produces, although some academics still argue as to whether these manuals are the cause or the result of the cloning process (see Zob & Braguette's seminal article: 'Which came first, the landscape format or the bullet point?'). The strange feature of these Clones is that, taken individually, they appear totally normal and, indeed, they may even exhibit a strong streak of individualism. However, when placed together, they turn a uniform shade of grey and become quite indistinguishable one from another. They are also risk-averse and shun confrontation. No matter how bad your business may be, a Clone will always report that 'there are opportunities for improvement' rather than simply saying that your product stinks, your sales-force would not know an opportunity if it bit them and the Plant Manager is smashed out of his brain at ten o'clock in the morning.

Evolutionary note. During the Middle Privatisation period (approximately 1985-88), the population of cons in the UK grew rapidly, due primarily to the warm moist currents of the Public Sector drift. The period was marked also by the spreading of spores from the larger forests of the American continent, leading to the sudden flourishing of alien species in unexpected locations and interbreeding between the cultures of the Old and New Worlds. It was left to natural selection to make sense of these anarchic genetic mutations. As groups of cons coalesced into larger and larger units, certain DNA became dominant within each until standard Clones emerged. In some colonies, it is only among the lowest ranks that Clones are to be found (c.f. worker bees) but in other cases the queen is surrounded by an elite Partnership of Clones. This serious shortage of fresh genetic material at the top may pose a threat to the continued existence of the hive.

Response. The presence of Clones can be detected quite easily at the proposal stage, if the cons bidding for the work are asked to put on a formal presentation at which all team members are expected to speak. Under these circumstances, if the firm has been contaminated by Cloning, it will be impossible to tell one team member from another. However, this should not be grounds for automatic disqualification. Clone infestation causes no overt damage to the healthy project, at least in the early stages. It may first be noticed if the work calls for the generation of a number of scenarios, when the various options may be found to be relatively unimaginative. At worst, in fact, there may only be a single scenario put forward for consideration, and this will be as uncontroversial as possible. For these reasons, Clones are ideally suited to public-sector projects where their ability to produce lengthy reports, guaranteed to offend no one, makes them ideal for the task. Horses for courses.

Type 9: The Old Hand

Population. Virtually extinct in the larger firms, but holding up in self-employment or smaller consultancies. Certain corners of the consultancy jungle still afford a comfortable living to Old Hands, in niches sufficiently unglamorous to deter the brighter species. They are often to be found with their shirtsleeves rolled up, on projects to do with trucks and tachographs, or plant maintenance, or work study, or security. Just what these things have to do with consultancy is lost on most other species of con, but the Old Hands have been doing them for the last forty years and they will doubtless carry on for the next forty. Good luck to them.

Plumage. Not for them the Armani or YSL favoured by Suits and Thought Leaders, nor the uniform grey of the Clones. Not even the Oxfam jacket and corduroy trousers of the true Guru. No, these are the blue suit boys. Nice, practical, navy with a preference for man-made fabrics. Old Hands are often mistaken for retired police officers. In fact, some of them *are* retired police officers.

Uses. Good, steady cons for good, steady jobs. Stick to their area of knowledge and they will give you a decent answer (the same decent answer that they have been doling out for years). Stray from it and they will make no secret of their unease. Old Hands are the only consultancy type incapable of bullshitting, which is one reason why very few are employed by large consultancies. Another is their unwillingness to work after 5.30. Perhaps, after all, the rest of the profession could learn something from them.

Type 10: What you really wanted

I have been known to feel sorry for clients. No, not often, of course: mostly, cons are too busy trying to extract work, data or money from their clients to worry about their finer feelings. But sometimes. It usually happens when a prospective client decides to invite bids from a number of consultancies and to have each of them present its proposals. It is midday, you are the third firm that they have seen this morning and there are two more to come after lunch. Faced with this beauty parade of pro after con, the luckless purchaser's eyes are glazing over. In these circumstances the client will have long since ceased to remember what it was that she really wanted.

If you find yourself as the client in that situation, forget about the project plan and the technical references and focus on the consultants as individuals. Ask yourself what sort of person you really want to work with on this job. What kind of skills will it take: not the technical skills but the *personal* ones? Do the consultants you are talking to have those skills? Do you respect them as individuals and how will others in your organisation react to them?

The trouble is, of course, that what you really wanted was a con with the brain of a Guru, the slickness of a Suit, the perseverance of a Grunt, the organisation of a Controller and the comfort rating of an Old Hand. I'm not sure that even Sir John Harvey-Jones could lay claim to that lot. So try to come up with a list of priorities, and then stick to them.

Never lose sight of the simple truth which I stated at the start of this chapter: consultancy is a 'people' business and what you get out of it depends on the calibre of those assigned to your job. Be very cautious in making assumptions about the team or its individual members. The fact that the consulting firm has undertaken several similar jobs to the one they are proposing for you does not mean that the *individuals* on the team have ever done a piece of work of this kind. The fact that they know the right buzz-words or the jargon of your industry does not prove that they have in-depth knowledge of it. The fact that someone has a fee rate of £2,000 ($3,000) per day does not make her the world expert in *your* problem.

It is important not only that the cons should have what it takes as individuals but that they should work together effectively as a team with each other and with your staff or colleagues. Try asking yourself the following questions about how they might fit into your project:

- Who is going to *manage* the day-to-day work? Do they have the right experience for this? More importantly, do they have the organisational ability and attention to detail which the role demands? A lot of cons can come up with bright ideas or an interesting model, but by no means all can be relied upon to tie up all the loose ends and make sure the job gets finished.

- Who is going to provide the necessary *inputs and ideas*? Do they have the knowledge base and the intellectual capability that this may demand? Can they show evidence of original thinking? Do you need someone who is creative or simply a good technician? How does this need match to the personalities on offer?

- Who is going to *interact* with your own staff, and at what level? Do you feel that their personality is right to enable them to build an appropriate relationship with your people and to find their way around your organisation? Particularly if they have to deal with senior management, they may need negotiating and political skills of a high order.

- Who is going to do the *donkey-work*, whether that means data collection, administering questionnaires or observation of the yard at 3.00 a.m. on a winter's night? Is there sufficient resource of this kind to ensure that the job will be done at the necessary level of detail? It is all very well staffing a job with senior cons but that is a very expensive (and possibly ineffective) way of trawling through five years of accounting data or undertaking a telephone survey of a thousand customers.

- Who will assure the *quality* of the job, adjudicate between conflicting ideas and sort out any problems that may arise along the way? Cons can get carried away with what may seem like a bright idea, or latch too rapidly onto a particular solution, and may need someone to pull them back. Any job, however small, needs an element of quality assurance to be provided by someone not directly involved in the work.

- Who will drive the team to get *results* and, if appropriate, be required to convince your boss, your colleagues or the Board that the solution is the right one? Do they have the energy and the weight of personality to do this effectively, meeting any objections that are raised? Do they have the integrity to tell the truth even if it is unpalatable?

These questions do not imply that there has to be a different con for each bullet point. The important thing is that the *roles* must be covered, even if the same person performs several or even all of them. Some roles may be performed by the client himself, in which case this needs to be explicitly agreed. On large projects, with big teams, there is more opportunity (and, indeed, a requirement) for specialisation in the roles that team members play but the internal chemistry of the team becomes critical. On a small project there may be only a single con although usually there will be at least a quality controller of some kind in the background. In this situation, the personality of the individual is particularly important, since she will have to perform so many roles.

Consultants are only human. You are used to judging your staff by what they actually achieve, not by the noise they make; you try to assess potential recruits in accordance with their real talents and not just what they claim on a CV; you have seen through your boss' little games a hundred and one times. You can and should assess cons as individuals in exactly the same way as you assess your own people. Never let a superficial flashiness blind you to what human instinct will probably tell you.

While the informal approach may be sufficient, it could be useful on large jobs to make a more formal assessment of the characteristics of the proposed team members. The inventory' devised by Meredith Belbin is one of the best-known tests for determining the roles that individuals play in teams and ensuring that the blend is right. In cases where the job is to be staffed jointly by cons and client personnel, the use of this or similar techniques should be considered seriously.

Finally, do not think that you have always to live with what you are given. If, after the first meeting or halfway through the analysis, you decide that the senior con on your project is not right for you, then say so. You do not have to put up with Suits and Slaves, and if the project needs a Controller then demand one. There are plenty of ways of saving face, if that is what either you or the cons feel you must do in making the changes. But there is only one way of getting a good result from a project and that is to have the right people on it.

CHAPTER 4: HOW MUCH DID YOU SAY IT WILL COST?

THE ONE THING THAT *EVERYONE KNOWS* ABOUT MANAGEMENT CONSULTANTS, by some kind of received wisdom or simple osmosis, is that they are violently expensive. To have any dealings with cons, the belief goes, is to risk the loss of at least one arm and one leg. Consultancy fees are supposed to clock up like the fare on a London taxi stuck on the M6 somewhere between Heathrow Airport and Marble Arch via Shakespeare's Birthplace, or one of those Tom and Jerry cartoons where Tom the cat gets metamorphosed into a petrol pump with spinning numbers in place of his eyes. In short, only those with a dumper truck full of used notes should even *think* about consultancy.

Like all popular myths, this one has a grain of truth behind it. Well, actually, more like a watermelon than a grain but, for all that, it is not the whole story.

No one can pretend that major consultancy support comes cheap:

- *Any* consultancy project of a more than trivial nature, by a big-name firm, will run up fees into five figures of pounds: say £20,000 ($30,000) just to give them a reasonable start at whatever the problem is.

- A piece of work of some substance, running over perhaps six weeks or a couple of months, is likely to have a price tag of several tens of thousands of pounds: say £50,000 or $75,000.

- Large scale projects, involving a team of several consultants more or less full-time for a few months, will certainly take you into hundreds of thousands of pounds.

- Major involvement with a top-flight strategy consultancy, or long-term re-engineering or change management projects using other big-name firms, can set you back *millions* of pounds or dollars in fees.

I have done jobs for as little as a couple of thousand pounds and I have worked on a number of assignments where the total billed to the client, admittedly over a series of connected projects, was several million. I am not talking about blue-sky strategy assignments which usually command top rates. For this sort of money, from the kind of operational consulting in which I was involved, the client received very substantial deliverables.

What matters in using consultants is not whether they are 'expensive' (whatever that means) but what you get for your money. To use a solicitor to help you buy a house may be 'expensive' but, if that lawyer saves you from buying a faulty lease or inadequate title, you will consider it money well spent. To equip your factory with the latest robotic welders is 'expensive' but what the shareholders want to see is a return on their investment. Consultancy should be seen as an investment in exactly the same way.

In suggesting this, I am not seeking to distract attention from the cost but to highlight the need for clients to review the potential benefits of a project, compare them to the costs of running it either in-house or using cons, and continually monitor the evolution of both costs and benefits as the work progresses. All of this is basic stuff which would apply to any investment: consultancy is no different.

Figure 4.1 shows that the clients in my survey were much less impressed by the value for money they received than cons seemed to think they should be. This may not be terribly surprising but cons need to be concerned that almost a quarter of clients felt that their work gave poor value for money.

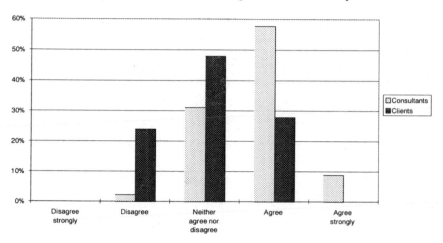

Figure 4.1: 'Consultants are good value for money'

In this chapter I aim to do three things. Firstly, I take a look at how consultants come up with a fee estimate for a project and the signals that this estimate gives to the client about the job and its value. Secondly, I try to explain why consultancy work costs as much as it does and the ways in which cons themselves have tried to deliver more bangs for the client's buck. This introduces some fundamental issues about the nature of consultancy and how it should be managed, which I will come back to later in this book. Lastly, I review the different ways in which cons can structure their fees, the advantages and drawbacks of these approaches to the client, and what clients themselves may do to reduce the cost of the support that they need.

It's worth what you pay for it

I gave above some benchmark figures for what a consultancy project might cost. These, by their very nature, are rough and ready. Moreover, I have no doubt that some cons will read them and start tut-tutting at the figures I have quoted. Those at one end of the scale may be appalled that I have even suggested that any decent job could cost less than $1 million. At the other end of the spectrum, freelance cons or those working in small firms may be thinking ruefully of all the times they have given their clients high-quality results and immediate cost-saving opportunities for less than £10,000. What this goes to show is that, in consultancy as in any other business, there is a 'going rate' for the job concerned and this rate varies across different sorts of work and different sizes of firm.

How do you, as a consultant, decide how much to bid to your client for a particular job? I am assuming for now that you are bidding on a fixed-fee basis: this is by no means universal and I will come back to the alternatives shortly.

With a fixed price job there are two ways of coming up with the price and the two overlap:

- What may be called the *reductionist* approach starts with a detailed project plan that breaks the assignment down into tasks. You decide how many cons are to work on it, then estimate the number of days of work for each con in each element of the plan. Adding these up gives you the total days that each member of the team will require on the job. You multiply the days by the billing rate which the firm has set for each grade of staff and out pops the total cost. All perfectly rational.

- The second way could be termed *holistic* which is a smart word for sticking your finger in the wind. It requires rather less time and arithmetic than method one. You take a metaphorical step back from the proposal, think about the client, the job and the deliverables and say, 'That feels like a bit less than a £50,000 assignment' or, 'I wouldn't pay more than 150k for this one.' In short, you are deciding what the price should be, based on similar projects that you have done and a subjective feel for the 'going rate'. Experience counts for a lot in this.

Usually, my experience was that the bottom-up calculator-crunching and the top-down tooth-sucking came out reasonably close to each other, although usually the former was a little dearer than the latter. A kind of well-oiled ritual used to go on in the Partner's office, as we cut down the days which we had estimated in order to fit them to our sense of what the client would bear.

Sometimes you can get this horribly wrong. You may overplay your hand and come up with a number which is twice the client's budget. You may err in the opposite direction and leave yourself with a woefully inadequate number of days to complete the job. Or you may find that your idea of the going rate is just totally out of step with the client's.

I recall visiting a knitwear importer in London's West End who had built up a business with an annual turnover of tens of millions of pounds. This was earned by buying garments speculatively in the Far East, importing them into stock in the UK, then reselling after the season was underway to a number of big name chain stores who might or might not need top-up merchandise to supplement their own pre-season purchasing.

Just describing the business in this way indicates that it was based on relatively risky trading in which the owner's 'nose' for a deal, and for the season's styles, was at least as important as any scientific forecast of demand. Although it had become quite a big business in financial terms, the company was in management and attitude still a small one. It called me in to discuss its planned expansion into Europe, and I brought with me one of our best fashion-industry experts from our Paris office. As we talked with the client, we convinced ourselves – and half-convinced him – that he really needed a full study of market opportunities outside the UK before going any further. We subsequently bid for this work, at a cost in excess of £100,000 ($150,000), only to see our proposal disappear into a black hole from which no further word ever emerged. Patently, our idea of what the job might entail and the going rate for it had been totally at odds with what the client had expected. It was not that the business could not afford the fees: simply that, to the owner, that kind of money was what you spent on a new Rolls-Royce and not on a pair of whizkids in suits. We should have realised.

It is all very well the consultant *knowing* from experience that a global strategy is worth at least (say) £200,000: if the client was expecting something under £50,000 then you are on a hiding to nothing. It should not be surprising that this happens: after all, cons are working on assignments of a given nature week in and week out, whereas (as with our rag trader) it may be the first time that the client has even thought about a project of the same type. This is one reason why it can assist both parties for the con to give some idea of the likely fees even as early as the first meeting with the client. It took me a few years, though, to build up the experience necessary to do this without risking giving all the wrong signals. In other words, to get a good feel for the going rate.

Where does this going rate come from? There are two parts to it. One, as already suggested, is comparison with similar jobs done in the past and what they actually cost to bring to completion. If you know that, last time, the job took two months and involved two people full time plus additional specialist inputs, this gives you a head start in your next bid. The second element is *what the job will bear* which is where client perception is so important. We all know that the pricing of beer in the pub or breakfast cereal in the supermarket is only partly a matter of its costs. So it is with consultancy: good quality or simply good packaging and branding may justify a higher price. More than that, as with consumer goods, there is a belief that if you pay a high price you must be getting the best. It's worth what you pay for it.

A few years ago, an article was published in a French IT journal under the apparent pseudonym of Arthur Leroy[1]. The title of the article was (my translation): 'I stitched up half of French industry and I'm proud of it.' The author, whoever he (or she) may be, claims to have relieved many clients of their money in return for information systems that gave them the illusion of understanding what was going on in their business. He recounts that, on one occasion, he sent out a proposal with an extra zero accidentally added to the total fees. Calling the client to explain, he was astonished to be told that his proposal had been accepted. He experimented further and each

[1] Arthur Leroy: 'J'ai planté la moitié de l'industrie française et j'en suis fier' – *L'informatique professionnelle*, November 1991. In France, Arthur Andersen is usually referred to simply as 'Arthur'. However, this does not necessarily indicate the provenance of the author.

time that he submitted a cost estimate ten times greater than it should have been, he won the job. His clients apparently felt that this inflated fee proved that he was the best in the business and that, if he could not help them, no one could. And so, of course, he continued.

The top-notch strategic consultancies (McKinsey, Bain, BCG and so on) have always maintained a premium pricing strategy that is itself part of the reason for their success. They offer a completely consistent package: they are only interested in advising the top level of the company, they charge the kind of fees that only the most senior management could authorise and they claim to deliver advice of a quality consistent with this cost and wasted on anyone below Director level. As an exercise in branding it could be a case study. In the late 1980s, faced with the chill breeze of a recession to which strategy boutiques were not totally immune, there was a lot of talk about them extending the range of their services into more operational fields. It never really seemed to happen, probably because it was hard for them to be convincing in these areas where, at the same time, the going rate for jobs was so much lower.

By the same token, the 'Big Six' accountancy-based consultancies have never looked really convincing in the strategy sphere. Image has become fundamentally important in the consultancy market and image is closely related to price. I can think of no example of success-ful entry to this market based on low pricing. The 1990s have seen the rapid growth of new competitors in areas including re-engineering and change management. Again, in these fields, the 'Big Six' strug-gled to shift their image in order to be credible against a new wave of firms (Gemini, CSC Index, Oasis and others) whose entry was based not on price but on product innovation. This was often enshrined in a proprietary methodology, preferably supported by a business book hyped as the next management revolution. One reason why methodologies have become so significant in consultancy is that, as Arthur Leroy realised, they underpin the 'going rate' for your work.

Brand names and 'ologies' serve the same purpose and compete with each other. In the supermarket, shoppers compare the price for

Kellogg's or Heinz or Nescafé products with the cheaper own-label lookalikes on offer. They tell each other, ruefully, that 'you pay for the name'. And so they do. As every good brand manager knows, the brand *is* still perceived as a guarantee of quality and reliability and part of the brand image is its price. With apologies to all big-name cons, the logic that applies to them is exactly the same as that which rules in the supermarket.

Never forget the U-word

'How much do you earn?' is a question which clients occasionally asked me, and others doubtless would have liked to. Almost invariably they were trying to reconcile in their own mind the disparity between the kind of salary they might have given someone of my age and experience and what they were expected to pay for a day of my time. The latter, incidentally, was somewhere around £500 ($750) when I started out as a pretty junior con and over £1,000 ($1,500) by the time I quit six years later.

In the UK it is common enough to see consultancy jobs advertised at 'up to £65,000' or even with the enticement of six figures, but this kind of money is normally reserved for those with substantial experience (once again, strategy boutiques have norms of their own which are well above the average). Once a large number of junior Grunts are taken into consideration, the average salary for a UK con is probably between £30,000 and £40,000, with the going rate for an experienced con in the order of £50,000[2]. Divide that by the number of working days in a year and you come up with a figure of say £220 per day. So how come that same consultant will be billed out at four or five times this rate? And who is getting the rest?

It is not hard to see where this logic falls down. The billing rate used by a consultancy, like the 'labour' rate charged by a car mechanic, has to recover *all* the costs of the business plus whatever

---

[2] US rates may be higher. According to the *Economist* (22 March, 1997), new MBAs can command salaries as high as $120,000 a year plus tuition fees and bonuses, but I do not believe this to be general.

profit margin is to be added on top. The sort of cost make-up that big firms have is shown indicatively by the table below.

Salary costs	£000s / year
Senior consultant's salary	50
Pension, Social Security: say 20%	10
Support staff (backoffice, secretarial, etc): say 10%	5
Management overhead (see below): say	15
Total salary related	**80**

The management overhead includes the substantial part of Partners' or other senior management's time which is unlikely to be chargeable to clients. Some Partners are very hands-on and will indeed charge a substantial number of hours to clients. Others may charge little or no time in this way, leaving it as an overhead to be recovered through other billings. Overruns on other jobs, and discounts of every kind, have likewise to be written off as overheads.

Other Costs	£000s / year
Car and other benefits	10
Office accommodation (central London / similar) and overheads	15
Selling costs (travel, entertainment, etc, not chargeable to clients)	10
General overhead (promotion, exhibitions, training[3], etc, etc)	10
Total non-salary	**45**
Total cost	**125**

---

[3] According to a recent article in the *Economist* (22 March, 1997), Andersen Consulting spends over 10% of its revenue on training. I have included a much more modest figure.

Rough and ready though this may be, it shows how a simple salary of £50,000 annually may build up to an average total cost of approximately £125,000 per year, including non-wage overheads of around 50% of the salary bill. Allowing for a profit margin on top, the firm will be looking to recover say £135,000 annually for an employee on this grade.

Now for the real crunch. There are some 225 working days in the year after allowing for holidays but some of these are likely to be spent writing proposals, marketing, selling, training, attending conferences or otherwise 'between jobs'. If our hypothetical consultant is chargeable to clients for 60% of those days, then the required recovery rate will be £135,000 / (225 * 0.60) or around £1000 per day. For junior staff the figure can be a little less. For senior managers (forget Partners), who may only bill out say 40% of their time, it is not hard to come up with figures of around £1,500 per day which is indeed what you might have to pay for them.

It should be clear from this simple calculation that one of the most important numbers for any consultancy is the U-word. To a consultant, *U is for utilisation*. This is the touchstone, the shibboleth, of consultancy. New recruits should have it branded on their foreheads like the mark of Cain to remind them that their destiny is to go forth and be utilised. Any con who fails to get a decent level of utilisation, be he or she the world's greatest living expert in their field, is liable to be treated as so much dead meat.

Harsh though this may seem, the logic is inescapable once you realise how highly geared the consulting business is to this single figure. If our theoretical con is billed out at £1000 per day and achieves not 60% but 70% utilisation, the firm will make over three times the planned margin from his or her work. If the con only achieves 50% utilisation, not only will his or her entire profit contribution be wiped out, but over £12,000 worth of overhead will go unrecovered – a loss which has to be made good from the contribution of other, more heavily utilised, staff. On this model, a change of just 1 percentage point in utilisation is equivalent to a 22.5% change in contribution[4].

---

[4] At 60% utilisation, the margin will be £10,000: calculated as revenue of £135,000 (£1000 per day * 225 days * 60%) less costs of £125,000. 1% utilisation is worth £2250 per annum (£1000*225*.01) which is 22.5% of this contribution.

Suppose you took charge of a loss-making consultancy (they do exist, by the way). You would set about looking for the key levers that could improve the firm's result, either by cutting costs or increasing revenue. From the above calculations, it can be seen that a significant impact may be had by any of the following:

- Increasing utilisation (always the first on the list).

- Cutting general overheads such as office costs, administration, training, etc.

- Reducing the management overhead by eliminating senior posts.

- Employing less experienced staff at a lower salary cost.

- Targeting the marketing effort more accurately in order to achieve greater sales at lower marketing cost and with less unpaid time.

If you were a con charged with producing a business improvement strategy for the firm, you might at this point take the money and run. No one could argue with any of the above points. The issue is how you actually achieve them.

Looking for the easy wins, let us start with the simpler items on the list. To attack general overheads always looks like a short-term winner, although in the longer term they have a nasty habit of creeping back in. I can recall my employer decreeing that the cost of biscuits had risen to such a level that they would no longer be provided for meetings (cries of shock). Even in my time with the firm, secretarial support became noticeably thinner on the ground and the consultancy marketing support team was disbanded (before being reborn under a different guise). Training budgets came and went in step with the firm's bottom-line utilisation.

More radically, consultancies practised 'hot desking' long before it ever became fashionable in the IT industry: under this system, staff who are supposed often to be out of the office are not given a desk of their own but have to find a work station each day on a 'first come first served' basis. This enables the number of desks (and the space that they occupy) to be perhaps half what it would otherwise be. The logical extension of this, of course, is for cons to work from home and seldom to visit the office at all. Some, although not all, consultancies try to operate on this basis.

Measures of this kind, although apparently sensible steps towards lower costs and greater efficiency, are of questionable long-term benefit. As already mentioned, overheads have a nasty habit of creeping back, once minds are elsewhere. There also comes a point at which further pressure on secretarial resources or desks can lead to *in*efficiency. A good graphics secretary can knock out presentation slides far faster, and to much higher quality, than most consultants: is it sensible for cons to do this themselves? Conversations at the coffee machine can enable staff to find out about the experience of others in the firm which may be relevant to their project, whereas when they work at home they may end up reinventing what has been done a dozen times by their colleagues. And so it goes. None of this means that efficiencies cannot be made but, in the absence of more profound change in the nature of the tasks performed, there is only so much blood that can be wrung from this particular stone.

What of the cost of marketing? Again, there is no denying the principle that good targeting and effective use of personal networks should enable cons to find the next job while minimising wasteful expenditure. The practice, however, is very much harder. The whole rationale of the creation of the 'Big Six' accountancy and consulting firms was to cross-sell additional services to their more or less captive audit base. This proved much easier to say than to do. My own experience was of a deep mistrust and lack of interest between the auditing and consulting sides of the firm, feelings which made cross-selling very much the exception rather than the rule. As a result, in my area we acted pretty much independently, looking for sales wherever we could find them.

However much we tried to identify the most promising sectors and potential clients, success in targeting proved elusive. At the end of the day, the work tended to walk in through the door from the most unpredictable directions. The biggest client that we had in my time was given our name by an unrelated firm of headhunters that he happened to be using. How we had come to the headhunters' notice I simply do not know, but the seed may have been sown by some recent piece in a magazine or may have been blown in years before by a chance conversation long since forgotten. All that mattered was that we were given the chance to bid – and we went for it.

Success is never guaranteed. Another chance enquiry came from an Israeli company which wanted a big project done in the Far East. Bidding for the work led us to meet them first in Hong Kong and, later, in Tel Aviv. On both occasions I flew over with my Partner for a couple of days each time. The total selling cost must have exceeded £10,000, quite apart from the time spent on the proposal, and we failed to land the job. Inevitably, such failures will happen. The traditional consultancy, trying to be jack-of-all-trades, is bound to fail more often than it succeeds in competitive bidding. That particular job was one for which we were *not* well qualified – but success could have opened the door to further work of a similar nature in the Far East. Justifiable ambition or excessive optimism?

The best way of marketing consultancy, beyond dispute, is through personal contact and personal recommendation. The bigger the firm, the harder this is to sustain. Why this should be is not entirely clear, but it has something to do with focus and something to do with the personal touch. Small specialists are known precisely for what they are good at and probably will not even get the call unless the job is well up their street. Large firms are known by general reputation and may be obliged to chase up every blind alleyway in an attempt to sustain their size and develop new kinds of work. Far from achieving synergies in marketing, they may be saddled with a level of costs stubbornly resistant to reduction.

Simply putting the squeeze on overheads, or trying to sweat the marketing dollar, is unlikely to make a substantial and lasting difference to the cost profile of a consultancy. What, then, of the other action items proposed above: improving utilisation, reducing senior staffing and employing less expensive labour? These need more fundamental changes to be made, if they are to be successful. Consider the following propositions:

- *Proposition 1*: utilisation is unlikely to rise significantly if cons have to spend time chasing after every two-bit job that comes along. Corollary: ignore small opportunities and concentrate on selling larger jobs.

- **Proposition 2**: trying to do the same type of work with less qualified staff is likely to mean more mistakes and a lower quality of output. Corollary: change the type of work in order to deskill as much of the task as possible.

- **Proposition 3**: building a bespoke approach for each new client is time-consuming and requires senior-level inputs. Corollary: produce a standardised approach and shoe-horn clients into it.

Reasoning along these lines has taken major consultancies down the related paths of attempting to increase the size of their jobs and developing methodologies. The advantage of the latter, in this context, is that 'ologies' allow a standardisation of the work which means both that the selling of it is simplified and that the doing of it is reduced to following pre-defined tasks. As a result, the level of expertise required to complete a project can be reduced significantly, while more experienced resources can be directed at client-management and methodology development. This, at least, is the theory as shown in Figure 4.2.

Figure 4.2 – advantages of changing the type of work

	Bigger size of job		Standardised methodology	
Increase utilisation?	✓✓✓	More time working, less selling	✓	Less time in designing ad-hoc approaches
Cut general overheads?	✓	Less time in office	✓	Standardised materials, etc
Cut management cost?	✓	Some economy of scale	✓✓✓	Standardised tasks need less supervision
Less qualified staff?	✓	If involves standardised task	✓✓✓	Work partially deskilled
More efficient marketing?	✓	If involves selling on to same client	✓✓✓	Methodology targeted at need or sector

One way in which cons have gone for bigger jobs is through the 'bundling' together of various service lines. IT-based consultancies have sold the concept of the one-stop shop, offering clients both the initial business strategy and the ultimate computer implementation, along with everything else in between. This integration can substantially increase the potential fees earned from the client and minimise marketing and selling costs. Not content with offering such broadly-based advice to clients, some consultancies have now also become major providers of outsourced services, particularly in the computing arena. The issues raised by this are whether it compromises their ability to provide impartial advice to clients, and whether it is taking the cons too far away from their core competencies.

In any case, camping out with major corporations in the hope of winning big-ticket work is not always successful. I can remember it being said, although it may not have been absolute policy, that our firm was no longer interested in jobs which did not offer at least the potential of earning £100,000 ($150,000) from the client. The trouble was that the juiciest-looking clients could quite often turn out to be complete dogs, while some very small acorns turned into mighty oaks. Moreover, one consultancy Partner with whom I discussed the trend to larger projects suggested that the investments required to achieve this objective may *increase* the overall cost of marketing. This diminishes the benefits of the approach, although it does not affect the key one which is increased utilisation.

If the pursuit of size has its problems, recourse to a standardised methodology is even more problematic. It is just not possible to ignore the near-infinite variety of clients' needs. Correction: it *is* possible but it may not be very helpful to the client. By instinct, cons – like prostitutes – have the habit of saying 'yes' when approached by clients. Getting cons to agree only to offer straight sex (that is, the standardised offering) is not straightforward, nor can you impose this unilaterally on clients. Cons might, however, usefully learn from their counterparts on street corners that deviant tendencies justify premium charges. It is not obvious that the price charged by consultants adequately reflects the difference in costs between different kinds of work and, on occasion, the bespoke customer is likely to be subsidised from off-the-peg sales. There are some good reasons for this – not the least being that the first small job for a client, which is probably the most expensive to win and set up, is precisely the one which the con may need to sell cheaply as a loss-leader.

The choice between 'bespoke' and 'off-the-peg' consulting is a critical issue both for cons and clients. Having introduced it here, I will develop it further in Chapter 10.

Before that, a comment is called for on small consultancies. This book is really about the big fish in the consulting pond. However, a challenge is posed by the fact that small consultancies are often so much cheaper than their larger rivals. How can this be? In part, it is a reflection of the way that the big firms price deliberately high in order to maintain their brand image. At the same time, though, most small firms have a much lower cost base. Factors that contribute to this include:

- Use of a network of 'associates' who may be called in for a particular job but who will only be paid as utilised. This avoids the worst of the problems of having expensive staff sitting around waiting for the work to come in.

- Lower overheads and much cheaper office accommodation – normally away from London or other capitals (in the case of independents, simply working from home).

- High degree of focus: small firms know to limit their ambitions and simply will not bid if the work is too far outside their core competence.

- Specialisation: they become known for a particular type of work or skill and rely on word-of-mouth networking within their chosen sector. At the limit, such specialisation delivers the same benefits as methodology-driven consulting, but without the bullshit. I know one firm of management trainers (admittedly a rather specialist kind of consulting) who have been teaching the same course – and *only* that course – for fourteen years.

- They are simply less greedy. I have alluded already to the cost of keeping Partners in the style to which they are accustomed. In large firms, Partners not infrequently become part of the overhead burden: 'high-priced help', as we used to call them. With a take-home averaging upwards of £150,000 ($225,000) – several times this figure in the case of the most senior – they certainly live up to that description. Figures from *Management Consultant International* show ratios typically around 1 Partner (or equivalent) to 15 consultants. This is a far higher proportion of top-level management than you would find in most types of business. In smaller firms, Partners are likely to be much more heavily involved in the work and, by implication, much less of an overhead. They are also unlikely to earn the same amount, except possibly as a real profit share when the business has performed exceptionally.

It is certainly interesting to reflect that consultants, who have so often preached to their clients the benefits of critical mass and synergy, appear to have achieved precisely the opposite in their own businesses.

So what are you going to do about it?

There is no disputing the fact that you are going to require a serious budget – possibly the kind of budget which will need very senior commitment – if you are to engage consultants to do a significant piece of work. There are few free lunches at any time and least of all when it comes to employing professional advisers. If you want cons you must expect to pay up. Thus far, you have no choice.

In almost every detail, however, clients have a great deal of choice and need to consider a range of options which will have a significant bearing on the amount that they pay. Consultancy is far from being a standardised offering (even today, despite the impact of methodology-based consulting). There is no single way to set up a project and no single way to structure the fees. In the remainder of this chapter I examine the issues that clients should think about when the time comes to talk money. All concern the way in which the consultancy support is structured.

Issue 1: Fee structure There are three classic ways in which fees may be structured:

- Fixed fee. A proposal is made for a certain piece of work; terms of reference are defined; deliverables are specified; fees are agreed for carrying out the job in accordance with those terms, whatever the outcome. If the cons take more or less time than planned to achieve the defined objectives, that is their bad or good fortune as the client still pays the same amount. The great majority of my consulting was done on fixed-fee terms (and it no doubt shows in my attitude to some of the issues discussed in this book).

- Time and materials. Where the terms of reference, or the deliverables, cannot be made specific or where the work involved in achieving the project objectives is impossible to determine in advance, consultants will usually look to charge on a time and materials basis. Every hour spent on the job will be logged and charged to the client.

- Contingency fees (no win, no fee). The fees paid to the consultants are assessed as a proportion of the client benefits that they are able to demonstrate. For example, if the job involves identifying cost savings, the cons may be paid a percentage of the first year savings that they achieve. In accountancy-based firms, the industry rules governing accountants outlawed contingency fees and we used to assert that this applied also to consulting. In practice, some element of contingency was known to creep in but we preferred to keep it quiet.

In theory, contingency fees sound very attractive. Why should a client pay if she does not get any benefit from the cons' work? Why shouldn't consultants be given a real financial incentive to perform, as many managers and workers are? Cons often argue that their fees are amply justified by the benefits they deliver, so why not expect them to put their own money where their mouth is?

In practice, there are various drawbacks to contingency fees. These include:

- Definitions: how do you define (and who determines) exactly what benefits have arisen from the consultants' work? If the client says 'That was something we were going to do anyway,' does it count or not?

- Control: unless the cons are going to be given complete authority to implement their recommendations, they can only be judged on the *expected* benefits of their work. Yet this leaves the client exposed to paying for recommendations which then prove impossible to implement. Turning this the other way up, why should a consultant end up unpaid just because the client's implementation, over which he had no control, was a shambles?

- Dysfunction: there is a real likelihood that the results of the project will be influenced by the need to achieve certain benefit targets. Consider a cost-saving project (the most likely scenario for contingency fees). If the cons are to be judged on first-year savings, they will favour solutions which cut every possible cost even if they have negative long-term implications. Out will go the training budget, the maintenance budget and every IT project in the company. Be very careful before you give an incentive to a con to deliver this kind of result.

- Risk: it is well recognised that risk has its price and, if the contingency fee involves a significant risk that the cons will go unpaid, they will expect a greater reward in the event of a successful result than would otherwise be the case. If the risk is trivial, so will be the advantage to the client from structuring the fee in this way.

Contingency fees are only really suitable for situations where the result is capable of crystal-clear definition and adjudication. Cost-saving projects *may* indeed fall into this category but the warning given above about dysfunction should be noted carefully. Other types of work may also qualify: what matters is whether you can define in advance the required benefits of the project and whether they can be measured precisely after the event. For instance, corporate financiers will often be on contingency fees when advising on takeovers: in this situation there are only two possible results (the takeover succeeds or it fails) and no risk of confusion of the two.

Despite the drawbacks of contingency fees, the element of incentive is still appealing. Fortunately, there is no reason for fee structures to be totally black or white. In most cases I would suggest that fixed fees are probably a better bet but, where certain tightly-defined results are involved, an element of the cost (say 10-20%) should be contingent upon their achievement. For example, in a manufacturing study, if a key objective is to cut equipment changeover times a fixed bonus of 10% could be paid to the consultants provided they can show at least a 30% reduction in the time lost.

Charging time and materials (cost-plus) is a nice deal for the cons if they can get it. I seldom had the luxury of working on this basis which requires either or both of the following conditions to apply:

- The consultancy input simply cannot be defined in advance with any degree of precision and, in consequence, it is impossible to price it on a fixed fee.

- There is a great deal of trust between client and con (probably the result of previous jobs) which makes the client entirely happy to allow the cons to decide for themselves how much work they need to put in.

I would urge considerable caution in deciding that the first of these applies to a given situation. The worst possible reason for entering into a time and materials contract is that you cannot be bothered to think through exactly what is going to be involved in the job. In *every* situation it should be possible to define the deliverables that you require. The only question then is whether there is sufficient information available to enable the cons adequately to estimate the work required to achieve these deliverables. If there is not, then time and materials may be the only option. Even in this situation, though, you should try to ensure both that there is an overall ceiling on the fees and that there are defined and specific interim deliverables from which you may gauge the progress of the work.

As an alternative to time and materials, there is much to be said for running an initial *scoping* project which then enables both parties to make a better estimate of the work required to complete the balance. Beware, though, of this being used simply to protract and expand the job.

Issue 2: Project structure The discussion of fee structure has started taking us, inevitably perhaps, into the issue of how the project should be structured. By this I mean the phases into which the work may be divided and how they relate to each other.

A lot of projects follow the classic three-part structure of:

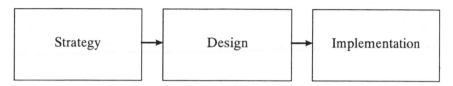

Where such a structure is proposed it is normal for each part to be costed separately; it is also not uncommon for the implementation phase to be left vague both in terms of its specification and its cost, pending completion of the earlier parts of the job. Phasing of this kind can be beneficial, if and only if it fits with the client's underlying needs. If you have already done the strategy, insist on starting with the second box. If your requirement is completely vague, but you are absolutely convinced that you need consultants to help you[5], consider adding an overview and scoping stage even ahead of the strategy and commit only to paying for that first element.

Carving a job up into phases like this minimises the client's up-front commitment and gives a chance to update the likely benefits at the end of each stage, before pressing on with the next. Suitably handled, it may also encourage the cons to price the first phase as something of a 'loss-leader', further minimising the client's exposure until he is quite happy with the consulting team's approach and expertise. Some cons, especially when pitching for major cost-saving or re-engineering projects, may even do the first phase without charge.

---

[5] The better option is probably not to do the job at all: see Chapter 1.

A free lunch, then? Hardly. Any loss that the cons make on the first phase they will look to recover subsequently. The more you chop a job up into its constituent parts, the more the cons will want to seek opportunities for loading the fees as close to the front end as possible.

Let me explain what I mean. If you are a con bidding for a £200,000 assignment, you will be prepared for a ride on both swings and roundabouts: on some parts of the job you may have to put in more hours than expected, on other parts fewer. If the same job is chopped up into five projects each worth £40,000, and you are asked to undertake the first with no guarantee of the rest, then you run a greater risk of being left out of pocket. If, in addition, you have to bid for phase one at £25,000 in order to get a foot in the door, you will be very sorely tempted to push up the price on phases two and three to perhaps £55,000 each in order both to recover your initial loss and cover yourself for the chance of not getting the last parts of the project. In this situation, the client ends up paying more (£15,000 to be precise), for the privilege of keeping his options open for so long.

Worst of all is the situation where the client shies away from giving the consultant a decent-sized piece of work to get her teeth into. A lot of the hidden cost of a project lies in setting it up, getting the team up to speed, understanding the client's business and so on. The cost of doing this is normally spread across the whole job. Priced properly, a series of small jobs is much more expensive than a single large one. The client who takes a cheese-parer to the job may get poor value as the cost is unlikely to come down as fast as the expected deliverables. My least favourite client would never give us a single project of any size: instead, over several years, they kept coming back for a few days more work, an update of the model or another validation of something they had done themselves, and ended up paying us far more for much less than if they had decided up-front to do the job properly.

Proper phasing can both help the achievement of the project objectives and ensure that the client pays no more than necessary. Distorting the project, by chopping it too finely or in a misplaced effort to avoid up-front commitment, does no one any favours.

Issue 3: Rate structure If the job is to be performed for a fixed fee, the cons' calculation of costs will involve estimating the days required and multiplying by the daily rate of each team member.

The way in which the job is structured determines the days which the consultants will budget to spend on it. The cost per day which is applied to this figure depends on the grade of consultants involved. Finally, the overall price may be adjusted by the application of a discount if the consultants consider this to be necessary or desirable.

Chapter 3 dealt with the selection of the consultancy team and I will not repeat it here, other than to reiterate that getting the right people on the job is absolutely fundamental. There is no point in striking a hard bargain with your cons if the result is a downgrading of the personnel deployed on your assignment. In general, the shorter the piece of work the more senior a con may be required to tackle it: a constrained budget (both in cost and – therefore – days) means that the consultant may be operating alone and will need to get up to speed very fast. With a bigger or longer piece of work there is more scope for deploying junior staff to undertake basic tasks or after suitable training. Large jobs based on methodologies enable a certain deskilling of the work and the use of less experienced consultants.

Having decided what resource you need, pay for that and nothing more. Even when fees are quoted as a lump sum you should request a breakdown of the estimated days of input from each team member, so that you can be confident of where the balance lies. And you do not *have* to pay for 'high priced help' from a Partner if you do not feel it is adding value.

If the u-word – *utilisation* – is a key one to all consultants, the d-word – *discount* – is sometimes regarded as a grave obscenity. In theory, we never gave discounts off our rates. In practice, it would all depend on how confident we felt in our proposal and how keen we were to get the business. We tended to fudge this: rather than show the appropriate number of days at a discounted rate, we preferred to reduce the estimate of days in order to maintain the appearance of full-rate pricing. This had negative implications for the cons deployed on the job as often they would then be leant upon, by the Partner or project manager, to book an unrealistically low total of days to do the work. The squeeze was put on the individual's utilisation in order to avoid showing an explicit discount or having to take a write-off on the project.

One client who always got a discount, however presented, was the European Commission. Work for the Commission tends to be high-profile: the kind of job that looks good on the firm's reference list. They are also very big buyers of consultancy. With these two advantages, they are able to set their own standard for acceptable daily rates and this was somewhere around half of our normal fees expectation. Bidding for European Commission work at full rates was just not possible. 'Losing' the discount by inflating the estimated number of days, and leaning on the cons to do the work in far fewer remained an option and one which we did our best to exploit.

Does this mean that other clients were subsidising work done for the Commission? Possibly, but not necessarily. European work can be large-scale, and any job which utilises the cons more or less full time for more than a few weeks should qualify for a substantial discount. Go back to the explanation, earlier in this chapter, of why *utilisation* is such an important measure. If a consultant who works on a series of small to medium jobs can achieve 60% utilisation, a job which ties him up full time or better[6] for (say) six months is a major bonus for the firm. The bonus is in fact worth a discount of 40% off the consultant's normal billing rate. Discounts on this scale are certainly not normal in large consultancies (except when market conditions are tough and the gloves start to come off) but perhaps they should be.

What tends to happen is that cons underprice small jobs, in order to get a foot in the door, and then try to sell on much larger jobs at full rate or only modest discounts in order to recover the difference. If you are asking cons to bid for a substantial piece of work you should try to reverse this logic and make sure that you get the kind of rate structure justified by the economics of the business, rather than the one dictated by the normal practice of the consultants.

---

[6] A con may be utilised in excess of 100% if the hours he works for the client (and charges for) come to more than the firm's standard hours per day.

Issue 4: Task structure There is really only one thing to say about the structuring of the overall task required by the client: it is cheaper to pay serious money for the right job, bought for the right reasons, than to get a bargain price on the wrong job done for all the wrong reasons.

I may be labouring this point by now, but I make no apologies as it is basic to any consideration of the way organisations use consultants. Go back to Chapter 2, if necessary, where three key questions were posed for prospective consultancy clients:

- What sort of change am I trying to achieve in my organisation?

- What do I need to happen if the knowledge, expertise and skills of my own people are to be used to best effect in this process of change?

- What do I need from outside because I cannot find it inside my organisation?

Answering these three questions should ensure that any consultancy inputs are adequately defined and correspond to a genuine need. If you can then get the right team onto the job (as discussed in the last chapter), and know the way that they will approach things (dealt with in the *next* chapter), you stand a pretty good chance of achieving your objectives. The money – however much it may be – will have been well spent if you get to this point.

Answering the questions will also point up the scope that you may have for limiting the cost of the work by deploying more or less in-house resource on the project. If you have staff capable of obtaining data but you are not confident of their ability to use it to the full, pay consultants to do the analysis while ensuring that they use your own people to do the leg-work. Deploying a 'mixed team' of consultants and client staff is in many ways desirable: one advantage, although not the complete picture, is the extent to which it may hold down the fees. Mixed teams can, however, fall down badly if the mix is not right or if either side (probably the client's) fails to deliver what it is supposed to. If pursuing this approach, keep it simple and make sure that the whole project is under single management, be it your own or the consultants'.

Above all, avoid moving the goalposts once the job is underway.

Nothing wastes more time and money than a client who is not clear what he wants or who changes tack partway through once she has seen which way the wind is blowing. If the fees are set on a time and materials basis, the on-cost will go straight through to the consultants' invoice. If you are running a fixed-fee project, everything may come to a grinding halt while the terms of reference are overhauled. If you have gone for a contingency fee, incentivised the team to achieve a given result and then changed your mind ('I know I said the objective was to reduce costs, but actually what we really want is for you to improve our customer service standard without increasing the cost'), you may have to pay up for the wasted effort before starting again from scratch.

Summary

This chapter has covered a lot of ground, from why consultants cost so much to how determined clients can make sure that they pay even more than they need to. Cons will price as high as they feel they can get away with and as low as they feel they have to. The moral for clients can be summed up as a set of dos and don'ts:

Do:

- Expect to pay serious money for serious consultancy support.

- Treat consultancy like any other investment, which has to produce a payback in the long, or preferably not-so-long, term.

- Consider carefully whether you really need to pay the premium rates commanded by big-name consultancies.

- Look for ways of giving the consultants an element of incentive to achieve the objectives set for the job.

- Divide the work into appropriate modules, with the later stages dependent upon a successful outcome from the earlier.

- In complex situations, consider starting with a scoping study which you may be able to get as a loss-leader, in order both to define the main project more precisely and to get a better feel for the consultants.

- Press for an appropriate discount if you are undertaking the scale of job that will keep one or more consultants busy for months on end.

- Pay only for the cons who you really want on the project team.

- Consider mixing your own in-house resource with the consultants, in order to hold down the overall cost.

- Make sure that you are absolutely clear why the work is being undertaken, and what it has to achieve, and monitor the progress of the project continually against these objectives.

Don't:

- Assume that you will necessarily get what you pay for.

- Be too quick to believe that the bigger the fee, the better the quality.

- Be pushed into accepting a methodology if it is not what you really want.

- Rush into demanding contingency fees unless the job and its benefits can be defined very tightly.

- Push too much risk onto the consultants: remember, risk has a price.

- Allow yourself to slide into fees based on time and materials simply because you cannot be bothered to define the job properly.

- Split the work up into so many parts that you lose any economies of scale.

- Move the goalposts once the job is underway.

In Chapter 3 I suggested that, with cons, what you see is not necessarily what you get. The message of this chapter has been that you do not automatically get what you pay for, either. As a client, it is your *responsibility* – not your right – to achieve this.

Alternatively, there are plenty of Arthur Leroys out there who would love to meet you.

CHAPTER 5: TRICKS OF THE TRADE

YOU'VE DONE IT NOW.

Having weighed up whether your reasons are good or bad, you have decided to bring in cons to help you sort out the business, reduce the cost base, set a strategic direction for the future, implement the latest fashion from the other side of the Pond or just get the boss off your back.

Perhaps you are just at the stage of reading the proposals that your shortlisted firms have sent you. Perhaps you are checking whether the team has too many Suits and not enough Grunts. Perhaps you are haggling over the budget. In any event, it is time for you to start thinking about the approach that your consultants are likely to take as they get down to work, and the techniques which they may deploy as the project progresses. To put it less charitably, you need to know what stunts they may pull as they attempt to deliver some of that elusive commodity, value added, as perceived by you, the client.

Alternatively, you may be a consultant yourself, about to walk through the client's front door for the first time on what is Day One of a 6-week assignment (in which case I suggest you stop reading this and take a look at the terms of reference for the job). It would not be surprising if the first thing you knew about the project was at 5 o'clock last Friday when a Partner rolled in from the first of what may be many lunches with the client, announced that she had secured a new piece of work, and looked around for some luckless fall-guy to start straight away.

Your mission (which you will accept whether you choose to or not) is to replace Jim Faraway, who was named in the proposal but unfortunately turns out to be in Kazakhstan for the duration, or Sarah Overburthen, the only person in the firm who actually knows anything about the client's industry but who has already been sold on three other jobs and won't even have a Sunday to spare for the next month. Having snatched a quick look at the proposal in the bath last night, you find that you are now the world's greatest living expert in the marketing of latex-based compounds, which is pretty good for someone who has always worked up to now on implementing manufacturing control systems in the petfood industry.

In short, the start of a pretty typical project. The chances are that the proposal appears to have been written by a victim of verbal diarrhoea but fails to make clear exactly what is expected by way of deliverables, and that – as far as it goes – it promises the earth without much heed for the practicalities of delivering a global-market analysis in the allotted ten days of consultancy input (inclusive of quality control, presentation to two half-day workshops and the Partner's second lunch with the client).

Tricks of the trade? You'd take any that were going, wouldn't you? From the con's point of view, the 'tricks of the trade' are often simply stratagems for survival or the accumulated wisdom of those who have passed before.

By the way, there is nothing particularly far-fetched about the scenario outlined above. To be wheeled into jobs at the last minute, to be dumped into a project whose terms of reference seem to you completely misconceived, to find yourself the 'expert' in a topic of which you know virtually nothing: these are run-of-the-mill challenges for a con and go some way to explain the particular pressures of the job (a subject developed at more length in Chapter 9).

It is far from unusual for the consulting team to walk into the kick-off meeting on Day One without having had any prior discussion about the job or their respective roles and – in some cases at least –

with only a hazy idea of what was in the proposal. The extreme case of this may be the consultancy equivalent of the 'Vanishing Hitchhiker', but the anecdote is repeated sufficiently often to give it some credibility. It concerns a new project where, on Day One, the cons are being introduced to various managers of the client firm. The consultancy Partner duly shakes hand with the Finance Director, the Marketing Manager and the Head of Production. Seeing someone else enter the meeting room, he turns to them with a smile and outstretched hand. 'Hello, I'm Peter Armani from Arthur Marwick Ross,' he says pleasantly. 'And you are . . ?' The new arrival, of course, turns out to be one of the consultancy team.

So, the subtitle of this chapter could be 'What every consultant needs to know in order to survive Day One'. Apart from a thick skin and an automatic bullshit generator, without which even these suggestions are unlikely to be of much use.

Starting at the beginning: the importance of structure

When I was fifteen or so, it dawned upon me that you could bluff your way through most examinations so long as you could produce an essay with some structure to it. It did not seem to matter much whether the content was right or wrong. It did not even make much difference if you got the odd date wrong or wrote the formulas back to front. The key thing was structure: a bit of an introduction, a touch of 'on the one hand', a leavening of 'on the other hand' and a good dose of 'so, in conclusion'. I even learned to write notes at the start of my examination answer (dutifully crossed out, of course), just to draw attention to the fact that I had got it. Structure, that is.

The technique worked like a dream at school. I then found, rather to my surprise, that it was equally effective at university. Some years later, when I got around to doing an MBA, I dusted it off again and – amazingly – it still seemed as good as new. From Modigliani and Miller's capital asset pricing model to Belbin's theories of group interaction, they all yielded to the good old structure of thesis-antithesis-synthesis.

It might be argued that one of the reasons why consultancy is so popular with recent graduates is its resemblance to the familiar (to them) world of essay crises and examinations. Whether you are assembling a proposal for a new client or writing the final report for an established one, the key element is the same as in any examination: structure. On one occasion, along with other colleagues, I had to rescue a project which had gone seriously adrift due to the key consultant suffering something resembling a nervous breakdown. We found ourselves in possession of a great many charts and tables which he had produced but otherwise pretty clueless about the job that had been done. Instinctively, we all took a leaf from the anatomy textbook: don't worry about what anything does, just get some backbone into the beast and then hang the charts and tables wherever they seem to fit on the skeleton. One way or another we got away with it.

I have described the situation where a con is parachuted into a job with very little preparation. On a luckier day, you may have the opportunity to pick things up from the first tentative contact, be the one who discusses the client's requirements with him and then find yourself writing the proposal. And the first thing you learn is that, however tangled the client's situation may be, however vague his requirements, you can and must knock them into some sort of structured project plan. Nothing impresses the vague client more than a consultant who seems to have just the approach to sort out the tangle.

Like my school examination technique, there does not need to be anything sophisticated about this. The simple ideas are the best, so start from:

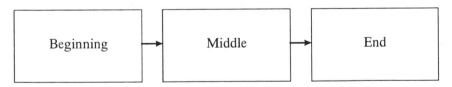

Surely (I hear the reader cry) no one could be impressed by something as trivial as this? Well, perhaps not; but try this version:

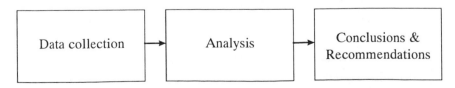

Now we're talking. There are plenty of consultancy approaches which amount roughly to that. Not that we need stop there. If you want sophistication then try the version that I already used in the last chapter:

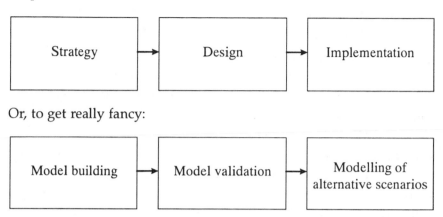

Or, to get really fancy:

It is wonderful what you can do with three boxes joined together by arrows. I am prepared to bet a Partner's profit-share that million-dollar assignments have been sold on nothing more substantial than this.

I shall probably be taken to task by those who argue that the market has become more sophisticated of late, that clients demand *methodologies*. Allow me to let the uninitiated into another secret. Most methodologies consist of three boxes joined together by arrows and given a fancy title. The use and misuse of high-falutin' terminology deserves longer discussion, so I will come back to it in the next chapter.

A headhunter-cum-remuneration consultant once told me of a bid he had submitted to advise the Government on suitable salary levels for senior executives in a soon-to-be-privatised industry. He informed me that, in the world of salaries, there is no real 'science', no hard and fast rules, simply a combination of pragmatism and horsetrading. However, when he went to sell his proposals to the Civil Servants in charge of the study, he found himself repeatedly grilled about his lack of a methodology. He realised at that stage that his presentation had been preceded by those of several 'Big Six' firms, who had wheeled out entirely plausible, if largely spurious, sets of boxes joined by arrows and saying things like 'Compile database from industry sources', 'Develop comparative model' or 'Construct skills-salary matrix'. It was no surprise to him to find that he did not win the work. It did, however, rile him when he later found out that the winning bid had been at roughly ten times the price which he had proposed. Remember, structure pays.

Perhaps the most entertaining proposal that ever crossed my desk was one that a colleague submitted to a UK police force. The subject was the distribution of stolen goods around the country, which the consultants were to investigate. What amused me was that the proposed approach followed to perfection the classic sausage-machine 'beginning-middle-end' structure. It included such old favourites as data collection, interviews with key players and model building. At every stage, however, the classic methodology had to be subtly twisted to fit with the fact that this was a study into criminality. So the interview programme was to be conducted with both 'reformed criminals' and other suitable trusties still in prison. Volumes of traffic had to be calculated from the quantities of goods seized by the police. A model was to be built of the flows between dingy railway arches and the inventories held in grimy back yards. The overall effect was of a looking-glass world where the normal rules of structure had been applied to a totally abnormal situation. Who am I to knock it? The con got the job and, for all I know, the client was delighted with the outcome. There is no situation so bizarre that you cannot fit a structure to it.

Upstairs, downstairs: find the right level

As you try to knock structure into a job, you need also to consider where to pitch it on an imaginary scale from pure strategy to direct hands-on action. Most jobs will fall somewhere between these two extremes.

There are various models which describe this continuum. Every consultancy has its own version but the one that was current among my colleagues was called GOSPA, after the initial letters of its five levels:

- The GOALS of the organisation;

- The OBJECTIVES set in pursuit of these goals;

- The STRATEGIES aimed at achieving the objectives;

- The PLANS to implement the strategies, and:

- The ACTIONS required to carry out the plans.

Why there should be five levels, and not four or seven, is (to my mind) arbitrary. So, to a degree, is the choice of terminology. The model is significant, however, because the concept of a hierarchy of levels is fundamental to a lot of consultancy. The client may not be aware of the concept at all, but the good con will take considerable care to scope a project at the appropriate level between what, for simplicity, I will call strategy and tactics.

Take the situation where a consultant is asked to fix a problem in the warehouse, which consistently fails to get goods out to customers on time. This appears to be a tactical problem: it concerns the fifth level in the GOSPA model, namely *action*. At the limit, the client may be expecting help with the fourth level, *plans* (for example, does the warehouse have the right manning levels?). But, in reality, the problem may lie far higher up the hierarchy than that. Does it actually have its roots in the company's marketing *strategy*, which has been to offer 24-hour delivery without heed to whether the goods are in stock or not? Or is the underlying cause the *objective* of double-digit growth which has been set by the Board without paying sufficient attention to the investments required to sustain it?

The client may be scared stiff if you leap straight in and suggest a review of the corporate growth objective when what he was actually expecting was a bit of time and motion in the warehouse. There may or may not be a way of swinging the project from being what the client thought he wanted to what he actually needs (see Chapter 1 for this distinction): for example, asking to talk to other senior managers before bidding, or proposing an initial phase of the work to confirm the underlying nature of the problem. In any event, there is little chance of a project succeeding if it comes in at the wrong level.

One way in which this is important is in specifying the kind of data to be obtained and analysed during the project. In my experience, it is hard for 'strategic' consultants to work alongside their more 'tactical' counterparts, even when they are from the same firm, not least because they are used to working with quite different levels of data. Operations consultants tend to look for wheelbarrows of detailed figures, of a kind which makes the eyes of their strategic colleagues glaze over. Conversely, strategic consultants think nothing of extrapolating huge conclusions from a few high-level numbers, in a way which frightens most tactical cons to death. Let us be clear: *either* approach may be correct, dependent entirely upon what the client is looking for from the study.

Attempting to run a project with the wrong level of data is a recipe for disaster. I once had to work alongside some US cons who insisted (in a relatively *strategic* project) on obtaining from the client their computer files of every single order fulfilled in the previous two years. This was hugely time-consuming in itself, made it extremely difficult to do anything useful with the data (which ran to many thousands of orders) and was in any event quite useless because, in a fast-changing industry, the future had very little to do with even the recent past.

Skilful use of the different levels of analysis can turn a single project into a whole series. I have already mentioned the classic style of information consulting, where you had to have an IT strategy before you could have a system specification, which was followed by a design phase before you could even begin to think about implementation. Such an approach *may* be appropriate. But it has often been oversold.

From the point of view of the client, the more tactical the study the more likely it is to lead to ready implementation. The frequent complaint that consultancy projects produce fancy reports that no one can implement may reflect a general tendency to commission (or an excessive zeal of consultancies to sell) work of a strategic nature. Certainly, if the cons are being wheeled in to flatter the vanity of senior management – by no means unknown as a scenario – then the high-sounding strategic 'ologies' are likely to be preferred. However, the converse danger is equally real: a tactical project in the absence of a firm strategy may lead to a brilliant implementation of a completely inappropriate solution. Both cons and their clients need to take care when it comes to selecting the appropriate level of intervention.

The different levels of analysis are reflected in the different language used to describe projects. An indispensable trick of the trade when it comes to writing proposals is the use of *weasel words*. Let us return to the hypothetical producers of latex-based products who have commissioned a marketing study. They require the consultants to produce a review of the global marketplace, an assessment of the strengths and weaknesses of the competition and an opinion as to the client's own capabilities. These they must analyse in order to come up with recommendations for the future. They also have a budget of no more than say £50,000 ($75,000) which is going to be very tight for the cons to cover all these points. What to do?

The answer is easy: the proposal commits the consultancy team to a *high-level* market analysis from *publicly-available* data, to deliver an *overview* of the competition, provide an *indicative* comparison of the client's capabilities, model *selected* scenarios and make *outline* recommendations for the future. The insertion of the italicised weasel words is not a trivial matter: basically, what they mean is that 'you the client will accept whatever detail we can cobble together in the time and budget available, and you will have no leg to stand on if it does not give you sufficient information to be able to implement the results'. The weasel words corrupt what may be seen by the client as a tactical, detailed piece of work into a high-level, relatively strategic study.

The use of weasel words is justified by the cons' need to protect themselves from unreasonable demands by their clients. Their potential for abuse, however, is self-evident.

It is all too easy for two people to think that they are using words in the same sense when in fact they are poles apart. If a consultant uses words like 'strategic' or 'indicative' in his proposal you had better make absolutely sure that you know what he means by them. At the end of the day, if the client buys a strategic project, he or she cannot expect tactical levels of detail. And if a purely tactical project has been sold, it is useless to complain later that the level of detail was too fine.

Building relationships: play the man, not the ball

I am going to have to come clean at this point. *I was not a very good consultant.*

When I worked on a client's project, I was always keen to understand the business in which I found myself. I was very concerned to add value to the client and I liked to feel that every stone had been turned in order to ensure that the result was correct. Whatever the problems of the job, my main concern was to deliver a quality result.

Isn't this what being a consultant is all about?

Frankly, no. The good con knows that you can deliver a product that is unadulterated rubbish and still end up with a happy client. More than that, the true pro knows that a happy client is the *only* thing that matters, and that if this involves totally misunderstanding the business and leaving all the interesting stones unturned, then so be it. Chapter 3 pointed out that consultancy is a people business and this works both ways. The con does not choose her client but the good con makes the client feel that he is the most important figure ever to cross her threshold.

This is not a matter of prostitution: it is just plain common sense. Human relationships are the bedrock of business. If a prospective client calls, the first thing you do is offer to *visit* him (without charge or obligation) for a face-to-face discussion. I have yet to meet a consultant who sells his services over the Internet, although plenty use it for advertising their wares[1]. On Day One you schedule a kick-off *meeting* for the teams to meet each other. When it comes round to delivering results, the most important format is usually the verbal *presentation*, whether formal or not. At every stage, building the relationship with the client is paramount.

One reflection of this is that every client likes to believe that you are working solely and at all times for her. I never ceased to be surprised by this: the client *knows* that she has only bought ten days of your input, spread over a six-week project duration, but this does not stop her expecting to be able to pick up the phone to you at any hour of any

---

[1] For the web-footed, try *http://www.expert-market.com* which contains some useful material and a directory said to contain over 200,000 consultants.

day and find you engaged in her project. I never quite worked out how to pull off this trick but, as I said, I was not a very good consultant.

Every meeting with the client has a dual purpose: it has a greater or lesser technical importance in taking the work forward, but it is always important in taking the *relationship* forward. I was presenting our proposal to a US multinational when, after no more than two or three minutes, the client thumped the table with a cry of, 'Bullshit!' I could have tried to ignore him; I could have meekly withdrawn my point; instead, I chose to argue back. As it happens, it was the right decision and it laid the basis for a 'no holds barred' kind of relationship that brought us a great deal of work.

You may deliver the best presentation in the world, but if the client dislikes your tie then you are in trouble. The same US multinational was the kind of business where everyone wore jeans and trainers. We persisted in turning up in smart suits, despite more than a few remarks from the client about this. After a few months, the client started coming to the meetings wearing a tie. It was a sign that the relationship was now so good that we had been allowed to win this trivial victory, but I would not recommend flouting the client's dress code as the normal way to win friends and influence people.

Once a relationship has been built, it should be maintained at all costs. This is one rule that brooks no exceptions. Normally, the con who first comes to meet the client will stick with the project (and its successors, if any) throughout. The same con may well project-manage a whole series of jobs for the client, even when some of them go well outside her normal technical competence, in order to maintain the relationship. Change of management at the client is a source of great concern to incumbent consultants, as it can disrupt or break relations. Similarly, replacing the consultancy Partner or manager dealing with a client is always tricky and usually only undertaken when forced by circumstances.

The Eleventh Commandment: Manage the client's expectations
And Moses said: 'Thou shalt at all times and in all places manage thy client's expectations'. Although this is an aspect of building and maintaining the relationship, it merits a section of its own.

Much of the paraphernalia which surrounds a consultancy project – proposals, project plans, milestones, Gantt charts, methodologies, flow diagrams, review meetings, sign-offs, interim deliverables and the rest – is aimed at restricting the element of uncertainty. It ensures that the project develops in the way that the client expected. At the same time, it leads the client's expectations to develop in a way that is convenient to the project or – more specifically – to the project team.

At best, progress can be checked off stage by stage as the cons deliver the various results expected by the client. At worst, the client is led initially to expect one thing (the world, probably) and ends up cheerfully accepting something much less, but a lot easier to deliver. The key word is *cheerfully*: it is embarrassing, at best, to have to deal with a client who feels that she has been robbed. So the good *project* manager will also manage the *client* and her expectations.

Let me give an example. I found myself called into a post-merger study for a French company and its main US rival who had decided to pool their interests. The proposal had two elements. The main one was to help the client put together the organisation chart for the new company. In addition, the proposal promised that we would make a 'validation' of the savings (running into many millions of dollars per annum) which had been predicted to arise from the merger. When I saw this, alarm bells started ringing. To validate such figures completely would imply a massive task of analysis of every figure in the business plan: for example, we would have had to pronounce on the accuracy of the proposals for reducing the cost of production in what was a highly technical fabrication process of which we knew virtually nothing. Interpreted literally, the requirement to 'validate the savings' could have made us hostage to fortune.

As it happens, my fears were groundless. The client's senior executive who had commissioned the project was not particularly interested in this validation. It had been included in the terms of reference to sweeten other, internal interests in the client business. A good deal of lunching went on between our Partner and various members of the client's Board. Some suitably high-level observations were made in our report about the expected savings; the spotlight was shone elsewhere; everyone was happy. But, without proper management of the client's expectations, the story could have been quite different.

The kind of disaster which can happen is shown by an information technology study carried out for a public organisation. The consultants *thought* they were bidding to deliver some kind of system specification. The expectations of the client were so different, however, and the proposal was so poorly written, that the cons ended up having actually to deliver the piece of software itself. The result was a vastly increased amount of work and a thumping loss on the project.

If all goes well with a job, the management of expectations is not much of an issue. It can become critical, however, when there is a mismatch between what is expected by the client and what the project can reasonably deliver, as shown in the above example. Such a mismatch can occur for various reasons. One of the most basic is that the specification of the work was not clear at the outset. The opening chapters of this book have alluded repeatedly to the importance of clarity in specifying what is required of the consultants. My research found that consultants rated 'unclear client objectives' as over twice as important as any other factor in causing projects to fail.

Usually, the specification can and should be enshrined in writing. However, certain 'strategic' projects may be initiated with a much looser brief: because of their wide-ranging nature, it may be felt inappropriate to define in advance exactly what they will deliver. This situation leaves the door open to all kinds of mismatch between the client's expectations and the consultants' ability to deliver. Cynical cons may be aware that the project is unlikely to deliver everything the client wants, but may go ahead anyway in the hope of winning follow-on work.

A mismatch can readily occur if the job was 'oversold': in other words, promises were made at the proposal stage by the consultancy manager or Partner which were simply unrealistic. In this situation, the chickens are likely to come home to roost sooner rather than later unless the client can be gently persuaded to expect less than was originally promised.

Another situation that causes expectations to go unfulfilled is when something goes wrong with the project along the way. For example, having found yourself unexpectedly elevated to expert in latex-based compounds, you may then discover that the published market data on which the proposal relied as a source is virtually useless, since figures including car tyres are not very helpful to your client in the rubber-gloves business. The client was promised a 'quantitative overview of the world market', or some such high-sounding deliverable; you are looking at an OECD document that is ten years old and a couple of articles from the *Economist* which the client has probably already read. So what do you do?

What you try to do is avoid the situation coming to a head. Tactics for managing your client's expectations, in roughly descending order of preference, include:

• Building the relationship between client and consultants to the extent that awkward questions can be smoothed over or avoided.

• Finding plausible reasons why, in fact, the analysis which has been promised in the proposal is of no conceivable interest or would not assist the rest of the project. 'There's really no point in doing *that*, is there?'

• Using the weasel words with which you larded your proposal, along with some careful dressing up of mutton as lamb, gradually to persuade your client to see the results of the project as a sufficient response to the original brief, even when they fall far short of what may once have been in his mind.

• Drawing attention elsewhere, so that the omission of certain deliverables goes largely unnoticed. For example, if you can distract the rubber-gloves maker into worrying about the incidence of missing fingers, they may lose interest in pursuing the global market analysis which you were supposed to produce.

• Coming clean and owning up to your inability to deliver what was promised, praying that the client may let you off. A technique only to be used *in extremis!*

A mismatch between what the client expects and what you can deliver occurs also when there is bad news to deliver. Suppose you find that, far from being able to expand in the latex market, your client has got such a poor reputation with his main customers that they are about to cancel their existing orders. Again, client management is vital in this situation. The experienced con will start dropping hints at an early stage, involve the client as much as possible in the analysis and seek to lead him towards drawing the clear, if negative, conclusion for himself.

The injunction written on every con's heart is *no surprises*: whether the news is good or bad, the worst possible time to break it is at the final presentation. The true pro will always prepare the ground, sound the client out, fly a kite, bounce some ideas around... In short, from the start of the project until its end, management of the client's expectations is paramount.

How should clients react? You should welcome being prepared in advance for the project's conclusions, especially when they are hard or controversial. You may have no objection to the team's work being refocused, as the project advances, if certain of the original objectives become inappropriate or unnecessary. The thing to watch out for is major or systematic slippage of the terms of reference.

Your best guarantee is the written proposal agreed between yourself and the cons at the outset. If something is important to you, make sure it is in the document, focusing on the results that you require rather than the means to achieve them. Then remind yourself from time to time, by reading these terms of reference again. If the consultants tell you that the project is too broad or open to allow for specific definition of this kind, then suggest that they conduct a first stage (as limited as possible in its duration and cost) which will scope the work and at the end of which a more detailed specification will be agreed for what is to follow.

There is a breed of con which simply hates being pinned down in this way, and which prefers to stress words like 'trust', 'commitment' and 'partnership'. As far as I am concerned, however, any project can be specified in such a way as to set the main deliverables in concrete. Provided this is done, managing the client's expectations is simply good practice. Without such a guarantee, it can become sharp practice.

Getting on a roll: sell in and sell on

Another of the basic tricks which all cons are supposed to master is that of selling on. Simply put, this means using one job as the basis for selling the next. In fact, there are three permutations of selling on:

- Using one job in a company to sell a follow-on or related mission.

- Using a project as a Trojan Horse, in order to scout around inside the organisation and look for other jobs of any kind.

- Using work of a given type for one business to sell on to similar work in another company.

When a client is reluctant to buy a major project in one go, it is often both easy and effective to split the work up and offer a first phase (usually with a weasel word like 'strategic', 'scoping' or 'overview' in its title) as a way of at least getting a foot in the door. This may even be done as a loss leader in order to smooth the way, although consultancies are usually reluctant to drop their rates too much in case they are then unable to get back to full rates in subsequent jobs. Some, though, may offer to do a certain amount of work up-front for no fee, after which they will supposedly demonstrate the extent of the benefits that can be obtained if you carry on into the next stages. There is nothing particularly skullduggerous about these approaches, but clients should be aware that a first stage, however small or cheap, is deliberately aimed at establishing a psychological bond between client and con and freezing out the opposition. Accept such an approach, if you wish, with your eyes open and never forgetting the old adage that there is no such thing as a free lunch.

The Trojan Horse technique is much harder than simply selling on successive phases of the same job, because it calls for the con to build bridges within the client's organisation. For example, an IT consultant may be working on a project when she hears that there are problems in the manufacturing area. To capitalise on this opportunity she needs to find her way (preferably via an introduction) to the Director or Senior Manager responsible for Production, with whom she will have no established credibility. This has to be done, too, without alarming her immediate client contacts who might feel that she is going behind their backs or diluting her attention to their needs.

Often, internal consultancy rivalries will make cons reluctant to call in their colleagues with other skills and this impedes such cross-selling. There is also a concern that the *new* job may go wrong in some way and that this will reflect badly on the cons still working on the original project. Despite these handicaps, some of the very best cons are brilliant at scouting around for work for their colleagues. Just bear in mind that, when you send for the cons, you may be letting a ferret up your trouser leg.

When it comes to selling on from one job to similar work for new clients, there is of course nothing illegitimate about this. One of the best ways of judging a consultancy proposal is by giving proper attention to references from previous clients. However, in this there is a substantial difference of attitude between different types of consultancy. I have not made much play of this up to now, but the term *consultant* covers a multitude of sins from telephone canvasser through real estate salesman and head-hunter to grizzled ex-Chairman. Even the recognised management *consultancies* cover work varying from blue-sky strategy to hands-on computer, manufacturing or distribution implementations. The basic skills, or tricks, of consultancy are mostly applicable across all sectors, but there is a clear distinction between consultancies who sell similar work to client after client and those who encourage their clients to think they are getting something absolutely unique.

In simple terms, the more strategic the con the less willing he or she will be to discuss their previous clients. Blue-chip strategy boutiques routinely offer or undertake not to work for any other company in the client's industry for a defined period. The reason given is that the *absolutely* confidential work they undertake, for the most *prestigious* senior management with whom they work in *intimate* partnership, makes it necessary for their lips to be sealed ever after. By the same token, then, you can hardly expect them to come armed with references from all your rivals. If you suspect that appealing to corporate vanity is as important here as a genuine need to avoid revealing competitive information, then I might find it hard to argue with you.

In any event, getting a strategy con even to name his previous clients requires what Kipling called 'infinite resource and sagacity'.

At the other end of the scale, cons who specialise in reducing your work in progress or shaving the cost of overhead labour will fall over themselves to tell you how much they saved for Oldrival & Co down the road. They know that their track record is their best selling point. When new methodologies appear on the marketplace (such as bench-marking or re-engineering did in the none-too-distant past) there is a mad scramble of consultancies trying to pick up their first client in the new skill area, so that they can start to sell on elsewhere. They will not, of course, admit that they are virgins in whatever technique it may be[2]. However, if you can spot one of these cases, and if you rate the team, you might just pick up a bargain as they will be very keen both to win the work and to make a success of it.

A hint and a spin: make a little into a lot

As a con you soon learn to make the best out of whatever experience you may have, however limited.

If you have never done a job before in, for example, 'Strategic Outsourcing' (whatever that may be) your prospective clients in the pharmaceuticals business may be understandably reluctant to let you loose on their organisation. What to do? The answer is pretty obvious: you find any previous projects that your firm undertook in some vaguely related area and you dress them up as well as you can to pass muster. So the two days that you spent putting together a list of haulage contractors for an audit client becomes a 'Supply Chain Outsourcing Strategy for a Major Consumer Goods Manufacturer'. And that old study into reducing the cost of pencils in the NHS suddenly resurfaces as a 'Competitive Review of Procurement Opportunities for Healthcare Equipment Supplies'. This kind of thing rapidly becomes second nature.

Exactly the same happens when it comes to individuals. Any con

---

[2] It occurs to me that this is a rather important difference between cons and prostitutes: in the latter market, I understand that real or feigned virginity commands a premium. Not so with cons.

will tell you that he has worked on a number of very similar projects for clients in your industry. Press him a bit and it may emerge that:

- Actually, it was just one job and it was about as closely related to your business as those outlined above.

- The con concerned *did* work on a major study for a similar company, but his role was simply inputting data to the computer and gave him no real insights at all.

- It was done ten years ago.

  or:

- The job was a complete disaster.

Of course, you might have struck lucky and found someone who really *does* know the business. Even this may be a mixed blessing. A former colleague came from the brewing industry and became a con mainly to get broader experience. Instead, he spent two years doing virtually nothing but brewing assignments. This is the kind of experience likely to give even the best con a bit of an attitude problem. More normally, things seem to work the other way round: if you know about something, the chances are in some big firms that you will never get to work on any project remotely connected to it. Instead, you find yourself dressing up your CV to make a lot out of a little.

In my time, I had to bluff my way in matters as diverse (and as completely off my map) as the storage of natural rubber, the market for computerised typography and the organisation of a platinum fabrication business. With hindsight, I spent quite a lot of my consulting career wandering around client organisations trying desperately not to look completely gormless. Occasionally they even seemed to fall for it.

It was one of my senior colleagues, a far more consummate pro than I could ever be, who summed up the business for me when he said: 'I didn't get where I am today by knowing what I was talking about.'

The professional fair and the professional foul
There is a whole range of other techniques which can come in handy. Some of them are summarised below, ranging in approximate order from the decently professional to the seriously underhand:

- Find some *easy wins* to hang your hat on as early as possible in the project. This is a well-worn adage of any change programme but is still valid.

- Always get your *assumptions* down on paper and get them approved, explicitly or otherwise, by the client. Once the client has effectively signed off the assumption that the market for lion manure will continue growing indefinitely at 10% per annum, you can carry on writing a business plan for the world's largest lion farm without any further need for justification.

- When presenting data, always have up your sleeve at least *one more level of detail* than you are initially going to show the client. This will help to cover up any areas where the data is seriously weak (bare patches are less noticeable when seen from a distance) and, if the client wants more information, it should impress her no end when you reveal (a little) more.

- If you have serious trouble with data, try the *gloves model*. This goes back to a spreadsheet used for calculating warehousing costs. I believe it originated with one of the supermarket chains, was taken up and used by a logistics contractor and was then pinched and adapted by some colleagues of mine. The spreadsheet ran to many pages, including costs often into the millions of pounds or dollars for rentals and capital equipment. Tucked away inside was an entry for gloves to be worn by the warehousemen: X pairs at Y pence per pair. Whenever a client was shown the model, it was a safe bet that he would get side-tracked into some irrelevant argument about the gloves while much bigger assumptions, about the size of the building or the cost of equipping it, would get overlooked. To divert attention, always have 'gloves' (choose your own variant) close at hand.

- Match the **thud factor** to the client. This was our term for the weight of a document presented to a client. Mistakes here can be costly. Some individuals or organisations really do seem to measure their consultants by the pounds of thud that they turn out. Others are wise to the old 'lovely report to put on your shelf' trick and will react very negatively to heavy documents. There used to be a rule of thumb among some of my colleagues that a proposal should have one page for every thousand pounds of fees expected. Before you ask, I *have* seen proposals running to several hundred pages – and that was just the Appendices. At the other end of the scale, strategy cons like to write very brief proposals on the basis that the less you write the less the client can hold you to.

- If you don't like the recent past, excavate a bit of **ancient history**. Curiously, although I have often known clients require you to give references of past projects, I have only once had to show the date when the projects took place. A quick search on the computer usually turned up some suitable past jobs. Ten years old? No matter. I have seen jobs quoted as references when they had been performed a decade and a half before by people who had long since left the firm.

- If in doubt, **make it up**. Of course you don't wish to be totally dishonest, but a combination of a few juicy assumptions with our old friend 'making a lot out of a little' can be used to fill almost any gap. This kind of thing is easier to get away with in a verbal presentation than in writing, especially if you have managed to establish some kind of authority over your audience. 'Ladies and gentlemen, as you can see from this slide the total cost of refuse collection is ten million per year. Now, if we can save just *ten per cent* of this, that will give us a straight saving of a million.' Wild extrapolations come into the same category: 'As we have seen, the cost of pencils can be cut by five per cent. If we can achieve that same level in *all* our supplies, then we will put a million on the bottom line.' Or try the temporary suspension (never to be lifted) of disbelief: 'Of course, Schmitt are operating from Malaysia so the cost base is not strictly comparable. However, they found that they could improve output by ten per cent without additional labour. So, *just supposing* for a moment that we could do the same . . .'

- Playing *bait and switch*. This is a well-known technique of street traders and hustlers. You advertise some fantastic bargain ('Video recorders for only £49.99') to bring in the public, and then switch them onto other, more expensive, merchandise. Potentially, consulting offers any number of ways of doing this although I think there is still sufficient integrity around to make it rare. One way that it does happen is the switch of personnel on a job. Cons have never shaken off a reputation for wheeling out the blue-eyed boys for the presentation and then leaving the work in the hands of juniors. The problem may be exaggerated and, in my experience, switches of staff were usually because the chosen con was tied up elsewhere, but they do happen. With this, as with every other tactic and trick that I have outlined, *caveat emptor*.

Summing up
The con who is a real pro will:

- Turn any old mess into a well-structured project plan.

- Take great care not to confuse the strategic with the tactical.

- Sprinkle weasel-words about like peanuts in a Snickers bar.

- Cultivate the client relationship assiduously.

- Manage the client's expectations at all times.

- Avoid springing surprises, even good ones, on the client.

- Sell on further work to the client, the client's colleagues, his wives, camels, concubines and dogs and as many competitors or similar organisations as possible.

- Make a lot out of very little.

- Look for easy wins.

- Use carefully signed-off assumptions, different levels of data, diversionary tactics, ancient history, the thud factor and sheer barefaced cheek as weapons for survival in the kidding fields of consultancy.

And what of the smart client? Above all, he or she should be aware of these practices and be prepared to ignore, challenge or counter them when they get out of hand. In particular, the client should:

- Be very clear about her expectations from a project – less in terms of what has to be *done* than what must be *delivered* – and ensure that these expectations are not compromised, irrespective of all the expectation management and relationship building that may go on.

- Make sure that she understands the significance of words used by the cons, especially terms like 'strategic'.

- Remember that there are a lot of shades of grey between the truth and a downright lie.

Finally, a thought to ponder from Howard Davies, a former McKinsey man who became the Deputy Governor of the Bank of England: 'I found it hard to understand why my clients were prepared to pay decent money to employ someone who knew so much less about their business than they did.'[3]

Perhaps he knew a few tricks.

---

[3] From a review published in *Prospect*, January, 1997.

CHAPTER 6: THE SIMPLE PERSON'S GUIDE TO CONSULTANCY-SPEAK

THEY SAY THAT WORDS ARE CHEAP. WHICH JUST GOES TO PROVE THAT *THEY*, whoever they may be, never met a con. Every con knows the value of words.

Words are valuable not for themselves but for what they convey to the listener and for what they confer on the speaker. While we use words to communicate information to someone else, we are also through our choice of words communicating something about ourselves. Like the information itself, this message about ourselves may be anywhere between absolute truth and complete fiction. Cons love to use words which confer on them a status of expertise and knowledge. By doing so, they are building their own image with the client and, in turn, building their power base.

We all do this, of course, consciously or not. But few professions require the individual to maintain the aura of personal expertise which is demanded of consultants. In their use of words, cons strive continually to reinforce the kind of status that can justify a billing rate often in excess of £1,000 ($1,500) per day.

To be a successful con, it may not be absolutely essential never to be at a loss for words, but it sure helps. One of the knacks that I picked up along the way was the ability to stand on a platform and address a conference: it is another of the standard ways in which cons reinforce their authority. At the limit, it hardly seemed to matter what it was that I was asked to speak about: conference organisers appeared much more eager to fill up the programme than to worry about matching speakers to topics. I delivered to a conference in France a paper hailed by the trade press as a 'brillant exposé' on a topic of which I had never even heard until they rang and asked me to speak. The value of words? You bet.

The words most favoured by cons are, of course, those which make the speaker sound as smart as possible. In short, jargon and bullshit. Although some may confuse these two, I make a clear distinction:

- Jargon is the use of language, be it normal words or specially-coined ones, in a way which is specific to a certain culture or line of business. So the word *server* means something quite different to the tennis player, the computer engineer and the restaurateur. Jargon means something – but its meaning will be opaque to the uninitiated.

- Bullshit is the use of language, which may or may not be jargon, in a way which is exaggerated and pretentious. Bullshit may be totally meaningless or, to the extent that it means something, falls far short of the grand pretensions with which it is dressed up.

Cons have a weakness for jargon, both concerning their own business and the client's. In this they simply mirror the industries where they work. It is just not possible, I fear, to have anything to do with information technology and not to have recourse to what – to the outsider – can be a pretty impenetrable jargon. What many people associate with consultants, however, is out-and-out bullshit: high-sounding verbiage which is designed to obfuscate rather than elucidate. They are not the only perpetrators of management bullshit. Academics and writers share the blame, but cons are probably best placed to make money from it. And too many cons (I was one) are inclined to ask: 'Why use one word when five would do?'

Good bullshit, for me, is characterised by three features. Firstly, it sounds reasonably familiar and not too technical. Terms coined out of familiar words are good from this point of view as they make us feel that we either understand them already or, with only a little effort, we might: *delayering* is a good example. Secondly, the word must have a resonance that ripples as wide as possible and suggests something really good and really big. Like *empowerment*. Lastly, the term must lend itself to being applied as widely as possible across any number of functions or activities. *Global*, for instance, can be attached to just about any business activity that you choose to think of (try manufacturing, finance, operations, distribution, procurement . . .). If a word passes all three tests, and is relatively novel, you could be onto a winner.

OK, so cons like talking bullshit. So what? There can be a problem, of course, if the client is foolish enough to buy the services of someone whose skills or experience turn out to be so much hot air. In addition, I have more fundamental concerns on at least two levels:

- Words mean what you want them to mean. If both con and client are using words like *re-engineering* or *optimisation*, do they mean the same thing by them? If not, whose meaning is going to prevail? If a consultancy proposal promises to *integrate your strategic processes*, is anyone capable of judging whether or not the project succeeds in this objective?

- Do words unite or divide? If Britain and America are divided by their common language, is this not also true of client and con? The con's desire to impress by using long words may get in the way of common understanding and true cooperation. Alternatively – and I have seen this happen – the client may feel obliged to match the consultant word for word, and falls into the trap of aping the con's use of bullshit. You can then get the bizarre spectacle of a client's project manager struggling to explain to his colleagues what on earth he, as a kind of honorary consultant, is talking about. This gives rise to a self-reinforcing group-think[1] in which both client and consultant may convince themselves that they are working on something far more profound than is actually the case.

Enough of this bullshit. The title of this chapter promised a guide to consultancy speak, so here are some examples from A to Z of the kind of lingo which may start in the business school but often ends up in the mouth of a con:

a is for *assets*, which is what consultants often talk out of.

Also, as in 'our people are our greatest *assets*' which is a turn of phrase much favoured by senior executives who are about to make a third of the workforce redundant. In consultancy, the idea that the staff are the key *asset* is so obvious that it seems to have been quite forgotten by those at the top of the tree. Contempt is the best word that I can find to describe the way in which some consultancy leaders regard the lower forms of life in their own firm. The best example occurred when one of our overseas firms had to declare a significant number of redundancies: the senior Partner (or Grand Fromage to give him his full title) chose to make the announcement at the staff Christmas party. The idea that this might have some impact on morale or on his retention of his better *assets* was presumably alien to him. Be warned, all ye who seek to enter the gates of consultancy: the minute you cease to be a bankable *asset* you become a liability.

action plans are an essential part of any consulting job. Cons use them as a way of listing all the things that they cannot be bothered to do

---

[1] Group-think is itself jargon, but rather a useful concept. It was coined by Irving Janis to describe the excessive cohesiveness that can develop in a tightly-knit group, which then becomes convinced of its invulnerability and refuses to accept any evidence that goes against its own selective version of reality. The Bay of Pigs blunder is usually cited as the prime example of group-think.

themselves and making sure that the client is made responsible for doing them instead. At the end of a project, an *action plan* is very handy for sweeping up all the loose ends which should have been part of the job but somehow got left out along the way. Agreeing them as *actions* will not get them done any quicker, but it does get the cons off the hook.

b is for *BPR*. Although this is popularly supposed to stand for Business Process Re-engineering, its real meaning is Bore the Punter Rigid. More or less the same thing, of course. Other sources claim that it stands for Bigger, Pricier, Richer. So no change there, either.

brainstorming is a very handy device for getting out of awkward corners. A *brainstorming* is a meeting with very vague purpose and outcome, at which participants usually go over the same ground they have covered fifty times before. The thing that makes it special is that it has been called by the consulting team. And the reason why it is so valuable is that it fills in very effectively when the cons have no clue what to do and fancy picking up a few ideas from the client, or when they are hopelessly stuck and need to pass the buck back to the client. *Brainstorming* is a great way of coming up with *action plans* (q.v.) of a size inversely proportional to their usefulness.

buy-in is what cons like to get from their clients. It falls somewhere between the abdication of all critical thought processes and the signing of a blank cheque. Once you agree to *buy in* to the consultants' approach, diagnosis or recommendations you are committed emotionally and, in all probability, legally. *Buy-in* will lead you (by the nose, if necessary) to sign-off.

brand valuation is a specialist consultancy niche. It consists in attributing large monetary values to *brand* names which supposedly enable their owners to charge higher prices or command a greater market share than they would otherwise deserve. Ever wondered where this idea came from? Of course, you wouldn't pay over the odds for a con just because she happened to come from a firm with a fancy name, would you? Thought not.

C is for *commitment*. You might imagine that this is what a con has to have for his clients. Wrong again. *Commitment* is what the client needs to have in order for the con to feel that it is worth his while getting up in the morning. In an article entitled 'Consulting: has the solution become part of the problem?'[2] an unnamed con is quoted as saying: 'Clients must be committed both financially and emotionally to the effort – with the financial side of such commitment running to $100,000 to $700,000 in fees per month for twenty-four to forty-eight months.' In my book, that makes between $2.4 and $33.6 million in fees. Who says you cannot put a price on commitment?

cross-ruffing was something which my one-time employers suddenly started urging all staff to practise, at the time that the UK end of the firm was cosying up to its counterparts in the US. We never did find out what it meant.

culture was one of the great management (for which read consultancy) buzzwords of the 1980s. It became very fashionable to talk about changing the corporate *culture* and building a *culture* of quality/success/innovation/apple pie/cross-ruffing (please delete as applicable). Various techniques, such as culture-mapping, were sold to anyone who would buy them. To borrow a line from a commercial, *culture* was 'hard to define but easy to recognise'. Which made it an ideal recruit to the lexicon of consultancy-speak, where it nestles yet. Unfortunately, talking about cultural change proved to be a heck of a lot easier than actually doing it. So once everyone had learned their lessons from this, along came re-engineering instead.

d is for *deliverables*. 'Now what were they? Oh yes, we may have promised the client a few charts and stuff in our proposal, but he doesn't really want them, does he? He does. Detailed recommendations? No, I'm sure we can't have said detailed. Which page? I wonder how that got in. Yes, I know it says costed plans but surely

---

[2] By Robert G. Eccles, Eileen C. Shapiro and Trina L. Soske, in *Sloan Management Review*. 1993, vol. 34 no. 4.

that doesn't include capital items, does it? Well, I never wrote that. Look, if we do all this we'll never bring the job in on budget. What do you mean, if we don't do this he won't pay? That's ridiculous: look at the time we spent brainstorming with his team. Oh all right, but I've got to go to New York next week. You'll have to get a junior in to finish things off. I've got the notes from the workshop, somewhere. She should be able to cobble something together from those.'

delayering. Cons and gurus of every kind have had a field day persuading clients to remove all the people in their organisation who know anything whatever about its day-to-day operation. The consulting version of a frontal lobotomy, it produces clients who no longer have the capability of working things out for themselves and therefore have no option other than to continue their dependence on the cons. Game, set and match.

downsizing. What happens to the corporate piggy bank when senior management gets hooked on the use of external stimulants.

WARNING: consolvent abuse can seriously damage your wealth.

e is for *efficiency* (usually, if incorrectly, interchangeable with *effectiveness*), the great bronze idol on whose feet far too many pale virgins have been sacrificed. Now, I am not going to argue for *inefficiency* as a corporate virtue. But if you are going to use the efficiency criterion then you have to know what you are measuring and to understand what is, and is not, an appropriate benchmark. The only possible definition of efficiency is a measure of output as a function of input. When done at a high level, which is where most consultants like to operate, measures of this kind will almost inevitably be too general to be meaningful. If you consider the drive for *efficiency* in the National Health Service you will see how easy it is to measure inputs in a way which ignores a mushrooming management overhead. Compare the *efficiency* of a plant in the UK to that of a German factory using totally different equipment and you will come up with a figure that tells you nothing about how well the operations are managed or how hard the labour force works. If I were an optimist, I would say that the current trend towards 'shareholder value' as the ultimate yardstick shows that businesses have realised the inadequacy of traditional concepts of efficiency. The cynic in me wonders whether the lessons have really been learnt.

empowerment is a near-perfect specimen of consultancy-speak. Everyone can think that they understand what it means, but no two people can define it consistently. It has all the right associations that make it impossible to argue against it as a concept, and none of the tiresome baggage of measurement and benchmarks that come with something like efficiency. It can be used in every conceivable situation ('Klingons on the starboard bow, Cap'n. What shall we do?' 'Set *empowerment* to factor three, Spock'). It is a perfect front for any amount of hard-nosed downsizing and an ideal excuse for senior management to know less about their business than ever before. In short, a real gob-smacker of a word and I just wish I'd been the one who thought of it.

f is for *fast-track*. Not quite in the same league as empowerment, perhaps, but a handy little term to describe whatever you happen to be selling to the client today. Try a *fast-track* paradigm shift. Oh, you did that last year. Well, how about this cute little *fast-track* supply-chain strategy? No? Then perhaps what you really need is *fast-track* empowerment. Terms like this fit just about anywhere. And mean absolutely nothing. Be honest, when did you ever hear anything described as slow-track?

focused has been another big hitter in recent years. I think it started with the vogue for books bemoaning the decline in US manufacturing, from which crept the concept of the *focused* factory. Like a virus, it started to multiply and mutate. Strategies suddenly needed to be *focused*. So did product lines and human-resource plans. Within a year or two, major corporations which had spent two decades diversifying suddenly decided that they needed to focus themselves. The corporate advisers have been so busy removing their wheelbarrows of cash that they have gone cross-eyed with the effort.

familiarisation is a bit of consulting jargon used to describe the first days of a project. Everyone has to sit in a circle on comfy cushions and hold hands. Then they say things like 'I'm a really important senior consultant specialising in the field of focused asset downsizing, but you can call me Nigel.'

g is for *global*. Another nifty little go-anywhere, all-terrain, good-with-children, melt-in-the-mouth, 3-for-$1, stop-me-and-buy-one epithet. The main point about this one is that consultancies love to apply it to themselves. They all have to have *global* vision, *global* competence, *global* reach, *global* capabilities, *global* networks, *global* scale and *global* support for their clients. Most confusingly, they all seem to claim *global* leadership of something or other. Just what all this globalisation really means, I could not say. But the word presumably comes from *glob*, which may tell us something about what it is worth.

h is for *helicopter vision*. I can no longer remember who came up with the idea that this is the defining characteristic of the senior executive, but it may well have been a consultant out to flatter his client. Whatever its origins, *helicopter-vision* has been reabsorbed by the consultancy profession as one of the key virtues for all strategy cons. It means being incapable of keeping your feet on the ground and whirling around at the kind of high altitudes that leave other mortals gasping for breath. Some people are impressed by this kind of thing. We used to refer to our more helicopter-like colleagues as seagulls: they flew in occasionally, flapped about, squawked a lot and dropped smelly stuff on everyone else before flying away again.

holistic is what every approach has to be in an age which has come to mistrust the specialist and in which too many executives simply do not understand the detail of their own businesses. Generalisations, superficiality and oversimplifications can all be justified on the grounds that they are part of a *holistic* method. Those possessed of helicopter-vision are naturally good at seeing *holes*. Sorry – wholes.
Not to be confused with **heuristic** which is a posh word for a rule of thumb. I'm more of an algorithm man, myself.

i is for *imperatives*. Change *imperatives* are part of the jargon of re-engineering and signify the reasons why you really need to spend more money than you have right now on yet another consultancy project. Not to be confused with Mint Imperials.

integrated goes along with *focused* and *global* as the sort of adjective that you can add to just about anything. But what does it add to the meaning? You wouldn't buy a *disintegrated* procurement strategy, would you? Or have much truck with a *disintegrated* systems architecture. Or put your efforts into a *disintegrated* product-development programme. So try not to be impressed next time you get offered the *integrated* version of any of these. Alternatively, if you insist, I'll give you an Integrated Consultancy Management Example (INCOME). But only if you keep reading to Chapter 12.

indicative is as fine a weasel-word as you are likely to meet. Figures, comparisons, models, analyses, recommendations . . . You name 'em, they can all be described as *indicative*. Unlike most bullshit, however, the term means one thing and one thing only. Namely, that if push comes to shove, the client can hold the consultant to *none* of it.

intrapreneurship was coming up strongly on the rails a few years back, then seemed to fall somewhere before the final furlong. It referred to the idea that small teams within large companies should be encouraged to behave as if they were a mini-business in their own right. Seen at the time as a way of rejuvenating the big corporation, I think it ran into our friend *focused* on a dark night and was left bleeding to death in the gutter.

investment. Something that clients do. See *commitment*.

j is for *just-in-time*. A useful example of how words can be taken out of context and expanded way beyond their original meaning and value. The term *just-in-time* originated from the Japanese motor industry and had very specific significance within their production systems. However, it has all the characteristics of good bullshit: it sounds meaningful, we can all think that we understand its significance and it can be adapted to virtually any occasion. And it has been. Every con who has ever dabbled in the availability of hospital beds, or the handling of cheques in a bank, or even the supply of pencils to his client's stationery cupboard has called for these to be managed on *just-in-time* principles. Which means . . . er . . . they should arrive, sort of, *just-in-time*, you know? Such has been the overuse of the term that cons have had to borrow an even more specific word from the same Japanese origins – *kanban* – and have then set about debasing that in its turn.

k is for *kanban*. Japanese for 'Big Mac and regular fries, please.' Not a lot of people know that.

knowledge. Rather an elusive commodity hereabouts, you may feel. Although innocent enough, at first sight, the word seems to be creeping into consultancy-speak. A recent newspaper announcement highlighted the recruitment of a 'Chief *Knowledge* Officer' by a leading financial institution. I have never met one of these, but assume that he or she sits in the middle of a darkened room containing some large brains floating in cylindrical glass tanks. These hum gently and occasionally flicker as their synapses fire up in response to requests from the dealing floor for *knowledge*. Or perhaps I've just been watching too many episodes of *Mighty Morphin Power Rangers*.

l is for *learning*. Presumably how you acquire knowledge (q.v.). Now, you might think that we all do this, quite naturally, much of the time. But no: our own unaided learning is no use at all; what you need is a consultant to show you how it should be done. It's rather like when I tried wearing contact lenses and found, after a few weeks in Hong Kong, that my eyes felt as if they were burning up. I went to a Chinese optician who examined me thoughtfully and pronounced: 'Mister Asford, you not brinking ploperry.' Apparently, the brinking which I had done for the previous thirty or so years of my life was just not good enough, but I never did learn how to brink collectly. The *learning* organisation was rather a fashionable concept for a while. I may have learned what it was once, but I seem to have forgotten.

leverage is as nifty a word as ever graced a con's lips. Again you can see the characteristics of the genre: good resonance, lets us believe that we all understand it, highly transferable. This one has the added advantage that it has for long been an established jargon word in US accounting practice: *leveraging* is what the Brits call gearing. So Wall Street gave us the *leveraged* buy-out. So far, so good: but why stop there? If we wish to make the most of a famous name, lets speak about *leveraging* the brand. If we think we are good at R&D, how about getting more *leverage* from our innovatory capability? If the cons have got us pinned against the wall, we might as well make the most of it and *leverage* the skills-base of our knowledge partners. The particular beauty of this is that you can never have too much of a good thing: our client may be the best in the world at some particular activity, but we can still tell him to *leverage* it more. Neat, huh?

lean is another word that has arrived from the East courtesy of manufacturing consultants. In a society which makes fashion icons out of superwaifs, who can argue against *leanness*? If *lean* goes with mean, isn't it what every Chief Executive wants his business to be? Less is more. *Leaner* means fitter. Words like this are perfect for dressing up every sort of economy measure and cutbacks or closures on any scale. At the end of the day, though, is the business going to be healthier as a result of trying to get down to a size six? The answer is, of course, that it all depends. What is the paradigm that we are trying to change, and why? *Leanness*, like Kate Moss, is not the only model in town.

m is for *methodology*. For some cons, venturing out without their *methodology* is as unthinkable as going to work without their tie on. More on *methodologies* later.

measurable: as in *measurable* objectives, *measurable* standards, *measurable* targets, *measurable* performance . . . If you cannot *measure* it, it doesn't exist. Since it is virtually impossible to argue against this view of life, limited though it may be, I advise anyone who comes up against a con who is a compulsive measurer not even to bother protesting. Unfortunately they are a bit of a pain, especially when they are human resource specialists. Their insistence upon measurement is probably the result of working in this 'soft' area where they will have been given some stick for the vagueness of their theories. In revenge, they start insisting that their clients must *measure* the effectiveness of their personal development plans and set *measurable* targets for increasing the learning capability of their organisation. Theoretically sound, practically tedious and quite unnecessary if management is doing what it's there for, namely managing.

matrix. A pretty diagram consisting of (usually four) squares in a grid. Nothing wrong with that but the name makes it sound smarter than it really is. Then again, I suppose that calling it a Battenburg Cake Diagram might have been a bit embarrassing for the Boston con who first thought of it.

multidisciplinary is a jolly handy word for making a committee sound important. *Multidisciplinary* Taskforce Coordinator is such a fine title for the minutes secretary.

n is for *network*. About the time that I ducked out of consulting, we were trying to come up with a new product in the area that everyone else calls the supply chain. A great deal of energy was expended on an attempt to get it rebaptised 'the supply *network*'. It was, of course, exactly the same animal as before but it sounded as if we had something new to talk about. *Network* is another relatively portable term. Neural *networks* are the kind of computer jargon which we can all use without having the first clue what we are on about, except it sounds clever. *Networking* is, of course, the bullshit word meaning to have a good natter with your mates down the pub. Which leads me to a favourite anecdote. In Bangkok there used to be a bar called the Other Office. When anyone called the boss in the afternoon, his secretary could truthfully answer, 'He'll have to call you back: he's in the Other Office.' *Networking*, no doubt.

O is for *optimisation.* I plead guilty to severe abuse of this one. I never proposed that I would improve a client's operation: I would *optimise* it. Strategies are always *optimal* (unless they are the existing ones, in which case they are *suboptimal*). Not only does the word sound suitably grand; suggesting that you can *optimise* things avoids the element of criticism which attaches itself to telling the client that her business has room for improvement.

outsourcing has been going on quietly since the beginning of time, but previously known as purchasing or contracting or subbing or buying-in according to the circumstances of the transaction. Now we have all learned to call it *outsourcing* and think of it as a strategic decision. Could it possibly be (a wild hunch, I admit) that cons may have something to do with it?

P is for *players*. I really dislike the abuse of this humble word. In case you haven't noticed, strategy cons never talk about the companies or businesses or competitors or participants in an industry: it's always *players*. Phrases like 'Let's take a rain check on the strategic competences of the other *players*' roll easily from their tongues. Is business just a game? Perhaps for the speaker it is.

process. One of the stars of the 1990s: *process* goes with re-engineering like toe goes with sucking. If you haven't found out what it's all about, this is not the book that is going to tell you. Just remember the mantra from *Animal Farm*: '*Process* good, function bad; *process* good, function bad; *process* good . . .'

parameters. The kind of con who wears specs and knows how to do more than play Solitaire on his laptop will get a buzz out of telling you that he has *parametrised* the model. Don't be fazed: it just means that he's stuck a lot of numbers into it. Take him down a peg by reminding him of the GIGO rule: Garbage In, Garbage Out.

partnership. (a) What you should have with your suppliers or customers, or both, according to a lot of cons. Unfortunately, in all the partnerships I have seen one of the parties came out the clear winner. (b) What you should have with your cons, according to a lot of cons. I wonder who the winner might be in this case?

positioning. What you do with your partner, in private. See also *market penetration* and *problems, mounting*.

q is for *quality*. Definitely a good thing to have. Whether or not it is a good thing for your cons to have accreditation to a formal *quality* standard is another matter. When one consultancy implemented such a standard, the only change at the sharp end was a requirement to produce a lot of documentation and put it in something called a *quality* file. Any connection between that and the work delivered to the client was pretty coincidental. At each stage of a project, a *quality* plan had to be signed by the Partner. This only really mattered when the auditors were due to come and inspect things, a threat which unleashed an avalanche of backdated signatures and forged documents carefully tailored to the needs of the *quality* file. Who gains from this? *Quality* consultants, of course.

quals is consultancy jargon for qualifications, i.e. the past work references which you use to support your proposal to a client. Arguably a bit of a misnomer, since half the time we had to bend a miscellany of only vaguely relevant experience to force-fit it into the new proposal. However, unquals does not have quite the same ring to it.

quantum leaps are what you are promised if you undertake a programme of re-engineering. Now, if someone claims that their fitness training course will give you a *quantum leap* in your track times, or that their latest paperback will deliver a *quantum leap* in your ability to organise your life, or that their diet will enable a *quantum leap* in reducing your waistline, you might suspect that you are being sold snake oil. So why does the mention of a *quantum leap* in organisational performance induce senior executives apparently to take leave of their critical faculties? No, I don't know the answer either.

r is for *re-engineering*. What more can I say about this? One can only stand and marvel at the gravy train that these 13 letters brought to the lucky few. R is also for rich, seriously.

rightsizing. Memo to all Chief Executives: if you have to give half your staff the sack in order to salvage your bonus, please have the decency to say so honestly. Dressing it up under a ghastly euphemism adds insult to injury. There is a good case for banning all forms of *sizing* (*down*, *up* and *right*) before someone is murdered for using them by the Campaign Against Misuse of the English Language (CAMEL).

S is for *synergy*. This can probably claim to be the granddaddy of all consultancy-speak. At one time, every merger or operational amalgamation used to be accompanied by a rationale based on *synergy*. Like all overused terms, the shine wore off it after a while and it has joined a select class of words that cons avoid using because they immediately make clients suspect that they are being bullshitted. A pity, because this one has – or at least can have – some real meaning behind it.

strategic, by contrast, seems to be as popular as ever even though it probably deserves a worse fate. Anything devised by a con can be made to sound grander than it really is by denoting it *strategic*. Too often, a *strategic* policy means one which the client is expected to adopt without any proper quantification of its benefits. For their part, client managers are not above passing the buck for poor performance by blaming it on *strategic* decisions which are, by implication, beyond their control.

shareholder value became the war-cry of the mid-1990s and looks good for a few years yet. It is largely what economists might call 'our old friend net present value' dressed up in new clothes. Its danger, as with *brand valuation*, is that it adds a possibly spurious aura of scientific measurement to an approach which, while intellectually appealing, raises real practical difficulties in use. Plenty of scope there for the cons.

scalable is another smokescreen word. Every con who has taken a small sample and then cheerfully extrapolated to the population, or done a short pilot study to justify a universal roll-out, has implicitly asserted that his or her work is *scalable*. And so it may be: but only if the facts support this and not just by virtue of attaching the word *scalable* to it. In computing, to be *scalable* is fast becoming one of the cardinal virtues (in common with *user-friendly*, *modular*, *integrated* and another half-dozen similar adjectives). Clients are well advised to probe behind such terms if they wish to be sure that a system, product or policy is right for them.

t is for *TLA*, or three-letter-abbreviation. Cons, and all perpetrators of management theories, have a renowned weakness for calling things by TLAs. To list but a few: BPR, EVA, MBO, SBU, TQM, JIT, MRP, CYA, DRP, ECR, CRP, DPP, NPV, DCF, ABC, MIS, EDI. Regrettably, there are no prizes for correctly identifying all of these. A related obsession is with catalogues where every item starts with the same letter, such as the 'four Ps' of marketing or the 'seven Ss' of the McKinsey framework popularised by Peters and Waterman. Interestingly, of this, the authors wrote: 'Without the memory hooks provided by alliteration, our stuff was just too hard to explain, too easily forgettable'[3]. Draw your own conclusions.

time-based competitiveness was a concept that came onto the scene a few years ago but never quite seemed to make it into the premier league. It fails on at least two of the three criteria of good bullshit, by not really sounding sufficiently big and by being insufficiently portable (it fits in operational disciplines, but is hard to transfer elsewhere). Academically, it was a good effort to define a criterion of business success that was not based solely on dollars and cents. Pragmatically, dollars and cents are probably all that the CEO wanted to hear about.

u is for *upside*. Recommendations always seem to have a lot of '*upside* potential' but only 'limited downside'. What this means is that the cons are not prepared to stake their name and fees on you achieving a better result than their central prediction but they would love you to feel that such an outcome is likely. Like most consultancy-speak, unsubstantiated *upside* is best ignored.

V is for *value-added*. A bit of technical jargon, when deployed by those who can actually define it, which has passed into being another multipurpose term for the bullshitter to use. Re-engineering is promulgated on the notion of eliminating non-*value-adding* activities. Who could argue against that? But working out what it actually

---

[3] Thomas J. Peters and Robert H. Waterman, Jnr: *In Search of Excellence* (Harper & Row, 1982).

means in practice is something else again: few wins are as easy as this makes it sound. Nonetheless, I do believe as an unshakable article of faith that consultants have to add value to their clients.

validation is what you are supposed to do to a model after building it and before using it to generate recommendations for the future. Basically, you run a historical or current scenario, using real numbers, and see whether it will produce a result close to the actual outcome. Unfortunately, it is difficult and time-consuming and there is a great temptation to skip it. In fact, while I did a great deal of spreadsheet modelling in my time as a con, I never did a proper *validation* of any of it. So, if you *really* dislike your consultants, ask to see the *validation* of their model. Tee hee.

virtual will be, I confidently predict, the top money-spinning bullshit for consultancies as we near the millennium. *Virtual* organisations and networks are already proliferating, at least in the literature of business. Predictably enough, we now are also living in the age of the *virtual* consultancy although please do not expect them to work for *virtually* nothing. The first firm that I have seen described in such terms is the exotically-named Z/Yen. I am confident that they will not be the last.

W is for *world-class*. Another motherhood and apple pie kind of concept.

warehousing used to be a grubby old shed where you stuck your production until you could shift it to someone else's grubby old shed. Somewhere along the line it transmogrified[4] into a sexy term for database computing. Never let it be said that cons cannot produce radical change.

X & Y are for two contrasting propositions about human behaviour in organisations, propounded in the 1950s by Douglas McGregor. The

---

[4] A great shame, I feel, that we got re-engineering instead of the infinitely jollier-sounding Business Process Transmogrification.

'theory x' person is indolent, prefers to be led, is not very bright and can be readily duped. Also known as the perfect client.

Z is for *zero-based*. Remember *zero-based* budgeting? Cons, academics and learned textbooks may come and go, but budgets based on what happened last year will be with us for ever. RIP whoever invented this one.

This lexicon of the good, the bad and the downright *global* terminology beloved of management consultants turned out longer than I expected. That reflects, I fear, the ever-lengthening list of such terms with new ones coming onto the market at regular intervals. By the time this book is published, I suspect words like *re-engineering* and *rightsizing* will have become sufficiently old hat, and sufficiently discredited, to have been abandoned by most cons. How are the mighty fallen?

This leads to the serious question which underlies this admittedly frivolous compilation of bullshit. *Why* is this stuff so popular and so successful?

The answer may seem obvious. Using words like those listed makes you sound clever and gives you political advantage over your client or the client's employees. You acquire referred power by drawing on the supposed wisdom of the term's author and evoke feelings of inadequacy in anyone who imagines that they should understand what you are talking about when in fact they have not a clue. So far, so straightforward.

There is, however, more to it than this. Many of the words that I have listed have their origins in (or, at least, owe their popularity to) consultancy methodologies. What has happened in the consultancy market is roughly what happened a generation ago to food retailing: we have moved away from the era of weighing out goods to fit exactly what the customer wants, or making up a mix to their own taste, and moved firmly into the age of packaged convenience. This implies standardisation of consulting work, an emphasis on product development and, above all, a preoccupation with brand names and glitzy packaging of the latest methodology. For consultancies, the benefits are partly economic (as seen in Chapter 4) and partly managerial (the subject of Chapter 10).

Has this been driven by consumer-demand or producer-push? Some of both, no doubt, but it is the push element which dominates when it comes to the business of continually reinventing the product and finding some new high-sounding name to excite the punter. Moreover, the growth in the consultancy business makes this imperative if the same Fortune 500 companies are to be continually recycled as clients. After all, there *should* come a time when a client has taken all the consultancy inputs that he needs. Were it not, that is, for the fact that by the time that day comes the cons will have invented a new product to sell the same client and start all over again.

Recent news stories have highlighted, with some glee, tales of companies who have downsized and are now busy upsizing again – possibly with the help of the same cons. Whatever the truth behind the anecdotes, consultancies are obsessed with the need to refresh their products before the expiry of their shelf-life. And each new 'ology' that comes along needs its own grand title to wear as a crown, even if its backside may be sticking out of its trousers.

The grand name which is used to denote a methodology (such as Business Process Re-engineering, Overhead Value Analysis, Strategic Outsourcing, Supply Chain Optimisation, Change Management, Benchmarking or whatever) represents a kind of linguistic code which only the privileged few are able to crack. Such codes may hide one or more of the following three secrets:

- Dressing up what is basically common sense in order to make it sound grander than it really is.

- Out and out obfuscation, such as passing off under a new guise the same old stuff that we did yesterday.

- Genuine insight.

My own feeling is that most 'ologies' consist 80% of the first of these, 15% of the second and possibly 5% of the third. The trouble is that such insight as there may be tends to get lost under the verbiage which for some reason cons feel it necessary to layer on top. The author John Mortimer, on a visit to Australia, once commented that the seafood was good but that you had to be at the quayside to grab it as it was landed, before someone deep fried it and served it with whipped cream and a maraschino cherry. I have nothing against re-engineering – honest! I do genuinely believe that looking at groups of activities as *processes* is a powerful tool and a source of real insight. I object, however, to the grand house of cards which cons have sought to erect on top of this.

Words are used to trigger not just thoughts but feelings, too. The marketeer who called a washing powder Daz knew what he or she was doing: the word, invented though it is, evokes a sensation of brightness which we feel rather than think about. But do you really want to buy consultancy in the same way as you buy detergent? In the more serious moments of Chapter 3 I drew attention to the funda-mental importance of the calibre of the individual consultants who will work for you. Fancily-named methodologies seek to replace the experience of the individual with the direction of a prescribed approach, adding for good measure some of the marketeer's emotional manipulation. Mistrust them.

If you are on the other side of the table, perhaps as a relatively inexpe-rienced con trying to survive in front of an awkward client, you have two choices in the matter of consultancy-speak. You can either:

- Decide never to bullshit your clients, always tell the truth, refuse to dress up the ordinary in fancy clothes and admit it when you are out of your depth;

  or:

- Survive.

On the whole, the latter is probably a better idea. And remember, clients like to be bullshitted up to a certain point.

For those who have yet to acquire the knack, what you need is a random bullshit generator. I make no claims for originality in this but it is a most useful device that you can fold up and take anywhere with you – which is more than can be said for some methodologies which are embodied in so many volumes of turgid prose that an articulated truck is needed every time you want to move them. So here, for the uninitiated, is a handy consultancy-speak generator.

Consultancy-speak Generator

Column 1	Column 2	Column 3
Business	Process	Re-engineering
Integrated	Knowledge	Heuristic
Global	Network	Commitment
Focused	Culture	Buy-in
Fast-track	Partnership	Leverage
Lean	Value	Empowerment
Multidisciplinary	Matrix	Optimisation
Strategic	Learning	Synergy
Scalable	Brand	Validation
Virtual	Quality	Delayering

All you have to do is select one word from each column, at random, and concatenate them: for example, *Fast-Track Learning Commitment*, or *Strategic Network Empowerment*. Who knows, you may come up with the next all-singing all-dancing TLA. And, if you do, you won't forget my royalties, will you?

CHAPTER 7: BEWARE OF FLYING BULLETS

Beware the bullet point, my son!
The jaws that bite, the claws that catch!
Beware the Jubjub bird, and shun
The frumious bubble chart![1]

A few years ago I was browsing through a computer magazine when I came across a review of the latest version of a popular presentation graphics package. Having outlined its various features, the reviewer closed with the throw-away remark that he supposed this might be of interest to someone but that he had never met anyone who actually *used* a package of this type.

I was somewhat struck by this because, as a consultant, my life seemed at times almost to revolve around presentation charts and graphics packages. Even when the firm had *downsized* secretarial resource to the point of invisibility, we still managed to hang on to a graphics assistant whose sole task was to put together the classiest presentations possible. In the course of my time with the firm these evolved from simple bullet charts to full-colour 3-D masterpieces well

---

[1] After 'Jabberwocky' from *Through the Looking Glass,* with apologies to the memory of Lewis Carroll.

hung about with clipart. Such was the volume of this work that, just to support an office of some thirty people, we ended up buying a very expensive colour photocopier to turn the stuff out.

Putting together a good presentation is a core skill which any decent con must acquire. In fact, my employers required staff to take not one but two courses in presentation skills, the only topic that was deemed important enough to require this. Although the technique of presenting material on a screen was only part of this training, it is a vital weapon to have in the armoury. By the same token, clients need to be aware that cons not only set out to impress them through the use of visuals of various kinds but may use these presentational techniques – from bullet points to bubble charts – in ways which can obfuscate or mislead as easily as they can enlighten.

It is obvious enough that presentation graphics are not used solely by consultants and that, if they have not spread very far among the writers of computer mags, they are nonetheless reasonably familiar to many managers. However, while few may admit to being impressed by the consultant who walks through the door with a slick sales presentation, managers are still vulnerable to confusing style with substance and allowing the smart presentation of information to distract them from its weak foundations.

Perhaps it is just a coincidence, but consider this. The growth of management consultancy has been a phenomenon of the last decade and a half, accelerating rapidly from the second half of the 1980s onwards. In this it has mirrored, almost precisely, the rise of personal computing and its widespread adoption in business. There is a direct link between the two in that a lot of consultancy has been concerned with the specification and implementation of computer systems. There is also, I suggest, a second and indirect connection: cons have used the power of the PC to keep one step ahead of their clients in collecting, manipulating and presenting data in ways that are considered meaningful. This has been an important contributor to their status as experts or value-adders. In some cases that status has been well justified and the use of computing power has simply helped the presentation of an important message. In other cases, the personal computer has given a spurious legitimacy to some very dodgy analysis and stuck a stylish facade on a jerry-built shack.

So did the personal computer develop to meet the needs of analysts and consultants, among others, or was it the machine that catalysed the consulting industry? I cannot prove it either way but, if the computer begat the con, it is something else to blame on Steve Jobs and Bill Gates.

The Jabberwock with eyes of flame

Presentations do not need to be sophisticated. The favourite tool of the consulting profession, whether presenting proposals or delivering results, is a simple, old, tried and trusted favourite:

• The bullet point.

Where would consultants be without bullets, those eyes of flame that jump off the page and burn themselves into the consciousness of the client? At their best, they convey information with a crispness and concision which is hard to match. At their worst, they line up by their hundreds across dozens of turgid slides, concussing the reader into the kind of persistent vegetative state that would have a doctor reaching for the off switch on the ventilator. Between those two extremes lie a multitude of wingdings.

Why do cons so love bullet points? To answer this question, what better than a bullet chart?

The value of bullet charts

- Concise: draw attention to the main points

- Forceful: give an impression of action

- No need to worry about substantiating your arguments

- Easy to pass quickly over negative points

- Quick to write and produce

The virtues of concision are real enough: the simple act of trying to put your thoughts down on paper as half a dozen crisp points concentrates the mind wonderfully and this is likely to benefit the client. The bullet style lends itself to conclusions, recommendations and action points and discourages woolly thinking.

The other advantages of the bullet chart, however, are much more weighted in favour of the consultant. It is the written equivalent of the sound-bite so beloved of politicians: it encourages statements that sound good, or feel plausible, or give an impression of dynamism and action, however little substance may lie behind them. Bullet points flatter bullshit. You can just imagine the first con who put up a chart saying something like:

Action plan

- Re-engineer the organisation

- Go home for tea

and his client swooning with ecstasy at the thought of it, even though he had not got the first idea what the con was talking about.

Writing bullet charts is a form of editing: out goes all the detail, all the complexity, all the subtlety, all the ifs and buts, all the arguments that could either prove or disprove the point. What you are left with is an invitation to take something on trust. If it suits the con largely to ignore the points which might disprove the argument being advanced, they can be reduced to insignificance or left out entirely. A few bullet charts can be knocked up quickly and it is easy, all too easy, to use them as a cover for sloppy analysis or a lack of substance.

Consider the following extract from an imaginary final report and a bullet-point version of the same recommendations. First, the report:

Overseas Expansion

In order to escape the constraints of the domestic market, the preferred
option is to seek to expand overseas. Compared to the UK market of around
£50 million per annum, the value of the US marketplace is estimated to be at
least $600 million annually, although two thirds of this is in automated
equipment which is not part of the company's range. Of the remainder, three
major competitors control some 85% and monopolise the distribution chain.
For this reason the US would be very difficult to penetrate.

In Europe there is no overall dominant player. The market is highly
fragmented and there are at least 1500 significant purchasers in Germany
alone, which makes marketing expensive. The German market has an
annual turnover in the region of $120 million. According to the OECD, total
sales in Europe are three times this figure although some press reports
suggest sales over $450 million. In both France and Italy, only national
producers are eligible to bid for Government contracts under an EU
derogation which has just been renewed for a further five years.

Expansion is unlikely to be easy, both because of the degree of existing
competition in the markets and because the company currently has neither
the language skills nor the systems capability to sell effectively in other
countries. More detailed market analysis will be required before a final
selection of targets can be made.

Entry into an overseas market would be facilitated by the acquisition of a
local company, but the high price which would have to be paid to acquire a
successful operation, if a candidate could be found, would give an
unacceptably long payback (in excess of ten years) unless exceptional
profits growth could be achieved. The alternative might be a joint venture
but this would almost certainly be at the price of giving the overseas partner
access to the company's UK customers.

Our recommendation is for gradual organic growth targeted on not more than

---

Now, the bullet chart:

Overseas Expansion

- Recommended option to escape UK limitations

- Market size: UK: £50 m

  US: $600 m

  Europe: $500 m (est)

- Need to strengthen our IT and language capabilities

- Options: acquisition, joint venture, organic

- Go for organic growth in European markets

- Undertake market research to confirm priority targets

On the face of it, the bullet version is far stronger: certainly it is crisp and concise where the full account is much harder reading. What should also be clear, though, is that the editing process has turned a cautious conclusion into a bullish recommendation, leaving out inconvenient details about how hard it will be to penetrate the new markets and what a large proportion of them is closed off to the company. A focus on action has been used to emphasise the need for a market-research project which the cons will no doubt be only too pleased to undertake as their next project. The second version may be true, after a fashion, but it is certainly not the whole truth.

Clients in the survey showed a firm preference for summary reports and action plans over full reports, as shown in Figure 7.1. Bullet charts and other summaries, along with verbal presentations to the client, were the clear favourites. Workshops were also popular but relatively few clients saw 'the process itself' as a significant deliverable.

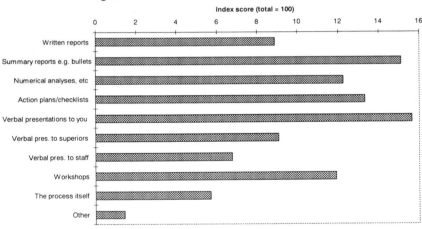

Figure 7.1: Most useful deliverables from project

How can clients take advantage of the good things about bullet points, while avoiding their perils? Three rules may help:

- Do not rely on consultants to take all the complexity out of an issue. Expect them to cut through it and produce a firm recommendation, but accept at the same time that some issues go way beyond the 'single page of A4' so beloved of senior management. You should not expect consultants to make things too simple for you. After all, why should senior managers only get to make the *easy* decisions?

- If you ask for a bullet-point proposal or report, be aware that a lot will have been left out. Do you understand what has been edited out and why? Do you know what options have been weighed up in order to reach the conclusion? One way of finding this out is to question and probe every bullet. An alternative is to insist on having the full report as well as the cut-down version, but there is no point in having the complete argument unless you are going to read and digest it.

- Far and away the best way of understanding the blank spaces between the bullets is to be closely involved in the project as it advances so that you scarcely need the report at all. The time to understand, and argue, the risks of expanding overseas is probably weeks or months before the report is going to be written. In a major project, get your own full-time resource working alongside the cons so that you – or at least someone in whom you have confidence – fully understand the issues being raised before they find their way into bullet points. On a smaller job this may not be appropriate but you should still almost be able to write the bullet chart yourself before the con puts pen to acetate. Decent cons should welcome this: remember that a con's basic credo is 'No surprises'.

A criticism of cons which I have heard more than once is that they seem very impressive while they are around but that they leave little behind when they have gone. To avoid this, the client needs fully to understand not only the cons' recommendations but the why and wherefore of how these were arrived at. This implies digging deep, challenging and questioning. Bullets, by themselves, are dangerous: get behind them.

Forever blowing bubbles

If bullet points are the simple mainstay of consultancy presentations, bubble charts are at the other end of the scale of sophistication. They came in the 1980s to be the leitmotiv of strategy cons, summing up their ability to deliver complex analysis of strategic issues to clients in a way that even the dimmest of non-exec directors could understand. Those in the know tell me that today they are seen as a little *passé*, but that has certainly not stopped their use as the stock in trade of some of the biggest names in the game.

The firm in which I was formerly employed had its own strategy boutique which, while owned by us, was very careful to keep a maximum of distance from our earthier style. There was a serious problem, in fact, with the prevalence of 'them and us' attitudes on both sides of the organisation. For 'us' this was crystallised into derision of bubble charts: it only needed the name of our strategic offshoot to be mentioned and you could be absolutely certain that, in the next sentence, someone would mention bubbles. This was always the cue for generalised mirth.

There was, in this attitude, more than a little envy and insecurity and I will not try to defend it. The interesting (if bizarre) thing is that everything we feared or disliked about the strategic guys came to be represented by a sheet of paper with a few circles on it. The medium triumphed over the message. It is hard to explain why this was so: my best explanation is that the bubble chart seemed to sum up a kind of intellectual pretentiousness that tried to pass off as profound something that we suspected of shallowness.

Perhaps at this point I should pause and say what a bubble chart is, for the uninitiated. Basically, it is a cross between a matrix and a histogram: while a matrix may be used to present purely qualitative information (refer back, for instance, to Fig. 1.1), a bubble chart requires it to be quantified in some way. Moreover, the bubble chart allows you simultaneously to present three dimensions of data (even four, if you use colours): in this it is pretty much unique, and clearly quite sophisticated, as a presentational tool.

Figure 7.2 shows a chart which I constructed more or less at random from some old data on UK retail businesses[2].

---

[2] Source: *FT 500*, 1995. I have deliberately chosen old data to avoid any sugges-tion that I am commenting on the current performance of these companies.

Figure 7.2: The UK retail sector - 1993/94

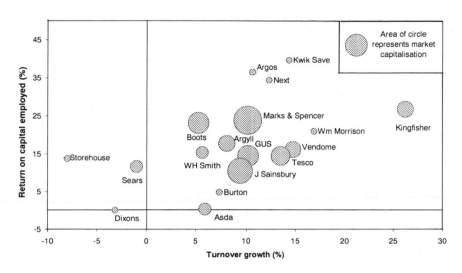

What does a chart like this tell us? It shows, clearly enough, whether there is any relationship between the growth rates of the businesses and the level of return that they are earning on their capital: the answer is that there is a fairly weak correlation. It shows, rather less well, whether there is any relationship between the capitalisation (market value) of the companies and their profitability: the answer is that there is none. And it suggests that big companies in a sector tend to produce broadly similar results. So what? Looking back at this old data, it certainly could *not* have been used to predict the future performance of the companies concerned: while Dixons and ASDA have recovered strongly from being among the worst performers, Kwik Save and Kingfisher have seen the shine worn off their once-proud reputations.

Figure 7.2 is pretty trivial but, despite this, it *looks impressive*. It also tempts the unwary, whether client or con, to draw conclusions supported by very little evidence. For instance, take a pen and draw *clusters* of retailers on the chart. Now, if you have drawn a 'high return' group consisting of Kwik Save, Argos and Next, reflect on whether there is really anything similar at all about a discount food retailer, a catalogue store and a fashion chain. It is nonsense but it sounds horribly plausible.

Like bullet points, any data chart is a heavily edited version of events. If I was to add to the data used in Figure 7.2 the earnings per share of each company, the dividend yield, the gearing ratio, the inside-leg measurement of the Chief Executive and a few more columns of data I could generate dozens of different bubble charts. Which ones are worth showing? Which actually mean anything? Are there other factors outside of my data that explain differences seen on the charts? These are good questions and, skilfully used, bubble charts can be an excellent way of exploring data and raising these sorts of issues. Equally, though, they can be used as in Figure 7.2 simply to look good. Selecting the axes to be used, and identifying clusters or trends that really mean something, are critical to the success of the analysis.

When you hand consultants the role of selecting and editing your data, be aware that you are giving them considerable power. If you have set up the right job, with the right cons, there is nothing wrong in this. If not, you may simply get a lot of your own data presented back to you in a way which adds nothing but a little gloss: the classic case of borrowing the client's watch to tell the time. It also makes for dull presentations: there is little more tedious than having to sit through a dozen bubble charts that tell you what you already know. Worse, the cons may present conclusions which are simply wrong, due to poor understanding of the data, or which have been manipulated to fit a version of the truth that suits them. In any of these situations, you will need to be good at challenging the cons when they come back with their bubble charts.

One of the very best questions that a client can ask is devastating in its simplicity: *'So what?'* Figure 7.2 shows that the largest businesses tend towards similar levels of growth and profitability. So what? Does this tell us anything that we do not already know? Any con presenting data should already have thought these questions through, but a little prompting may not go amiss.

The 'so what?' question does not apply only to bubble charts: it is a useful test of almost any analysis or conclusion whether produced by cons or not. My colleagues and I were not given to bullet charts, but we did have a great love of the so-called Pareto curve. Figure 7.3

shows an example for sales of a given product in a sample of retail outlets.

Figure 7.3: Pareto curve for sample retailers

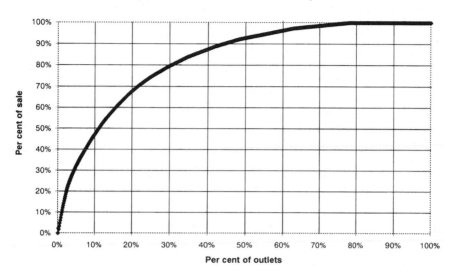

This shows that 20% of the retailers in the sample contributed some 70% of the total sales of the item concerned. The classic Pareto effect is 80:20 (or 85:15 in other versions that I have seen) and it can be found in all kinds of situations: for example, we could hypothesise that 80% of railway passengers are carried by 20% of the trains, that 20% of ambulance callouts contribute 80% of the waiting time or that 80% of the talking in Parliament is done by 20% of MPs. Our sample of sales through retailers is similar, although not exactly in line with the 80:20 rule. So what? Is the difference meaningful? If so, *what* does it mean: that we have fewer really strong sales points in our sample than we would expect, or that we have fewer poor sellers? If it means something, can we do anything about it? Should we be pruning the retail base or opening new stores? Or can we not say for sure?

I frequently presented a Pareto chart to my clients and I confess that not once was I really sure what it proved. No one ever said, 'So what?' and, in the absence of this challenge, the chart served the purpose of suggesting that I had done some clever analysis and that I knew what I was talking about. Quite frankly, this is not good enough. If more clients learned to ask 'so what?' there might be fewer bubbles in the air.

Lies, damned lies and consultancy reports

Getting a firm of consultants in to do the number crunching sounds pretty safe. It is also something that many consultants do very well. Do not imagine, however, that data analysis is a neutral activity that simply produces the *right* answer. The examples already shown have indicated how much is contributed by selecting and editing the information.

The presentation of information in pictorial form (charts, diagrams, matrices and the like) is particularly powerful because it can short-circuit some of the audience's critical filters. Most readers will be familiar with the distinction of the left and right halves of the brain. Analysing a rational argument falls to the left side of the brain but pictures may strike directly at our more intuitive side, the right, and this may explain why they can sometimes get round the 'so what?' reaction which words alone may elicit. The old cliché that 'a picture is worth a thousand words' can be as true in consultancy as elsewhere.

The question is, what is the story that the picture tells and whose interests does it serve? Data is not neutral. Data which is being deliberately manipulated is downright dangerous. But surely, no consultancy would actually set out deliberately to manipulate the numbers? Perhaps not, but *anyone* will look for the information which confirms his beliefs and no con can be expected to be beyond selecting and editing data in a way which strengthens her case. Something like manipulation can occur for all sorts of reasons short of downright dishonesty:

- The cons are, as usual, under considerable pressure on time or other resources. The client is demanding an answer, fast. Having decided what that answer is to be, they need to present it as convincingly as possible.

- The cons are rolling out what, to them, is a more or less standard solution to a familiar problem. They have assumed that your case is similar to those which have come their way before and, by the time they have finished looking for the numbers that support this argument, they will have made sure it looks that way.

- This is one of those jobs where the client knows what the answer is and is determined to get it, or where the political interests are so clearly in favour of a particular outcome that the cons have decided that it is not worth their while disagreeing. Integrity can be difficult to maintain in such situations.

- The cons are having trouble with what is a complex set of issues in a business with which they are unfamiliar. Or they may simply not be very good at their job. Or the data which they were given was poor. In any of these events they can end up presenting a very biased picture.

What does this amount to? It can be terribly simple. Take Figure 7.4, for example:

Figure 7.4: Sales performance since 1994

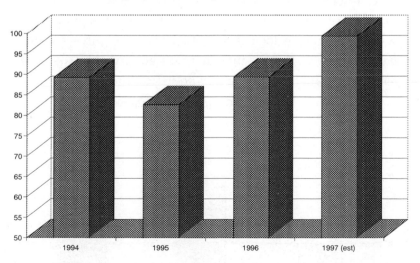

Clear enough, surely? A business where sales were declining but which has turned the corner. But what if we saw the longer-term pattern? Figure 7.5 shows just this:

Figure 7.5: Sales trend since 1980

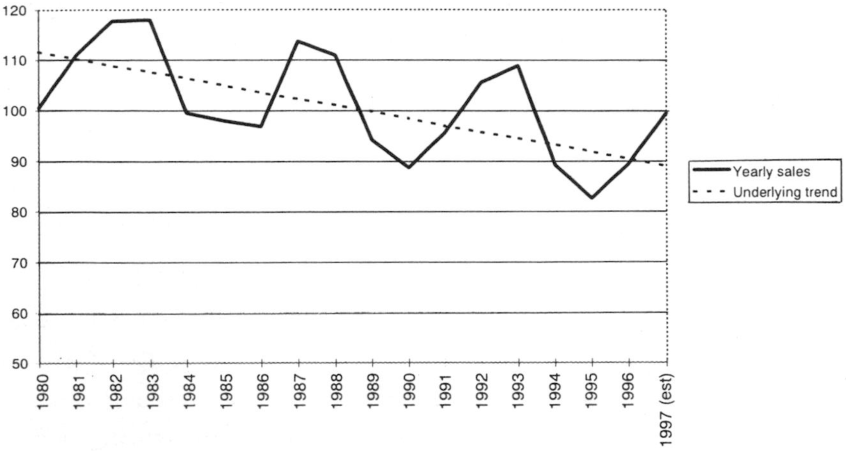

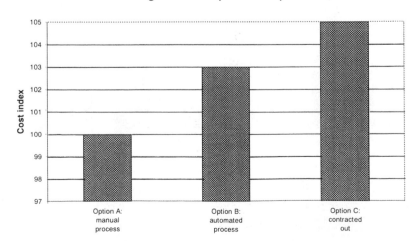

What we can now see is that the business is cyclical (with rather neat five-year cycles in the data, which I have invented to prove the point) and that the underlying trend has been, and is still, firmly downwards.

Which chart is *true*? Both are, clearly. They present different versions of the truth, however, and selecting the version which the client sees is a critical way of controlling the outcome.

At other times, the data may be exactly the same but just presented in a way that makes it look different. Compare Figures 7.6 and 7.7 which show exactly the same information comparing the cost of three different ways of manufacturing a hypothetical product:

Figure 7.6: Comparison of options

This version shows that Option A – a labour intensive process – is the clear favourite. But what would be the conclusion if the cons showed the same data in the following version:

Figure 7.7: Comparison of options

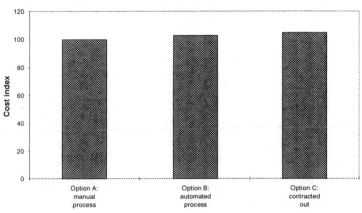

The only change is in the Y-axis scaling: now, the difference between the three options looks so slight as to be irrelevant. What the cons probably should be doing is digging out the critical sensitivities which underlie the charts: what happens if interest rates rise, or if the estimate of factory rents is out by 10%, or if labour productivity has been overestimated? The trouble is that these questions may not even get asked if the client has called for a simple solution or the cons are just being lazy. Figure 7.8 may be a much better way of provoking consideration of these issues, but it may never be shown to the client on the grounds that it is 'too complicated':

Figure 7.8: Comparison of cost breakdown

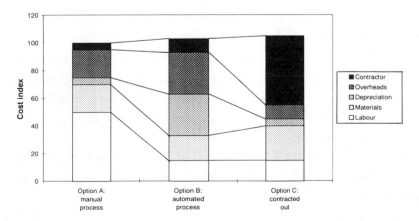

Whatever may lead the cons to present one version rather than another, there is certainly nothing neutral about the choice.

All of this may seem pretty basic but simple distortions can very easily slip into what may seem to be a sophisticated analysis. One of the worst errors, but also among the most frequent, is the comparison of apples with pears. Rolls-Royce make cars and so do Toyota but a comparison of output per man in their respective plants is unlikely to have any real meaning, given the very different nature of the products and the processes involved in making them. While it is easy to see that such a comparison would not be like for like, in other cases the differences may be subtler but no less damaging to the validity of the results. How many benchmarking projects have set out to compare apples with apples and ended up with a couple of pears and a lemon? What is of concern is that the client may simply not be in a position to know how flawed the underlying data is.

In my experience, clients have very little awareness of statistical issues and often overestimate the consultants' own knowledge of these. I found myself not infrequently dabbling in relatively technical areas where my little knowledge was probably a very dangerous thing. If, for example, a client needs advice on how much of a particular product should be kept in stock in order to meet a certain pattern of demand, this is a minefield for the unwary and the cons should be chosen with great care. Otherwise you will end up with consultants trying to mug up the subject from a textbook (I speak from experience) or with the blind leading the blind.

An example from my managerial present, rather than my consultancy past, will illustrate how a statistic that seems to the uninitiated quite clear can be profoundly misleading. Following a report in 1993 by the Monopolies and Mergers Commission, the retailing of newspapers in the UK was opened up to anyone who wished to enter it. A code of practice was agreed by the industry to ensure that this could happen. It allowed new entrants to enjoy the same terms of trade as existing retailers, provided they could achieve sales of newspapers equivalent to *not less than half the average sale* of existing retailers in the area. Before reading on, decide whether or not this sounds onerous as a threshold.

You will have decided, I imagine, that to achieve just half of the average should be easy enough as most retailers could be expected comfortably to exceed this level. In fact, only a minority of existing news retailers did so: far from being easy, the threshold was set at a challenging level for the new entrant. A few very large outlets in any area can have a major impact on the mean (average) sale. In this situation, the median (the sales value mid-way through the list of existing retailers) might have been more appropriate than the mean as a yardstick. Use of the median would certainly have made the threshold much easier to achieve. Whether all the authors of the code of practice were aware of this distinction, and whether they meant to set the bar where they did, is a matter for speculation.

Confused? Bear in mind that the mean, median and mode are basically Chapter One in any simple textbook of statistics. Using more sophisticated tools may be an essential element of a project or it may lead cons into more and more dangerous territory. An example is the use of regression to show how, for example, the cost of production is related to the output of a business. I have used regressions in my consulting work on various occasions but I have only a hazy notion of when the technique is valid. My clients were never known to challenge me on this, probably because they knew even less about statistics than I did.

Or take the related topic of correlation. I suggested earlier in this chapter that the rise of consultancy in the 1980s was in proportion to the spread of personal computers. With some suitable data, I might be able to show a close correlation between the two trends. This could lead me to claim that I had proved a causal connection: that PCs were indeed fuelling the growth of the consulting business. In truth, the data would mean nothing of the sort. Not only is the direction of causality unclear, but both trends may have been generated by a third, for example the rise in international competition forcing companies to seek every possible way of improving their operations. A good statistician will always check for this kind of thing. A con in a hurry may not.

The personal computer can give an illusion of cleverness simply by producing high-quality bullet charts or bubbles. It can also suggest analytical sophistication and statistical insight where none exists. The bubble chart seen earlier (Figure 7.2) was produced on a standard spreadsheet. With two clicks of the mouse I could add a 'trend line' to the data; I could even select whether I wanted it to be logarithmic or polynomial, without having the first idea what these terms imply. The trend line would look meaningful and I could make all sorts of claims for it, but it would almost certainly be complete nonsense. Nothing, however, would warn the foolish con or the unwary client of this. PCs are powerful machines and I for one would not be without one. But they can put powerful statistical techniques in the hands of people who can barely add up.

If the reason you are using consultants is because you need expert analytical support, make very sure that you have found the right con to deliver it. Because, once the job is underway, *you* won't know if *he* doesn't know.

A way through the minefield
This is beginning to sound like a *Catch 22* for clients: you need to know enough to tell when your consultants are wrong, but if you knew that you would not have needed them in the first place.

Fortunately, a large dose of common sense can get you a long way in understanding and challenging the consultants' work in most (although not all) projects, the exceptions being those of a deeply technical nature where the client herself may well be more of an expert anyway.

I have already suggested various ways in which clients can avoid the worst dangers of bullets, bubbles and charts of all kinds. Summing up, clients are recommended to:

- Accept that they need to get to grips with the detail of the consultants' work, and not expect simple one-line answers to difficult issues.

- Expect back-up details and full explanations to supplement summary presentations and recommendations.

- Get involved, or get one of their team involved, with the close detail of the work such that the results are developed jointly with the cons and based on a shared understanding of the real issues and their analysis.

- Remember that a flashy picture or chart is neither better nor worse than the data or analysis on which it is based. Just because something is in a bubble chart does not make it right, or even intelligent.

- Use the 'So what?' test to decide if an analysis adds anything to the project and what it is really saying about the issues being examined. Question, challenge, probe.

- Understand the power of the editor in putting together data and consider what information has been selected, what has been left out, what format is being used to present it and why.

- Be very careful that any comparisons are made on a strict like-for-like basis.

- Discourage the use of statistical techniques that you do not fully understand yourself and, when such techniques are necessary, take particular care to ensure that the cons are qualified in their use.

There is one other thing. I suggested previously that cons may have recourse to some fairly dodgy analysis when they are put under pressure to deliver a result almost before they have done the work.

A common vice of clients, and an understandable one, is to want the answers without going through the process of analysis. Sometimes this is caused by real time pressures. More often, I suspect, it is the result of a mismatch between the available budget for the work and the cost that would be incurred if the job were done properly. I was not enamoured of clients who wanted the answer but were not prepared to pay for me to reach it.

One reason why I left consultancy was that I felt I was seldom able to 'do the job properly'. This sentiment can betray the kind of obsessiveness that leads to paralysis by analysis. While this pitfall is to be avoided, so too is the opposite extreme of flying by the seat of your pants. If you are going to use consultants, you should expect them to take an analytical approach. Accept this and let them do the job right.

The kind of probing that I have talked about, asking, 'So what?' and looking for the causes of apparent trends or other features in the data, is precisely the sort of thing that the cons themselves should be doing. Given a bit of time and space, most will and probably very well. I am not suggesting that clients remove all budgetary constraints, nor that they just leave the cons in a room for a few months to see what they can come up with, nor (most emphatically) that they relax the discipline of the specified project deliverables. What I am saying is that you should not put a con in the position of having to short-circuit the analysis and fit the facts to a hastily conceived conclusion.

Or, as Lewis Carroll would have it, allow your consultants time for a few uffish thoughts by the Tumtum tree.

CHAPTER 8: WHY CLIENTS GET THE CONSULTANTS THEY DESERVE

'WHO'S THIS GUY THAT KEEPS TURNING UP AT ALL THE MEETINGS?'

The speaker was our client: not just any client, either, but one who was shaping up to be a very large client indeed. As for the guy he was talking about:

'That's the project Partner.'

'Yeah, but what's he here for?'

A tricky one, this. The Partner in question was in the throes of enhancing his reputation enormously by taking the credit for bringing in one of the best clients we had ever had. In fact, his contribution to selling the work had been virtually zero (or less, since at the very first meeting we had been obliged to cover up for his lack of confidence in presenting our qualifications). As the client had spotted, his contribution to the work in progress did not amount to a whole shed of chickens either.

'Get him out of here. We don't want him on the job.'

'Erm . . . Well, it's not quite as simple as that.'

How do you set about explaining to the client that the Partner comes with the project and that they simply *can't* not have one? How do you argue convincingly that the Partner is a major linchpin of quality control when he was clearly way out of it? The project manager did his best.

'OK. But we're not paying for him. He can turn up if he wants, but we're not paying.'

A compromise thus established, the project manager asked the accounts controller to set the Partner's billing rate for the job to nil. It was at this point that a major problem was encountered. Our computer system simply did not allow for anyone to be billed at a rate of zero pounds per day. And so it was that, for the weeks and months that followed, a Partner was building his reputation on the back of a job for which his own charge-out rate was . . . one penny per day. It's tough at the top.

Why do I relate this anecdote? Well yes, it's a good tale. But, more than that, it shows one of the basic rules of the game for consultancy clients: if you don't like what you are getting, you don't have to put up with it. Moreover, achieving a successful result from a consultancy study is up to the client as much as it is up to the cons. If you are not happy with the project team (or even the Partner), it is up to you to do something about it. I have no hesitation in repeating a remark that is far from original but no less valid for that: good clients make good consultants.

Figure 8.1 shows that there is nothing automatic about success: while the majority of projects were considered to be successful, by both clients and cons, a significant minority still fell short. Less than a quarter were rated 'completely successful' by clients.

Figure 8.1: How successful were projects overall?

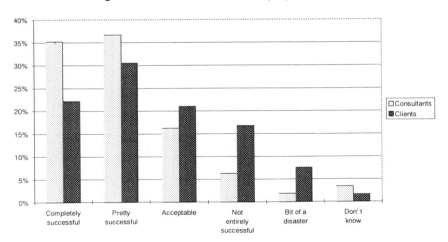

As we will see later in this chapter, projects can go wrong for all sorts of reasons, some of them genuinely beyond anyone's control: for example, unexpected action by a competitor may render a market study totally irrelevant. But for a project to go seriously adrift, plunging on past the danger signs into ever deeper abysses of failure, reflects as much on the client as on the cons. If nothing else, surely the client should have called a halt as soon as the truck left the road?

One client, who shall certainly remain anonymous, gave the following answers to my questionnaire:

- He had run 6 or more projects with a value of £100,000–£500,000 per project.
- He felt that consultants did *not* give good value for money.
- He rated 80% of his projects as *less* than 'acceptable' in achieving their objectives.
- In implementation, 80% of his projects had been 'a bit of a disaster'.
- He was 'very likely' to use consultants again.

There are two terms that I can think of to describe this manager: *eternal optimist* is the polite one. But you cannot sensibly use consultants on a wing and a prayer.

According to the consultants who participated in my research, as Figure 8.2 shows, around 30% of clients do not manage projects effectively and only some 40% are rated better than 'acceptable'.

Figure 8.2: How effectively do clients manage projects?

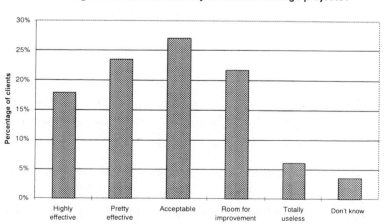

There is plenty that clients can, and should, do to ensure that a project delivers what they are looking for. Employing a consultant is a form of subcontracting: a specialist form, certainly, but not beyond comparison with other kinds of *outsourcing*, an approach that is currently in vogue. Outsourcing seems to offer scope for getting rid of the nitty gritty stuff, no longer having to bother about managing the cleaning, or the canteen, or the delivery trucks, or the computer room, or the order processing, or the after sales service . . . So why not your strategic thinking or change management as well?

Whether or not it is healthy to outsource your corporate thinking to consultants is the subject of Chapter 11. At this stage, all I want to say is this: whatever you are trying to subcontract (or outsource) it is *not* a fire-and-forget decision. Any contract needs managing. Partnership with a supplier may devolve day-to-day decision making but it does not absolve the principal of responsibility for the work. Just how involved the client should remain depends at root on the type of activity. The simpler or more repeatable the work, and the more marginal it is to the life of the principal, the less does it require to be managed. The more complex the contract, or the more vital it is to the client, the less can it be left to run itself. From which it should be pretty clear that consultancy is far too important to be left to the cons.

This chapter is all about getting the best from your consultants. At times that may mean calling the consultants' bluff. It can involve laying down the law but also, at other times, it may be a matter of shutting up and listening. What it *always* means is managing your management consultants.

Top Ten Tips

If you want to be an effective client – that is, one who manages consultants successfully and gets the cons that you want, not just the ones you deserve – here are my tips for success.

Tip 1: Focus on deliverables. I still carry with me a little card that I was given once on a presentation course. The first step it recommends in preparing a presentation, after deciding on the overall objective, is to 'design the close'. In other words, start at the end. It strikes me that this is also good advice for running a project with consultants.

In Chapter 2, and elsewhere, I have dwelt at some length on the importance of defining your objectives: deciding what it is that you need to change and what support (resources, skills, knowledge, process facilitation . . .) you need from consultants. You should be pretty clear about this before you even make the first phone call to the nearest con. However, you need to go further, whether this is done during your preliminary discussions with shortlisted firms or not completed until after you have chosen who you intend to work with. The task is to define the *deliverables* that you want from the job.

By deliverables I do not simply mean a list of documents or other material that you expect to receive: in most cases it is probably a waste of time trying to define these too precisely. What should, however, be set down with as much precision as possible is what you need to get from the consultants in a broader sense: what you need them to tell you, or what decisions they must make, or what changes they must have helped *you* make, before they can consider the job finished. Avoid generalisations. For example, if the required outcome of a project is defined as 'recommend a location for a new European factory', this can mean anything from a few qualitative remarks about national characteristics to a specific site search backed by a detailed cost model[1]. Decide what you want and stick to it.

The best way of sticking to it is to write it down. Projects can have a horrible tendency to creep away from what you originally wanted. Once you have decided on your objective for consultancy support, write it down if only for your own reference. When you have firmed up the deliverables that you want, and agreed them with your cons, write them down too. You may wish to make these part of a formal

---

[1] The example is not purely hypothetical. A colleague of mine once presented a client with an overview of national characteristics which he came up with by asking us what we most associated with each country. It seemed to amuse him greatly that none of us could think of anything much to say about Belgium. I am not sure what this all amounted to, but it probably was not great consulting.

contract or simply append them to a letter but, whatever their form, they will be the basis of your relationship with the cons.

This may seem obvious enough but focusing on the deliverables is too often lost behind a preoccupation with the approach to be taken. At the proposal stage, cons need to show that they have understood what you want and that they have the ability to deliver it. *How* they will actually do the work is perhaps the least important thing. They will almost certainly produce some kind of overall project plan. Rather than worry about the detail of which arrow leads to which box, look for the deliverables that you, as client, can expect from each stage. If there is no deliverable for you, the plan has probably been drawn at too detailed a level.

Tip 2: Think what can be done internally. A question which is always worth asking is: 'Can we do some of the work ourselves?' There is no single answer to this: it depends entirely on your situation, the nature of the job and the cons with whom you are working.

Martin Wilson, in a book[2] which deals in more detail with running a project from the client's viewpoint, recommends: 'Do not let or cause a professional adviser to take on basic tasks that any competent clerk, or indeed manager, could do. Allow your staff and colleagues time to do the detailed work themselves, wherever possible.'

I do not entirely agree with this. Wilson is coming from the perspective of a small consultancy where doing the Grunt work may be more trouble than it is worth. For larger consultancies, with a scattering of bright analysts to chuck at basic tasks, this is relatively straightforward. There are projects where much of the work consists of rounding up data already held within the organisation and cons may be playing a valuable role in doing this if the business was unable to find the resources to tackle it in-house. Wilson is quite right, however, when he goes on to suggest that cons are rather an expensive resource for doing straightforward data collection.

I confess to being ambivalent about this: in my own experience,

---

[2] Martin Wilson: *Getting the Most from Consultants* (Pitman, 1996).

whenever a client promised to take care of getting the information I needed this tended to be a recipe for disaster. However, the use of internal resources – if they are indeed forthcoming and if they are properly managed – can be a sensible way of limiting the scope and cost of a project.

Tip 3: Review progress regularly, against milestones. I suggested already that you should focus on *what* is to be produced (the deliverables) and much less on *how* this is to be achieved. This does not mean, however, that you should let the cons go away for three months and trust that they will come back with the right answer.

Milestones are essential. A milestone is a key point in a project: the completion of a particular phase, the delivery of a planned output or a significant decision point which will influence the rest of the work. Leave it to the cons to plan the work but then insist that they give you specific milestones, with attached dates. If at all possible, each milestone should represent either a deliverable in its own right or at least a very clear contribution to the required deliverables. If the milestone is not hit, on time, you need a clear explanation of why and of what is being done to get the project back on track.

One advantage of setting milestones is that they force proper project planning. Without them, it is rather easy for cons to start a piece of work in the hope that 'something will turn up'. A degree of this is inevitable. For example, I was asked to take a look at some French hypermarkets because a senior manager had a hunch that they were not handling their stocks of clothing in a very effective way. Neither of us knew, until I almost literally fell over it, that deliveries were being rushed in to meet certain pre-ordained dates only for the goods then to sit in the backroom for a month and a half. I had no idea what I would find when I looked at this operation, but this uncertainty would not have prevented me building into the project plan a milestone for reviewing a given number of stores and identifying practices requiring improvement.

Set targets, plan how to reach them, review progress. Basic stuff that should be second nature to most managers. If you do it with your staff, do it also with your cons.

Tip 4: Never move the goalposts. This is the ultimate sin.

If there is one thing that is guaranteed to cause trouble with your cons it is trying unilaterally to redefine the job once it has started or – worse – when it is already largely complete. Moving the goalposts can imply changing the objectives of the work, changing the assumptions which you have previously agreed with the consultants or changing the level on which you are expecting them to operate. Whatever it is, don't do it.

I mentioned in Chapter 1 the problems I had with a job for a paper manufacturer (in Spain) where the client's project manager (in France) was off sick for virtually the whole of the project. When he returned he set about systematically overturning almost every assumption that I had agreed with his Spanish subordinates while insisting that we should redo a large part of the analysis. Given that we had already incurred substantial overruns in time and cost due to the difficulty of getting buy-in from the local management, even relatively minor new demands like the production of a French-language version of our report and presentation were enough to concern us. When it came to starting the analysis again almost from scratch, with new assumptions but no new budget, we simply had to refuse.

It is true that the circumstances of this job were unusual. Unfortunately, though, the sight of the goalposts wandering around the pitch is far from uncommon. It can reflect the fact that the client has some hidden agenda about which he has not been honest with the cons. More usually, though, it is simply that the client has not properly thought through the objectives of the work and the required deliverables. The moral is obvious.

Tip 5: Be involved, and be available. In the last chapter I recommended clients to get fully involved with the work being done on their behalf. If the client's project manager is constrained by pressure of work or shortage of time, one or more of her staff should be immersed in the project and should act as channels to keep everyone involved and informed.

This is not an alternative to formal milestones. The progress of the project needs monitoring against these irrespective of the mix of the team. Indeed, if you take the view (as I do) that running a joint client-consultant team can only add to the complexity of the task of managing the project, formal milestones may be even more important than when the cons are on their own. In between these milestones, though, there should be regular briefings, workshops or other points of contact. The minimum involvement should be roughly weekly informal meetings (or even telephone calls) between client and con. More than this, if at all possible, there should be client staff working directly as part of the project team, whether full or part-time. This was recommended, without prompting, by many of the clients who took part in the research.

Involvement is not just a matter of the client watching what the cons are up to: it is also valuable for the consultants to have a relatively senior point of contact easily available to them. As I said before, bringing consultants in is not a fire-and-forget decision. Part of the reason for using them may be the fact that you are overloaded and desperately short of time. Nonetheless, you must allow them adequate access to you if they are to be able to practice the 'no surprises' consultancy which is in everyone's best interests.

I was asked by an old contact, who had recently been brought in at the top of a large company in a turnaround situation, to give him some advice about their distribution. It was a 'quick and dirty' piece of work but I was pleased that, in the very short timescale I was given, I came up with what I felt was a sound analysis of the situation and a good way forward. The problem was getting anywhere near my client in order to take him through my results. Dealing as he was with banks threatening to foreclose on many millions of dollars of loans, his mind was unsurprisingly elsewhere. In the end, frustrated by his inability even to return my calls, I submitted my report in writing and moved on to my next client. He paid my bill but it was hard not to feel that an opportunity had been lost.

The real value of deep client involvement is two-fold:

• The quality of the work should be improved by having continuous input from one or more individuals who really understand the business. Few cons are arrogant enough to forget that the client knows this far better than they do.

• If involvement leads to buy-in, there is much more chance of the project getting the deep-seated client commitment which is a prerequisite for a successful implementation of the outcome.

Tip 6: Probe, and probe again. I have already discussed at various points in this book some of the less desirable practices of consultants. There remains a category of 'consultancy vices not otherwise enumerated' which includes:

• Prejudging the answer: whether out of laziness, arrogance or a desire to fit a standard solution to the problem.

• Unsupported generalisation. A good example of this was given earlier in this chapter: my colleague's attempt to write Belgium off on the grounds that no one could think of any famous Belgians[3].

• Anecdotalism: picking up tales, from staff or others interviewed in the course of a project, and treating these as hard evidence. If, for example, a single customer complains about the client that 'they always deliver late', some cons will latch onto this and ignore statistical proof that 99% of all deliveries were made on time.

The lesson for the client is clear: challenge the cons, question their assumptions, probe the analysis that they have done and expect them to produce the evidence on which their findings are based. If you have been fully involved in the work yourself you may not need this but, in most cases, clients cannot probe too much.

This process needs to start early on, which means at the time of the consultancy presentation or proposal. If the cons claim experience of a particular type of project or client sector, probe to find out what it really amounted to. If they make proud boasts of a methodology, probe to see if there is more to it than a fancy name. If they say they will use their database to provide inputs, probe what this is, where the data came from and how up to date it is.

---

[3] It is also a gross slur: everyone has heard of Tintin.

Just because something sounds plausible, it is not necessarily true. And just because something looks clever, do not rush to assume that it contains genuine insights. Remember the acid test of any presentation: ask 'So what?'

Tip 7: Do not be afraid to look stupid. This is a corollary of the last tip.

Cons have a reputation for being pretty clever. Some clients react by trying to knock their consultants down a peg or two, which is not a great basis for a working relationship. Other clients can be overawed by the arrival of the smart suits and this can make them hesitate about probing in the sort of way that I have just been discussing. If the con uses a high-sounding term, and everyone seems to nod in agreement, are you going to look stupid if you ask him to explain?

Some of my best work was done for Americans. Compared to the British, they tend to have far fewer scruples about making themselves look foolish, and are less inhibited when it comes to butting in with awkward questions. Presenting to one of my best clients involved continually stopping as he interrupted with: 'Can we just go back here for one moment . . .' He was right to demand this.

The underlying point is that you, as client, need to retain your sense of judgment at all times. The cons may say what they like and add whatever sophistication they possess, but ultimately the judgement on their work has to be yours just as the commitment to its results can only come from you. Looking smart, while failing to acquire more than a superficial understanding of their work, serves no purpose at all.

Tip 8: Be prepared to take decisions along the way. This one may be more of a surprise to some clients. Surely, the consultants are there to follow the instructions that have been given to them and come back with a result? Isn't the client's only decision the final one of either paying or not paying the bill?

In practice, few projects really work like this (and, I am tempted to add, a good thing too). As already seen, clients should be involved throughout the job and cons should welcome this. Involvement implies understanding what the cons are doing and learning from them, but it is not a one-way street. At each stage in the project the client may well also have to make choices and take decisions that can be fundamental to the final outcome.

For instance, almost any operationally-based consultancy project is likely to need clear guidance from the client on the future business requirements which the operations are to serve. It would be impossible to plan a manufacturing operation without some understanding of future products, volumes and batch sizes, for example. Similarly, it does not make sense to design a computer system for handling orders in the absence of a vision of the number of orders and number of products that may be involved. Some of the data for this may be in the corporate plan, but it is quite likely that the manager running the project will have to sign off some significant assumptions along the way.

Many projects involve a phase of data collection up-front, followed by some kind of design or planning stage. This second part may take its overall direction from the earlier stage: for instance, data may be collected on a wide range of markets before selecting the most promising and developing a specific entry strategy for them. In this situation, the client will again have an important role in deciding which of the markets are to be selected or, at very least, in signing off the cons' recommendation. If the client's project manager is not senior enough to do this, or shies away from the decision, the result may be a continued search for more and more data to refine the analysis already presented. This kind of data collection for its own sake leads to analysis-paralysis.

I had a client who spent literally years changing the assumptions underlying the business requirements while repeatedly coming back to us for further bits of analysis. The company seemed incapable of ever deciding to 'freeze' things and get on with the implementation. When, finally, they took the plunge, the implementation included some frankly bizarre decisions (in which we were not involved) and they came back to us again in the hope that we could supply a justification for these. When we suggested doing things differently, the client's project manager told us that any change was impossible as he had already informed the Board. In this case, the client had lurched from indecision to poor decisions but the former is probably the worse evil.

Tip 9: Refuse to accept easy options. Another vice that cons may fall into is that of putting forward to the client proposals or recommendations that can be described as 'easy options'.

The recommendations may be easy for the consultants themselves, such as advising the use of a system or technology with which the cons are familiar, without really bothering to decide if it is the best for the job. Or the proposals may be intended to be easy for the client: ideas which are broadly in tune with what the client was thinking or which do not seem to require too much effort to implement.

It is a soft option for cons to slide into telling the client what they think he wants to hear. It is also difficult not to be swayed when collecting data or interviewing client staff by those who offer a friendly welcome or present a coherent argument, closing your ears to the sullen mutterings of a manager who would rather you were not there. Unfortunately, the latter might just happen to have right on his side, but this can be overlooked if he is perceived as hostile. In other words, consultancy studies may be more than a little subjective. Cons, like managers, are only human.

How can the pitfalls be avoided? Firstly, by refraining as far as possible from feeding solutions to the cons: give them the questions, or explain the issues, and make them come to their own conclusions. Secondly, challenge the analysis to ensure that it really has gone through all the options and not just picked a convenient one. Thirdly, where complex choices have to be made based on a range of criteria (for example: choice of a new location for the business, selection of a computer system, closure of one or more factories), insist that these are backed up with a proper scoring system to weigh and assess each of the factors involved. This should bring at least a minimum of rigour into a decision which might otherwise be too influenced by gut feel and the cons' perception of what you as client are comfortable with.

Tip 10: Neither expect, nor accept, miracles. In one version of a popular business cartoon, a monumentally complicated flow chart – full of boxes and arrows going in every direction – is somehow resolved into a single neat output. At the node where the maze of complexity is resolved, the chart reads 'Here a miracle is required.'

There are many things that clients should expect, even demand, from their consultants. Hard work, creative thinking, technical expertise, outside ideas, business acumen, process facilitation . . . These are all reasonable expectations. But do not expect miracles. If your data is absolute dross (not infrequently my experience), no con is going to transform it into dazzling gold. If your warehouse is full because no one wants to buy your products, do not expect an inventory study to fix your business.

More than this, do not *accept* miracles either. If the cons' proposal looks like the cartoon flow-chart that I have described, throw it out. If they have spent three months on data collection and analysis and then produced conclusions seemingly drawn from a hat, without any connection with what went before, challenge them. If they have performed a SWOT[4] analysis which correctly identified certain weaknesses in your business, and they have then put forward recommendations which imply turning these weaknesses into strengths, think long and hard about how realistic this is going to be.

Every project is different. There is no easy way for clients to ensure that they will always get the consultancy support that they want and need, but if these ten tips were followed in every case there would be fewer dissatisfied clients. I also believe that there would be fewer frustrated cons.

You do not have to take this just from me. In the research, both clients and cons were asked to suggest up to three pieces of advice for clients. The comments that were made tended to fall into a number of groups. The most commonly-offered advice from clients themselves was, in descending order of frequency:

- Have clear objectives and required deliverables.

- Be involved a lot with your cons and work as a team.

- Get your own staff working on the job, alongside the cons.

[4] Strengths, Weaknesses, Opportunities and Threats: this way of breaking things down should be familiar to almost all readers.

* Have a proper plan.

Consultants most frequently offered clients the following suggestions:

* Have clear objectives and required deliverables.

* Be involved a lot with your cons and work as a team.

* Select carefully the individual consultants for the job (not just the firm).

* Manage your consultants.

The small cog in the machine

So far in this book, whenever I have talked about what clients should do, I have been thinking of the project manager or other senior member of the client organisation. This person, it is assumed, is either directly responsible for procuring and managing the cons' services or is at least in a position to exercise significant influence over them.

Most client staff who have dealings with consultants are not in this position. Most are small cogs caught up in the machine built by the cons. Few will have been consulted about the decision to bring in external help and many will be nervous that their own jobs or careers are on the line if the cons recommend rationalisation, closure or other major change. What advice can they be given?

Consultants are only human. I know, it *is* hard to believe. But true, nonetheless.

Too many people are far too respectful of consultants. They do not have a monopoly on expertise. They are not possessed of X-ray vision. They are certainly not infallible. And, crucially, they do not know your business and your organisation anything like as well as you do.

There is another side to this, too. Cons are not immune to anger, impatience or spite. They have a job to do and are unlikely to tolerate pieces of grit getting into the mechanism which they have assembled for the purpose. They can also be quite powerful, if they have the ear of senior management. Think very carefully before you cross them.

Don't stand in front of the train. There are ways of stopping a train, and ways of diverting it onto other lines. But people who stand in front of trains are liable to painful and rapid lamination.

If senior management has brought consultants in to work on 'flattening' the organisation, are you seriously going to stop this process by arguing directly for maintenance of every level and sublevel within your department? If the project team is firming up the business case for a centralised telesales centre, a project to which the Board has already given outline consent, are you going to achieve anything by telling them that it will be an ivory tower and a complete waste of money?

I presented the result of one piece of work to quite a large group of the client's staff. One senior manager had been less than helpful during the project and he chose this final presentation as the moment to stand up and argue against our findings. It was a mistake. Not only did he have to take a return of fire from the consulting team, he seriously embarrassed his own boss. He should have followed our rule: 'no surprises'.

There is a time to argue and a time to keep your head down. Clashing directly with the consultants is unlikely to achieve much and you may get hurt. If you want to take them on, guerrilla warfare is likely to be far more successful than direct assault.

Making friends and influencing people. The way to a con's heart is to cooperate fully with the project team.

Provide data if it is asked for, make yourself available to be interviewed on request, ask (a few) questions but never allow yourself to be branded as 'uncooperative' or 'unhelpful'. If the cons come to see you, always offer to help them further if they want to come back or if they need additional information. And allow them to set the agenda and dictate how much time they spend with you or your staff.

If this sounds like grovelling, you could be right. If you want to influence the project, being seen to cooperate is important. You may be fully in favour of the consultants' work, in which case there is no reason not to assist it. Do not fall into the trap of thinking that the cons are trying to catch you out, as this is unlikely.

At the other end of the scale, you may disagree totally with the project's aims. In this situation, you are more likely to be able to get your arguments across if you start from a position of cooperation. To be seen to oppose the work exposes you to being ignored and makes it less likely that your views will be taken seriously. At worst, if you are too obstructive and capable of seriously hampering the project, the cons will be almost forced to ask for your removal.

Being economical with the actualité. You have kept your head down, avoided direct confrontation and generally brown-nosed the consulting team. How can you then influence the outcome of their work, particularly in situations where you disagree with the way it seems to be leading?

Cons can suffer all too easily from information overload. Feeding them one or two carefully selected ideas, or a nicely edited version of the data, may be a good way of leading them in the direction you choose. As I noted in the previous section, easy options can be tempting. So give the cons some easy options of your choosing:

- Avoid giving them too much undigested data (although if they ask for it, do not refuse to provide it).

- Present the numbers in a way that assists your case (see Chapter 7). If they have asked for specific formats to be followed (for example, requiring a questionnaire to be filled in) you may still be able to attach this to a summary of your own choosing.

- Resist the temptation to display your knowledge of the industry by raising scores of issues that you 'feel they should be aware of'. Keep things simple if you do not want the cons mentally to switch off.

- Put forward coherent and justified arguments. They may not always succeed, but they are almost certain to be better received than gut reactions like 'It can't be done' or, 'That's just typical of the shortsighted approach of management here.'

- Avoid personalisation of your arguments, for example criticism of specific individuals.

- Add a little spice through relevant 'anecdotes' such as comments made by customers or incidents which have occurred recently, assuming these help your case. Such anecdotes are often more memorable than facts and figures.

- Have one or two key messages that you reinforce at intervals throughout your time with the cons, in the hope of getting them to buy into these as their own.

The thing to remember is that, at the end of the day, the consultants will probably be basing their own conclusions on a heavily edited version of the situation. You can influence the outcome if you can get *your* editing accepted, rather than leaving the cons to perform their own. Tell them the truth, but that does not necessarily mean the whole truth. I do not recommend to anyone deliberately hiding information but there is a difference between concealment and judicious selection of the facts. Stick to the latter.

Remember who will decide in the end. In most situations, although the cons will be making recommendations, the ultimate outcome is in the hands of the client. In many ways the key relationship is not the one between the small 'cog' and the cons, but between the cog and her boss (or whoever is the client's project manager).

If the work of the cons is leading to a result that you regard as damaging (to the organisation or to you as an individual), and your attempt to influence it has been unsuccessful, you will have to try the other avenue of putting your case directly to those in your organisation who can affect the final outcome. Whether or not you are in a position to do this and how it can best be done, given the politics of your organisation, are matters which will depend on individual circumstances.

Remember that your boss may not be able completely to overturn the consultants' views, either. Whether you are seeking to influence management in your own organisation, or the cons themselves, diverting the train to a parallel track ('Yes; but also . . .') is likely to be far more successful than trying to build barricades on the line ('No, we can't . . .').

I was involved in recommendations to a client which led to the closure of a lot of small operations, scattered across Europe, in favour of a large centralised facility. The managers of the UK operation were opposed to this plan; to their credit, they argued their case strongly but without attempting to obstruct the project team. When it became clear that they were losing the argument, they took it directly to their European headquarters to whom we were answerable. They were well within their rights in doing this and they won a further review of our work, to which we could hardly object. At the end of the day, they did not get the reprieve that they wanted but they did secure special protection for themselves and their workforce and an attractive relocation deal for those who wanted it. It may have been a limited victory, but it was not a bad result for them.

What to do if things go wrong

Some of the things that can go wrong with a project are ranked in Figure 8.3. There is no doubt at all what cons see as the most likely cause: unclear client objectives. From their side, clients agreed with this but considered other factors – a weak plan, poor proposal, unreasonable expectations, moving the goalposts and poor work by the cons – to be of almost equal importance.

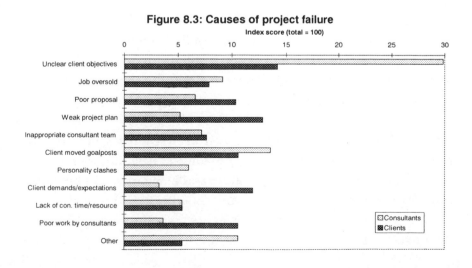

Figure 8.3: Causes of project failure
Index score (total = 100)

If clients focus on the deliverables, agree appropriate milestones with the consultants and remain involved throughout the project, most problems can probably be avoided or dealt with before they become major issues. Inevitably, though, there are times when things just do not work out as expected and when a project can go seriously off-course. I have known a situation where the main con on the job simply cracked up under the strain. I have seen other cons dig themselves so deeply into data analysis that only the tops of their ears were showing. I have seen client management split into factions and take sides for and against a particular set of proposals. I have known new Chief Executives arrive and call into question all that has already been completed, and I have seen companies go into receivership while the cons were still at work. In these situations, damage limitation and finding a way forward become high priorities.

Catch the problem early. This may sometimes be easier said than done but, in a project with proper milestones and adequate management, it should not be so hard to spot when something is going seriously adrift.

If the data was due to have been collected by the end of June, check if this has happened. If not, why not? Is it the cons' fault or the client's? Wherever the fault lies, it is better corrected in early July than left until September.

Remember, focus on the deliverables. Never mind whether the cons look busy or not (or even if you have seen them on site at all): look at progress against the required outputs. Slow progress may be the result of any number of problems, some minor and some serious. Find out which is the case and respond accordingly.

Document the problem. Make sure you keep a written note of any problems, the action taken, promises made and new dates set.

On a substantial project, keep a diary and note down anything that comes up, day by day: points to discuss with the cons at the next meeting, concerns expressed by colleagues, assumptions agreed with the project team, telephone conversations with the project Partner.

These things may seem trivial at the time but the record can be valuable if something does go wrong, and gives you the means to look back at any earlier discussions. If things start getting heavy, and you are going to make representations to the consultancy Partner, having a list of specific issues and problems is far more useful than just voicing general concerns.

Communicate the problem. If 'no surprises' is a vital rule for cons, it is a pretty useful one for clients as well.

If you are not happy with the way the work is going, do not sit on your concerns until the day the final report is due. Discuss them with the cons on the job. Bring them up with the project manager. If necessary, give the Partner a call and suggest it is about time he bought you lunch. For one thing, just showing the cons that you have your eye on things may make sure they get back on track. At the same time, if something is seriously amiss then this needs to be reviewed jointly.

Communication leads to diagnosis. If the symptoms are understood, the solution to the problem should follow. It may involve changing the plan, changing the team or clearing away obstacles. These are considered next.

Change the plan. Changes to the plan may be minor, such as putting the completion date back by a couple of weeks, or they may involve substantial change to the terms of reference. This is undesirable but can happen for all sorts of reasons. On a computer system implementation these could be:

- The consultants' fault: they may have selected a piece of software which simply does not meet the operating specification which was provided to them.

- The client's fault: the operating specification which the client provided for the new system may turn out to be seriously flawed, hence the implementers have put in a system which does what it was supposed to but not what the client actually needs.

- No one's fault: partway through implementation, the client buys its main competitor and thereby doubles its volume. The new system will be inadequate for the enlarged business.

In all of these situations the project can be rescued, but only with substantial replanning (and additional cost for someone). The system can be modified to make it fit the needs, a proper specification can be drawn up and the process begun again, or a whole new piece of work may be needed to look at the implications of the business merger. Whatever the case, there is only one way that the situation can be resolved: by client and con honestly working together to respecify and replan the project. Do not confuse mutually-agreed changes to the project plan with unilateral moving of the goalposts, which is quite a different matter.

Change the team. Sometimes the problem is not the plan, but the cons who have been assigned to the job. They may not have the necessary technical skills. They may not have the ability to deal with the people on the client's shop floor. They may simply not have the experience and weight to be able to bring their proposals to the Board. I have said before that consulting is heavily dependent upon the people on the team, and that getting the right cons on the job is more important than almost anything else. If this did not happen at the start, clients should not be shy in getting things put right when problems start to occur.

On the other hand, changing the cons will not improve things if the problem lies elsewhere. If the reason for a delay is that someone in the client business is obstructing progress, renewing the *dramatis personae* may not help a lot.

Change the constraints. If the fault lies with the client, and particularly if it is in a lack of cooperation between client staff and the consultants, the blockage must be cleared before the project can continue.

Have you provided the resource you said you would? Is the data available as promised? Are staff making themselves available for interview? Is someone in your organisation obstructing the project for political reasons?

This chapter is about how clients can manage things most effectively. However, it is worth pointing out that if the constraints are too severe, and if the project is being jeopardised through the fault of the client, the consultancy Partner may choose to call a halt until things are sorted out. Requiring changes to be made is not the sole prerogative of the client.

Change the consultants. At the end of the day, though, clients do hold the ultimate sanction in their hands: they can fire the consultants.

I am pleased to say that it never happened to me, although I may have got close on occasions. To ditch one firm of cons and (presumably) turn to another tends to suggest that there was something seriously flawed about the original selection process. I am not saying that there is never reason for cons to be shown the door, but it is a measure that begs more questions than it answers. Certainly, any firm coming in to pick up a job from which another consultancy has been removed is likely to want a pretty clear idea of what went wrong last time and why.

If sacking the cons is a smokescreen for problems elsewhere, think again.

Implementation: the final frontier

The implementation plan is the bit that the cons tack on at the end of the report, having written it over a beer on the night before the final presentation. It is fitting, therefore, that I should address the subject in this last section tacked on at the end of the chapter.

Time after time, clients complain that consultants leave them with a piece of work that they cannot implement. Among the unprompted comments made in response to my questionnaire, clients complained of:

- Consultancy work that was too theoretical to carry into practice.

- Over-complex recommendations.

- 'Standard' solutions that did not meet the client's real needs.

- Shortfalls in transferring skills and know-how to the client.

Complaints of this kind prompt all sorts of questions. What did the client actually commission the cons to deliver? Why was the complexity not resolved before the job was finished? Would the consultants have stayed on and managed the implementation if the client had been prepared to pay for this to happen?

Some consultancies lay great stress on their commitment to implementation and a few consultants, in responding to my questionnaire, declined to separate the work they produce from its implementation (see *Appendix*, Questions B2 and B3). Nonetheless, failure of implementation is unquestionably the Achilles heel of the consulting profession.

What is the solution? I am not arrogant enough to pretend to offer a simple fix to the problem, but I do contend that the same 'tips' that I offered earlier in this chapter for the running of projects are equally valid in assisting implementation. In other words, if in the course of the work you follow the suggestions already made, implementation should become a natural extension of the project and not some nasty bump at the end.

Go back and review my Ten Tips. In particular:

- *Focus on deliverables*. If you are clear about what you want out of the consultancy project (which may or may not include an element of implementation), and if you keep that firmly in front of you throughout the job, there is no excuse for saying that you cannot make use of the result.

- *Be involved, and be available*. Involvement implies understanding and learning. If you and your team understand the cons' reasoning, have learned all you can from them, and (preferably) have yourselves been involved in coming up with the result, you will be fully prepared to carry out the next stage. The classic 'go away and come back with an answer' image of consulting is a recipe for implementation failure.

- *Probe, and probe again*. This is something of a subheading within the overall concept of involvement. By probing, by questioning and by testing the answers you are given you will come to make the consultant's recommendations your own. The more you do this, the more you will be committed to the outputs. Commitment is a large part of implementation.

- *Neither expect, nor accept, miracles*. To implement a miracle is rather a tall order. Start from reasonable expectations and insist that your cons stay within them.

All of these tips can perhaps be summed up in a suggestion made by one client in response to my questionnaire: 'Think before you start the project about how you will implement its results.' If you do this, you will be truly focused on the deliverables. You will get involved and expect to understand fully where the cons are coming from. And you will *not* expect miracles.

All of the management textbooks will tell you that success in change management involves two key elements: there needs to be a champion for the change programme and there has to be real commitment to it, from a sufficiently senior level. To ensure that both of these are in place when you come to implementation, you should focus on the deliverables and on achieving the real involvement of client and con throughout the project. Working alongside the cons should build the commitment of your core team well before the final presentation. It will also allow either you or one of your team to develop into the necessary champion. At the same time, if the project has been done for the right reasons and has remained focused on the deliverables, the result should give you everything you need to secure buy-in from your boss or from the Board.

By this stage you may be ready to proceed on your own, or you may still need some consultancy help as the implementation proceeds. Whichever is the case, you will need to replan and refocus on a new set of deliverables. Only you will know when the time has come finally to call a halt to the work of the cons. If you have managed the project effectively, you will by then have got not just the consultants but also the *result* that you deserve.

CHAPTER 9: SO YOU WANT TO BE A CONSULTANT, SON?

WHY DID I BECOME A CONSULTANT?

I intend this as a serious question, although some readers may by now be asking the question rather more sarcastically, or at least wondering why I stuck at the job for six years if I have such a low opinion of some of its practices. My only answer to them is that my view of consultancy is one which I formed, through experience, during my time as a con. If I look at the profession now with a certain cynicism, I certainly did not start from that point. When I began as a junior consultant I had already had a lot more business experience than many of today's new joiners fresh from first degrees, but I was still largely ignorant of what consulting really involved.

I am not sure whether I was asked at interview why I wanted to be a consultant: the question is so obvious that probably no one thought to raise it. At any rate, if I was asked, the answer might have included:

- I wanted a challenge – the standard textbook reason for applying for every job that I have ever even considered. It is corny but I think also perfectly valid: most of us do not do well if left to vegetate and we need new challenges to motivate us. Consultancy sounded like a pretty good challenge: different clients, different jobs, lots of new

183

situations to handle and new things to learn. That, incidentally, was about as far as my notion of consulting went.

- I wanted to make use of my own skills and experience. I like to think that I have an analytical mind and a good way with words. I had acquired a level of knowledge about a particular industry, in which I had worked previously, and a then newly-minted MBA. I did not want to sit in some back-room planning unit when I could be out at what I perceived as the sharp end of business.

- I enjoyed working as part of a team. During my MBA I had found myself often working alongside others on group assignments. Rather to my surprise, I enjoyed the experience. Consulting seemed to offer something of the same team-based environment.

- I thought it might be a good way into senior management in industry, at some later date. I found this harder than expected, probably because I stayed a con for too long. By the time you have been there for a few years, recruiters start acting as if you are a Martian with three heads. But that is another story.

- It sounded vaguely glamorous. This is, of course, the great lure of consultancy to those unacquainted with its pressures and pains. Status, foreign travel, something to brag about at dinner parties . . . Sounded good to me.

- I liked and respected the people I met from the team of which I was to become a member. Of all the reasons, this was definitely the best.

One other thing. I went into consultancy, partly, because it was an easy option. I had done a good stint in industry before taking my MBA but it was from business school that I became a con. This is a route so well-trodden that it has a deep groove running down the pavement. Indeed, it is now possible at one business school (there may be others, for all I know) to take a Masters degree specifically in consulting[1].

---

[1] MSc in Organisation Consulting at Ashridge Management College.

A recent survey of European business graduates found that the top three employers for which the students hoped to work were McKinsey, BCG and Andersen Consulting[2]. From memory, over a third of my classmates went into consultancy, many of them into strategy boutiques. I decided that strategy cons were of a different breed to me, a view which remains unchallenged. My rejection of their values did not make me turn away from consulting altogether. It did, though, take me into a much more operational kind of consultancy and that is something I do not regret.

I duly found myself at my new employer's door on my first morning, raring to get stuck into the first challenge that came along and to start deploying my skills and experience for the greater good of my clients, if not humanity at large. I asked for the Partner who had recruited me. He was not present. I asked for the senior manager to whom I had been assigned. He was with a client. Having run out of names to ask for, I explained that I had come to start work and surely someone knew about me? Ah yes, the secretary had seen something about it so perhaps I'd like to sit over there and maybe someone could be found to have a chat with me. And so it was that my consultancy career started, flicking through a pile of past client reports and waiting for something to turn up.

In retrospect, it was my first lesson in some of the most basic truths about consulting. Assignments do not drop into your lap; things have to be done when it suits the client, not when it suits you; being there is not enough, you have to be *utilised*. Others learned similar lessons through totally different routes. I later met colleagues who had received a message, on the day before they started work, telling them to report at a client's premises; some of them went for months before they even set foot in our own office. They may have had more of a challenge than I did on Day One, but they took a long time to work out who it was that they were supposed to be working for: the client, or a firm whose name appeared on their contract but which they scarcely knew.

---

[2] 1996 *European Graduate Survey* conducted by Universum of Sweden – as reported in *Financial Times*, 15 May, 1996.

The overriding lesson that we all learned, as all cons must, was that consultancy is not having challenges or using your experience or helping clients. Consultancy is a business. The job of the con is to *do the business*. If along the way he enjoys the challenge, fine. If all that experience helps her to be fully utilised, so much the better. But doing the business – winning work, doing work, getting paid for work – is what you are there for.

Figure 9.1 illustrates the divided loyalties from which cons may suffer. In response to the suggestion that their first loyalty is to themselves or their firm, not the client, consultants were split although more disagreed than agreed. Clients, by contrast, overwhelmingly agreed with the proposition. I think the clients are right: cons are there to *do the business* on behalf of their firms. They forget this at their peril.

Figure 9.1: 'Consultants' first loyalty is to themselves/their firm and not to their clients'

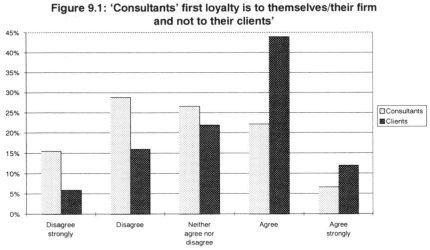

So what is it like to be in this *business*? What does it actually mean for the people who have to do it; and what kind of people do they need to be if they are to make a success of it? The balance of this chapter will concentrate on these questions. It is for anyone who thinks that they might fancy trying their hand at consultancy. If you have stars in your eyes about the men and women in smart suits, perhaps I can disabuse you. And for those who, at the end of this chapter, still think that you would like to be consultants, I hope I will have given you a better idea of what you are letting yourselves in for.

The image and the reality: scenes from the life of a con

How did my experience of consultancy score against my reasons for entering it as a career? Well, not too badly, on one level. Of challenge there was plenty; I certainly had to use any skills I could muster; and I ended up with so much foreign travel that I have to this day a suitcase of unused airmiles. Six years into the job, I still enjoyed the company of my colleagues. But these various facets of the consultant's job, although true, are still only half the story. The purpose of this section is to lift the curtain on the other half of the picture.

The glamour. In so far as there is glamour in consulting, it is pretty shallow. There is a 'bluffer's guide' in which would-be cons are recommended to turn up at the client's front gate in a chauffeur-driven stretched limo. In my experience, the consultants' entrance is more often round the back.

Scene: a railway station in Eastern Europe; midnight, late winter. I arrive not in a limo but in an ancient post-van. I am there to see newspapers being loaded onto overnight trains. Out on the exposed platform, snowflakes are blowing about as I try to look intelligent. A few downtrodden individuals are hanging around the train doors. 'Are those the loaders?' I enquire. The translator does his stuff and elicits a snort of derision from the client. 'No,' comes the answer, 'they're Romanian refugees.'

The travel. I confess that I did, just once, get to ride around in a private jet with a plentiful supply of champagne. That was when I somehow got co-opted onto a project with a consortium of bankers and venture capitalists checking out a prospective bid target. It made up for the occasion when striking Air France workers blockaded the runways in Paris with blazing tractors. I thought I was clever, taking the train to Brussels, until I found that every business traveller in Europe had had the same idea and all the flights out of Brussels, as well as every hotel in the city, were booked solid.

Scene: Heathrow Airport, 7.00 a.m. For the fourth time in as many weeks I am on the early flight to Paris. As I live west of London I 'only' have to get up at 5.30. Drive to the airport, park, check in, quick coffee. Boarding now. Arrive Paris 9.30 local time. Queue for taxis. Crawl down the A1, round the Périphérique. Reach the office around 10.45: on the go for five hours already, with a day of meetings ahead and then the return home by the same route. The client is already in the office: 'Could you get here a bit earlier next time?'

The challenge. Which one? There's the challenge of trying to solve all the problems that the client can think of in the space of the three days work which is all you've been allotted. The challenge of trying to look like a credible expert in anything that comes up: like the time that I went to sell a job to a firm of bookmakers, despite the fact that I have never placed a bet on a horse, dog or even snail in my life. The challenge of making sense of a stack of printouts a foot high, and the challenge of coming up with strategic recommendations for a client who seems to have no data at all. Or the challenge of just surviving.

Scene: suburban Dublin; an office block over a supermarket. We have appointed a new recruit with an excellent background in line management. It is his first consulting job and I have brought him to meet the client's Financial Director. As we walk through the door, the FD glowers at my new colleague and demands, 'Now then, what do *you* bring to the party?' He has, perhaps, sixty seconds to justify his existence.

The skills. A popular image of cons is that they float around at some ethereal level while letting words of wisdom drop from their lips. Such is their level of skill that they can sum up any situation at a glance and come up with a brilliant insight which the client, despite having spent his life in the business, has never thought of. What this image conveniently overlooks, of course, is the sheer hard grind that normally precedes the flash of inspiration.

Scene: the European headquarters of a US multinational, outside Brussels. My colleagues in the States have built a very elaborate model of the client's multidivisional business. Today we are to show it at a half-day interim presentation. Two of our team are flying in overnight from the US and, because the model is so big, they are bringing with them as hold baggage two top-spec Pentium PCs to run it on (this is in the days when a 386 is still the standard in our office). Time ticks away. I run out of polite conversation. We have drunk the coffee. Two hours late, my colleagues show up, *sans* Pentiums. OK, so who forgot that they would need customs clearance?

The teamwork. As I said, I respected my colleagues and usually enjoyed their company but they, like me, were only human and humans can let you down.

The scene: somewhere in Europe. The team: half English, half French. The project: trying to sort out a major nationalised industry with a desperate need for change. We have just five weeks to deliver a blueprint. The French work for four and a half weeks trying to analyse the costs. At each stage they burrow deeper and deeper into the detail until they have forgotten what they were there for. We are really sweating now, with a deadline fast approaching. I have completed all I can do without costs and have got half the report already written. But where are the numbers? The French decide that perhaps they should have used a different technique and, if I can give them a few more days, they will try a different model. I am not a violent man but could be about to break the habit of a lifetime. Voices are raised. French yields to Anglo-Saxon. 'Numbers, *now*. Just give me some f***ing numbers.' Miracles happen. Numbers appear. The report is completed. Entente cordiale.

The right stuff

I mentioned already the reactions I received from a number of recruiters when, after five or so years as a consultant, I started looking for a job back in industry. I stress *back in* because I had previously had seven solid years of commercial experience and, to me, it was a perfectly natural transition. After all, I had made the jump from management to consulting so why should I not hop equally easily in the reverse direction? I discovered that my own confidence about this was not widely shared. Would I be able to work within the confines of a corporate structure? Was I prepared to actually see my ideas through into implementation? Would I stick around for long enough to do this? Wouldn't I get bored after the first month? Could I relate to 'normal' people? These and similar questions all seemed to reflect a belief that consultants were somehow not like other men or women.

While not agreeing with this, I take the view that consulting is more or less unique as a job and that it requires particular talents and characteristics to make a success in it. This is not the same thing, however, as saying that you cannot be successful both as a manager and as a con. Personally, I feel that migration between the two is beneficial to all concerned. Nonetheless, consultancy places demands all of its own on the individual.

So, what makes a good con? This was a question that the research addressed with both clients and consultants. Figure 9.2 shows the responses:

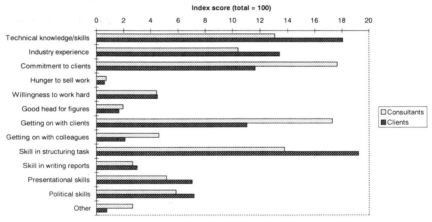

Figure 9.2: What makes a good con i.e. one who delivers good results to his/her clients?

The interesting thing here is that clients tend to emphasise technical knowledge and task skills whereas cons themselves give a higher rating to commitment and an ability to get on with clients.

Cons were also asked to rank the same factors on the criterion of achieving success within the consultancy firm. The result is shown as Figure 9.3:

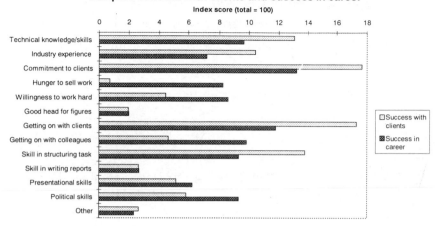

Figure 9.3: What makes a good con (according to cons) --
compare success with clients and success in career

Commitment to clients still scores highly, but so do more political skills, including the ability to get on with your own colleagues. Having a hunger for sales, and a willingness to work hard, also shoot up the rankings.

Taking this evidence one stage further, consultants and clients were also asked to give unprompted advice to the new con. Consultants themselves suggested (in decreasing order of frequency):

• Listen to the client/admit your weaknesses/be humble.

• Build a network of contacts, within the firm and externally.

• Get broad experience/learn as much as you can.

• Develop a specialism or niche role.

From their side, clients suggested:

• Listen to the client/admit your weaknesses/be humble.

• Give practical advice/keep it simple.

• Show innovation and creativity and avoid the 'standard solution'.

• Focus on deliverables.

• Work as a team with the client.

These are tough challenges for anyone. What they call for is a combination of task skills and people skills. Getting the right blend of these is a high priority for any consultancy. In the following sections I offer some of my own suggestions for what makes consulting work special and what it takes to succeed as a con.

Working under pressure. Cons are almost always under tight time pressures. I recall the delight which I felt after getting back into industry and having what seemed the luxury of being able to do things properly, rather than having to come up with instant solutions. This argument should not be pushed too far, however. It did not take very long in my new role for the pressure of deadlines to catch up with me again and for that luxurious time buffer to be used up. Cons work under pressure but this is hardly unique in business.

I am not sure that the hours that cons work or the stress that they are under are particularly unusual either. A lot of people work long hours, and many of them are far less well paid than consultants. There are plenty of small shopkeepers who put in over twelve hours a day, six or seven days a week and without a holiday from one year to the next: by those standards I would not claim to have done too badly. As for stress, I am not convinced that the average consultant is more stressed than the average broker or even the average front-line factory supervisor. I am absolutely certain that there are plenty of teachers and healthcare professionals, many of them earning far less than consultants do, whose stress levels are way off the scale of the cons who may occasionally walk past them in the corridor.

I had a colleague who used to pick up his tennis racket and head for the door regularly at 5.30 p.m. in summer, which reflected the fact that he was good at his job but also good at keeping it in perspective. I knew other cons who regularly worked well into the night. Some were very determined and successful, others were just badly organised or compulsive worriers. Of course, the approach of a deadline such as a final report tended to concentrate minds somewhat and lead to the burning of some midnight oil. But so it is in any organisation.

Living out of a suitcase. A lot of consultants spend a good deal of time travelling. The experience of quite a few cons can be summed up as a routine of packing your bags on Sunday night, heading to the airport, and returning to your home late the next Friday. This was particularly true of my colleagues in the US whose family life seemed to be under tremendous pressure. My own experience included, for a time, something resembling weekly commuting between London and various capitals of Europe and it was at the airport that I was once intercepted by a message that my wife had gone into labour. Others avoided the flying and a proportion of the overnights but only by virtue of long hours on the motorway, often tagged onto an already busy schedule. Once more, though, this sort of routine is not confined to consultants.

'Tomorrow? No problem'. In isolation, neither the hours worked by consultants, nor the pressure they are under, nor the miles that they travel are enough in themselves to be claimed as a special feature of the job. The thing which brings them all to a head is the sheer unpredictability of the demands placed on the individual, based entirely upon the whim of actual or prospective clients.

What ultimately I found a grind was not being able, ever, to plan my life outside work in any confidence of honouring the commitments which I might make. If the client wanted me in Budapest the day after tomorrow, Budapest is where I had to be. Too bad about the wedding anniversary or the dinner party. If there was a hot prospect in Aberdeen, out went parents' evening at school. When an old customer in Spain wanted a bit of follow-up work, it was back to the airport. No matter that my wife would have to cancel her evening engagement for the third time in as many weeks as I would not be home to babysit. Once you have done this a few times, you begin to feel a complete heel.

Essentially, then, consultancy *is* stressful but the hours and the deadlines and the travelling are really just a reflection of the client-consultant relationship which drives everything you do. The stress has much less to do with workload than with politics. Getting the cons to drop everything and rush across for an unscheduled meeting is one of the ways that clients assert their power over you.

As a pro, you do it because you feel you have to; until the day comes when you decide to find a cooler kitchen.

Spinning plates. Chasing your tail to satisfy the client is further complicated, very often, by multi-client working.

Some consultants get assigned for long periods to a single client: this can mean up to several years of steady work, day in and day out. The good news about this is that your utilisation is guaranteed for that time; the bad news is that it may not accord at all with your reasons for going into consultancy and it can leave you with a bumpy return to earth when the time comes for reintegration back into the firm for which you really work.

I never had the luxury of this sort of long-term involvement with a single client. The whole of my career as a con was spent in rushing from one job to the next, always trying to find time for the next sale and often having to keep several clients happy at once, much as in a plate spinning act the juggler rushes about the stage keeping all the plates in the air. In six years I was involved to a greater or lesser extent on at least 55 projects. If my average utilisation over that time was around 60%, that equates to an average of less than three weeks on each job and many amounted to just a few days' work. In addition, I was involved in many other proposals and selling activities, both successful and otherwise.

Unless your allotted time on a project allows your involvement to be more or less full-time, you need to find additional utilisation elsewhere. Suppose you have a substantial involvement in a major project: say eight weeks of your time but spread over a six-month project. Then you pick up another ten days of input to a second job, which has a duration of just a couple of months. Next, a colleague asks you to find two or three days to help him out with a problem he has hit. You are now up to around 60% expected utilisation for the next two months, dropping to around 30% thereafter. So you still need to be looking out for another piece of work, and when you hear of a new contact with a prospective client organisation you volunteer to visit them and scope out the job.

You are now involved in three actual jobs plus a large slice of developing a new opportunity. This may not sound too bad until the project manager on the first job decides to move all your eight weeks to the first two months of the project, the second client calls up to ask why you haven't been seen on site yet, you find that the two days of chargeable time promised by your colleague will require a whole week's effort to sort out and the new contact leaves a message to say that he wants you to present your proposal to his CEO next week and to send it to him in writing at least two days before.

This situation will sound familiar to almost any con. In most organ- isations you may have conflicting priorities but you will usually also have a pretty fair idea of who your real boss is and which of your tasks you can afford to ignore for a week or two. In consulting, you have to proceed on the basis that all clients are equally important because, large or small, *they* will always think so. And most cons find it very hard to say no. The Bible says that no man can be a slave to two masters but consultants spend their lives trying to please two, three or even more clients at any time. The plate-spinning tends to get worse as you move up the consultancy ladder, if only because you become a very expensive resource and therefore tend to find yourself spread ever more thinly.

It is a good question whether, at the end of the day, a con needs to be able to draw a line and refuse to go beyond it. Always saying yes becomes a habit as well as a state of mind. I found it hard to say no (and still do) but I saw a number of colleagues taking this to the point where they were very close indeed to physical or mental collapse. Being a consultant is not a great idea for those who suffer from insecurity: you need to have the confidence to lay down the law to a client as well as following whatever rules the client chooses to set. If I had been better at this I might not have had to chase so often from plate to plate.

Doers and sellers. Another feature of consulting is that you have both to *sell* the work and *do* the work. This is something which the business may share with some other professional advisers (lawyers, accoun- tants, even doctors) but it marks it out clearly from most other indus- tries. In manufacturing, not only do sales people never get involved in producing the product but the gulf between the two functions often gapes widely. Few consultancies, though, can firmly split the selling of their work from its doing even though they may allow some degree of specialisation.

There are sound reasons for this:

- At the proposal stage, clients want to meet and discuss the project with the cons who are going to do it. I have encouraged this in earlier chapters.

- It would be far too easy for a full-time seller to commit to delivering everything under the sun, at an attractively low price, in the knowledge that she would not have to carry the can for actually delivering on these promises.

- Except where a standardised methodology is deployed, assessing the scope of a job and developing an approach tailored to the client's needs is not something that can be entrusted to a sales person who does not have substantial hands-on experience of doing the work.

The consequence of this is that *selling* tends to be the specialism of senior staff. A junior con may have no involvement in this part of the process at all, but as she progresses and gains experience she can expect to get drawn into writing proposals, presenting to prospective clients and scoping simple jobs. All of this, of course, has to be learned alongside *doing* the work for other clients. The further you progress, the more time you are likely to spend selling and the less will you spend doing the work. At the limit, some Partners or their equivalents are more or less full-time sellers.

This is an unusual transition. Selling is often one of the lowest-level jobs in a business, one where you cut your teeth and then grab any opportunity to move to a decent desk job. For consultants, who may come into the business because they genuinely want to put their skills and experience to work for clients, the reward for success is to spend less time doing this and more time trying to flog the next job. Even in consultancies where there is a greater specialisation of roles, any middle-ranking con still needs to be able to sell as well as deliver successful projects. Not only does some sales skill enable you to sustain your own utilisation, if you are not needed on other work; it is also vital if opportunities to sell on further work to the same client are not to be missed.

Problem solving. It is hard to define the kind of intellect that it takes to be a good con. It is not necessarily a question of sheer intelligence. Nor do you have to be an expert in lateral thinking or advanced business theory. When interviewing candidates, I found myself looking for people who really knew their specialist function or industry but who were also capable of standing back from it. There are plenty of brilliant 'operators' who would be lousy consultants because they are not capable of rationalising what is good and what is bad about the way they do things. It is this capacity of detachment which every consultant needs.

Another way of putting it is to say that cons must be skilled at telling the wood from the trees. In a lot of projects, the answers may already be within the business or its people. Trying to unearth them takes a willingness to burrow into the detail but also an ability to stand back and see the broader picture.

In Chapter 5 I discussed the importance of finding the right level for a job, between the stratospherically strategic and the terrestrially tactical. Cons may need to analyse a huge amount of detailed information but it is the ability to make sense of complexity which will deliver results from it. This ability marks out the good con.

Something else that seems to be in short supply, judging from clients' responses to the research, is genuine creativity. What turns a good con into a great one (and I count myself out) is the ability to deliver not just a workmanlike solution but the truly creative one. Is it reasonable for a client, who knows the business inside out and who has failed to hit upon such a solution, to expect one from the consultant? Frankly, no; but a few, rare, individuals may be able to deliver this originality and they deserve to succeed.

Managing the business. Consultancy is a three-legged stool. The first leg is selling the work. The second is doing it. The third, all too easily overlooked, is managing it. Any business has these three elements but, in consulting, the same people are required to do all of them, in varying proportions. As you progress through the ranks and take on a bigger involvement in selling, so you can no longer be the one who is going to *do* the nitty-gritty of the work. The solution is obvious enough in theory: you need to *manage* projects by delegating. Delegation, though, is not a straightforward matter in consultancy. On complex projects or in a politically-charged environment it can be difficult to delegate without loss of quality and difficult for junior staff to understand what they have to do and where they fit in.

It is too easy, though, to blame complexity or politics for preventing effective delegation when the root of the problem may lie in poor project management. Those who see consultancy just as a way of deploying their own expertise may be poor at defining tasks for others to undertake. Highly individualistic cons are much better left to work alone. Unfortunately, as in other businesses, the reward for success is too often promotion to a rank beyond your abilities and this can lead to such individualists being responsible for the work of others. The result is seldom a happy outcome for anyone.

To be really effective as a con, you have to develop management skills to go along with your technical and selling abilities. Gurus who just want to pursue technical excellence may do well on their own, but they are not much use to large consulting firms. To sustain their growth, while maintaining some consistency of quality, major consultancies have had to become more professional. In some cases this has meant adopting a more methodology-driven approach. In others it has meant formal tools for internal quality control and rigorous staff appraisal. The overall message for the individual is clear: to succeed as a con you have to see consulting as a business and show that you can manage a part of it. This requirement strengthens my belief that migration between management and consulting is perfectly natural and beneficial to all concerned.

Individuals and teams. The essence of management lies in relating the work of individuals to the mission of the organisation as a whole. The relationship of the individual to the organisation is particularly complex in consultancy, where the nature of the work demands a high level of flexibility:

- You may be working totally alone on one job, responsible for every aspect of it, and as a part of a large team on another job where your role will be specified by someone else. Cons have to be team players on demand but solo performers as well.

- You have to understand your place and role in several parallel structures: the firm's structure through which you relate to your superiors and colleagues; the project structure which relates you to your manager on a given job; and a structure of relationships with any number of the client's personnel. These various parties will compete for your time and may see you in totally different ways. In turn, you need to respond differently to each and adapt to changes in the structure as you move from one job to the next. Consultancy is not an environment for those who need a fixed hierarchy and clear reporting lines.

- Similarly, you need to be able to work to tightly defined objectives but also to cope with high degrees of uncertainty in the tasks you undertake. It will all depend on the job you are working on and how it is managed (if at all). You may be given firm instructions or may need to pick up 'delegated' tasks that are hopelessly vague. I was sent to one client (actually, a famous receivership case) with the instruction just to hang around for a few days and see what I could pick up. I was assigned to another project (which went under the grand name of *Re-engineering the Marketing Process* for a very large client) and found myself, two months later, still asking the project manager what it was that we were there to do. I never did work it out.

The good con will cope with this variety of situations and relationships and adopt an appropriate style – directing, catalysing, team working, challenging – for each one. This calls for highly developed personal skills. It does not follow from this that you have to hit it off personally with every client or indeed every colleague. What you have to be able to do is drop into a completely new environment, peopled with individuals that you have never met before and who may have no particular respect for you, and rapidly build an appropriate relationship with them to start taking the job forward. You also need to create your own network of contacts both within the firm and with prospective clients, in order to give yourself the best chance of pulling in the work.

Standing up for yourself. The time to show what you are really made of as a consultant is when your back is against the wall and you have to defend the proposals or recommendations that you have put forward. You may have dug yourself into a bit of a hole and there is no one but yourself who is going to get you out of it. In management, you may from time to time be called upon to initiate major changes or lead a presentation to convince the CEO that your plans can really work. As a consultant you are doing these things, if not every day, pretty regularly; and then perhaps jumping in the car to sell the next one. It gets scary.

I have had to stand up and defend my position against all-comers in situations ranging from a room full of American Vice-Presidents to a hall packed with Hungarian trade unionists, not forgetting jerky Transatlantic video conferences at which I might as well have been communicating with a team of astronauts. You need to be able to enjoy the adrenaline buzz of these occasions because in many ways they are what makes the grind of project work fun.

A certain assertiveness is essential to a good con. Some clients will challenge you in order to probe your reasoning, some simply to find out what you are made of. In both situations you need to be able to stand your ground. Wilting violets need not apply.

Influencing people. In a lot of line-management positions, assertiveness can be replaced by (or is often confused with) aggressiveness: some managers like nothing better than to bark at their subordinates and rule by fear rather than respect. In consulting you rarely have the luxury of this and *influencing* has to be the order of the day. I cited earlier an occasion when I completely lost my temper with a French colleague, but this was a rare luxury.

The first skill required for influencing people is that of listening. Time after time, in their free responses to the questionnaire, clients stressed that they want cons who can listen and understand their issues. Only once you have done this can you hope to build credibility, propose solutions and begin to guide your client.

Within the firm, dealing with your peers or subordinates is much more about coaxing the best out of a self-motivated professional than about command and control. With the client, you have a relationship which is always ambiguous: in some ways it is the client, as holder of the purse, who is the boss but in other ways the consultant holds a lot of power through her status and through the importance of the task over which she has more or less complete day-to-day control. This can lead to some jockeying for position between con and client.

A client that I worked for in France was always trying to find ways of challenging my position and reinforcing his own. This was, perhaps, partly because he himself was an intermediary: part of a state-owned agency that was managing the job on behalf of another official body. At any rate, he made great play out of the occasions when he tried to call me in the Paris office but found that I was not even in the country; he agreed elements of our approach and then denied ever seeing them; and he told us who we should interview and then scoffed at their views when they did not accord with his own. At the end of the job, we reached conclusions with which he did not agree and this provoked a long argument. Fortunately, as we had done our homework thoroughly, we were able to prove the validity of our case several times over. In the end he simply refused to listen: 'That may be so, Monsieur Ashford,' he said, *'mais ce n'est pas la volonté de l'état.'*[3] Hard to argue against that.

Relationship management. You may have to stand up to clients but, ultimately, getting into a head to head with them is likely to be futile. The really good consultant will make sure this does not happen, through managing his clients and their expectations. I was not as smart as this and locked horns too often in sterile argument with my clients. If the client has changed her mind about what she wants, you may have to put your hand up and call a halt but there is no point in simply having an 'Oh no, I didn't' . . . 'Oh yes, you did' sort of argument. You have to find a way of taking the job forward, suitably redefined.

Consultancy is hard because you have to be firm and yet you have to be flexible. You need to recognise when to shut up and get on with it, because it is what the client is paying you for, and when to stop and argue. A good con wants to say yes but knows when to say no. A good

---

[3] It is not the wish of the State.

con is not afraid to put on a mask of being the world expert in any topic, but must know down inside what his or her limitations really are. As in any relationship, a little honesty can help.

Respecting yourself and your colleagues. At the end of the day, the good con will be respected by the client as an individual. Does the same thing apply within consultancies themselves? Certainly, I respected the *professionalism* of my colleagues. But it tends to be with cons as it is with sales people: you are only ever as good as your last sale or your last job. Because cons operate under pressure and often to tight deadlines, it is vital to them that everyone delivers what they are tasked to do. There is little sympathy for those who fail to come up with the goods, however difficult or misconceived the brief may be. In the same way, because cons are fighting hard to keep their utilisation up, they have little respect for those who fail to achieve this.

A lot of my colleagues felt that they were not respected or valued as individuals by the firm for which we worked. On reflection, although this was perfectly true, I can see that *we* also did not respect each other enough as individuals. It is in the nature of the job to reduce individuals to productive assets. If they do not produce, it is not long before their fellows start to see them as dead wood. Small wonder that the organisation is liable to spit them out. I saw this happen at regular intervals in my time as a con, partly, no doubt, 'to encourage the rest'. One might have thought that some, whose skills were regarded as no longer saleable, could have been retrained in new areas of expertise, but I never saw this happen. Many consultancies want to recruit their productive assets fully-formed, and only under extreme pressure will they train them in skills other than in the business of consulting itself.[4]

In my pre-consulting career I worked for a shipping company. In the container business we measured loads in units equivalent to twenty-foot or forty-foot-long containers. A Forty-foot Equivalent

---

[4] According to the *Economist* (22 March 1997) Andersen Consulting spends over 10 per cent of its revenues on training. However, the thrust of this is apparently on training consultants to apply the Andersen approach – what others would call, less charitably, turning them into Andersen androids.

Unit was known as an FEU. In consultancy, this was redefined by my colleagues as Fee Earning Unit. And that is precisely what we were.

In summary, to succeed as a consultant you need to be able to:

- Put up with long hours, under pressure, but not perhaps to such an unusual degree as some may make out.

- Live out of a suitcase when, and where, required.

- Cope with never being sure where you will end up and who you will be working for from one week to the next.

- Work at the same time for several 'masters' (of either gender), all of whom may feel entitled to your time whenever they choose, and whose needs you have to juggle with the pressure to sell the next job.

- Always go the extra mile for your client but, if you are to survive, learn also to say no.

- Sell work as well as doing it yourself.

- Work effectively both on your own and within a larger team.

- Handle vague and unstructured tasks that may be passed to you by others.

- Make sense of complex information, finding the right level of analysis that will enable you to extract meaning from the detail.

- Manage projects in situations of uncertainty and where delegation is not just a matter of passing out standardised tasks.

- Cope with the conflicting and changing needs of multiple organisational structures defined respectively by the firm, the project and the client.

- Develop relationships fast with colleagues and clients, enabling you to pull in work through networking and to get on with the job as quickly and smoothly as possible.

- Stick to your guns and argue your own corner when challenged, but deploy also the negotiating skills needed to get the best from both clients and colleagues.

- Stay flexible and creative, finding in all circumstances some way of taking the job forward.

- Achieve the respect of the client for you as an individual while coping with the knowledge that, for your business, you are simply a productive asset and only as good as your last job.

The last skill which the con needs is the sense, and good fortune, to get out at the right moment. Not everyone will have much choice about this: consultancies are famous for their 'up or out' approach to career development. Moving on after a few years may be no bad thing, anyway. Figure 9.4 summarises the views of consultants themselves, few of whom suggested remaining in consulting for more than ten years.

Figure 9.4: Consultancy as a career – recommendation of cons

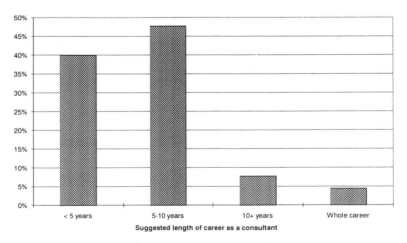

My experience was that you can end up so busy as a consultant that you never have time to apply for other jobs. The skilful manage to find attractive niches with clients. The rest of us, if we want to get out, take our chances.

It could be you

If you still think you would do well as a con, try testing yourself with the following *Consmopolitan Quiz*. Study each situation and decide which course of action you would follow. Then check the answers and see how you score against the pros!

Situation 1. Your utilisation, and that of your team, is looking a bit low. An opportunity to bid for a new job comes to you but you realise that another con is much better qualified to do the work.

Do you:

a) Agree to stand aside on condition that the other con puts one of your team on the job?

b) Grab the prospect for yourself and claim as your own the previous project references done by the other con?

c) Pass the lead on to the better-qualified con with a note saying that you hope she'll reciprocate at some time in the future?

Situation 2. You are presenting your proposal to a prospective new client but you are conscious that it goes beyond your previous experience. The client asks: 'Have you ever done this sort of job before?'

Do you:

a) Admit honestly that you have not?

b) Bullshit about a vaguely-similar job which can be dressed up to sound relevant?

c) Look the client in the eye and say, 'Yes, several times'?

Situation 3. After your presentation, the client tells you that he likes your proposal but that you are 30% dearer than your competitors.

Do you:

a) Give him what he wants then skimp on the analysis and take short-cuts without telling him?

b) Say 'I agree that our fee-rates are high but I'm afraid they won't let me do anything about it'?

c) Agree to cut your fees without changing the work content, then squeeze the time allotted to the team by 20% all round in order to balance the books?

Situation 4. A Partner in your firm has put you on a project which he has just sold. When he gives you the proposal you realise that the job has been hopelessly underscoped and cannot be completed within anything like the proposed number of days.

Do you:
a) Work really hard in your evenings and at weekends to get the job done, without booking more than your allotted time to it?
b) Tell the Partner that you cannot do it?
c) Get through the job as best you can but make sure you get your own back by booking extra days to the next job that the Partner puts you on?

Situation 5. The project manager has given you such a vague briefing that you have no idea what you are tasked to do. All that is clear is that you are supposed to be spending time at the client's premises 'getting a handle on the issues'.

Do you:
a) Do nothing until you are given a clearer brief?
b) Put in a week's work, write a specification for what you think is required next, then cease work pending agreement to this plan?
c) Hang around the client's offices for at least a month and book every minute of this time to the project?

Situation 6. The client promised to put one of her own staff on the project to do the donkey-work. The person selected is a bit slower than you would wish.

Do you:
a) Tell the client that the job will be a disaster unless you are allowed immediately to bring in one of your own juniors, to be paid at full rate?
b) Work harder yourself to try to compensate for having such a weak link on the team?
c) Say nothing but blame the client when things go wrong.

Situation 7. Halfway through the job you realise that it is a complete waste of the client's money. The client needs help, but has commissioned the wrong job.

Do you:
a) Carry on, then sell the client the job he really needed as an extension to the current project?
b) Tell the client that the job is wrong for him and suggest it be halted?
c) Carry on with the project while trying at the same time to do at
   least something of the job which the client should have bought in
   the first place?

*Situation 8. You have a client who is confident what the 'right' answer is.
When you crunch the numbers through a spreadsheet model, the 'wrong'
answer comes out.*

Do you:
a) Warn the client and look for a way of reconciling the differing
   views?
b) Fix the model to produce the 'right' answer?
c) Announce the answer that came out of the model at the next
   presentation to the client?

*Situation 9. You are working for a CEO on a review of his company's
computer systems. You are impressed by the Head of IT but realise that her
department has been seriously under-resourced which has made several
projects late. After two weeks the CEO asks to see you, explains that he has
been intending from the start to fire the Head of IT and asks you to endorse
this.*

Do you:
a) Agree that she should be sacked, realising that there will be a lot
   more work for you sorting out the resulting mess?
b) Say 'I'm afraid I cannot comment: it would be unethical'?
c) Defend the Head of IT and tell the CEO that she has been doing a
   good job?

*Situation 10. You have finished a one-off job but the client has not paid up.
When you go to see her she claims that, 'It wasn't what I wanted.'*

Do you:
a) Offer to do another week's work to put things right, leaving it up
   to her whether she pays for this extra time?

b) Threaten to sue unless you get an immediate follow-up assignment?

c) Look embarrassed and say you'll have to refer it to the Senior Partner?

Situation 11. At the end of the project, there remains the boring task of writing the report. As you are leaving the final presentation to the client, your Partner tells you to see to this and adds that the budget is all used up so you cannot book any more time to the job.

Do you:

a) Take the client out for a beer and persuade him to accept a copy of the final presentation slides instead of a full report?

b) Spend all weekend writing the report instead of taking the children to Alton Towers?

c) Have a good bitch to your mates in the pub?

Situation 12. You have finished a first job for a client and are hopeful of a follow-up assignment. Unfortunately, the management of the first job was a bit of a shambles and the client has noticed this. She suggests that your manager should not be in charge of the next phase of the work but that you should manage it yourself.

Do you:

a) Apologise but explain that you cannot ask your boss to step aside?

b) Assure her that things will go better on the next phase, then make sure you put your own time into doing the routine tasks that your manager ignores?

c) Promise to bring the job in for 10% less than budget if she insists that your manager be removed?

Scoring

Situation 1: A=5, B=10, C=0
Situation 2: A=0, B=5, C=10
Situation 3: A=10, B=0, C=5
Situation 4: A=5, B=0, C=10
Situation 5: A=0, B=5, C=10
Situation 6: A=10, B=5, C=0

Situation 7: A=10, B=0, C=5
Situation 8: A=5, B=10, C=0
Situation 9: A=10, B=0, C=5
Situation 10: A=5, B=10, C=0
Situation 11: A=10, B=5, C=0
Situation 12: A=0, B=5, C=10

Do you have what it takes?

Score of 40 or less. On this showing, you're a bit of a wimp. There's nothing to be ashamed about: the world probably needs hairdressers and telephone cleaners more than it needs another con. But no con is going to succeed by ducking the hard issues and just hoping they will go away.

Score from 45 to 80. You are honest, hard-working and concerned for your clients. You seem to have the right stuff but, frankly, you're just too conscientious. Your desire to meet your client's every need is very touching but you are clearly incapable of saying no. You are likely to get dumped upon by your clients and your colleagues and end up with a nervous breakdown. Are you *sure* you want to be a con?

Score of 85 or over. You are a cynical bastard, determined to come out on top even if that means taking your client for a ride and shafting those you work with. Perfect material for a few consultancy firms I can think of, but clients should be warned about people like you. In short, you are a real pro.

CHAPTER 10:
CONSULTANCIES ON
TRIAL

In the research that was conducted for this book, both consultants and their clients were asked whether they agreed or disagreed with the suggestion that 'Consultants are good at managing everyone's business except their own'. Figure 10.1 shows that, among clients, some 26% either agreed or agreed strongly. Half had no view either way.

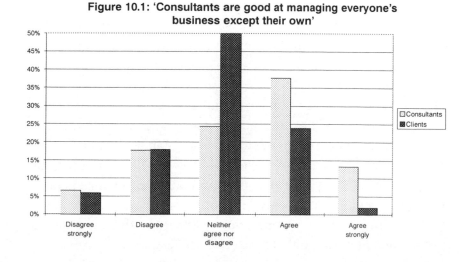

Figure 10.1: 'Consultants are good at managing everyone's business except their own'

Of consultants themselves, however, over half (51%) agreed with the proposition. Of these, 13% were in strong agreement. Among those employed by major consultancies (that is, omitting the self-employed and consultants in small practices) 60% agreed.

I find these results quite remarkable. The question asked in the research was a leading one and I rather expected to find that a significant proportion of clients would agree with it. It seemed to me that everyone would *know* that consultants are lousy at running their own business just as everyone *knows* that cons borrow your watch to tell you the time and, by the way, charge you an arm and a leg for the privilege. It is part of the mythology of consulting that the smart suits who claim the right to teach you how to do things are themselves incapable of running a Sunday school tea party. Apart from anything else, we like our idols to have feet of clay. It is satisfying for all concerned to be able quietly to mock those whom we are forced to respect.

But clients, in large part, are indifferent to the question. Perhaps they feel unable to judge the internal workings of the consultancy firms that they see only from the outside. Perhaps they feel that to criticise their cons on these grounds would somehow belittle their own selection of them as advisers. Or, perhaps, they are genuinely impressed with their consultants' management acumen and assume it applies internally as well as externally. Always excluding, of course, the 26% who agreed with the proposition.

It is the views of the cons in the survey that strike me as remarkable. These are the men and women who can reasonably claim to *know* how consultancies run their own businesses and only a quarter of them actively disagree with the suggestion that they are useless at it. What is going on here? Maybe consultants are incredibly modest about their own abilities and achievements (no, I don't think so, either). Maybe they have particularly high standards and feel that they fall short of them (hum . . .). Maybe all of us who work for corporations of any kind take the view that our bosses are a bunch of bozos and that euthanasia is the only kind way to change senior management (a grain of truth in this one, I fancy). Whatever the reasoning, the survey leads pretty strongly to the conclusions that:

- Consultancy businesses have a real problem in the way they are managed.

or:

- At very least, those employed in them *think* there is a problem, which in a people-dependent business amounts to much the same thing.

The issue is a serious one, for at least two reasons. Firstly, if cons really are so bad at running their own affairs, does this not undermine their right to advise others? Secondly, is there not a concern that poor practice management will spill over into poor project management? In other words, do clients stand to lose out because of poor direction of the consultancy effort?

To answer these questions, we need to examine the evidence of management failure in consultancy firms and decide if there is a case to answer. The reader must be the jury. Will you find the cons Guilty or Not Guilty?

Evidence for the prosecution

Lack of focus. It is certainly the fashion at the time of writing for businesses to be *focused*. Sprawling conglomerates have been stream-lined into tightly defined structures; shareholder value has been maximised (we are told) by breaking up unwieldy divisionalised dinosaurs; diversification, once the driving force of many corporate strategies, has become a dirty word.

By contrast, the large consultancies have gone on swelling in scope as well as size. Forget the fact that many of them are also auditors, corporate financiers and insolvency practitioners: sticking purely within the consulting business they have laboured to offer services ranging from blue-sky strategy to oily-rag implementation, to every sector of business plus the public sector, across all continents of the globe. Latterly, they have been falling over themselves to extend their activities into the direct management of outsourced services, primar-ily computing. They are still chasing synergies long after most of their clients gave up the race. Focus is not the word which most comes to mind.

For the individual consultant, lack of focus means never being sure where the firm is heading. Should you, as a con, be trying to consolidate your position in the knitwear industry or develop new clients in the aerospace sector? Are you still supposed to be selling benchmarking studies or should you have moved on to change management? It also means, in my experience, chasing your tail bidding for every opportunity that comes along regardless of whether you are really qualified. Because I used to do distribution work for manufacturers and retailers, I once spent a week of my life assembling a doomed proposal to advise an international agency on how to distribute food aid in the third world: a brief which encompassed channels as sophisticated as the porter network of Nepal. Was this focused? Was it even remotely sensible?

Feast and famine. It is easy for consultants to become overburdened. As described in the last chapter, I was often trying to undertake two or three projects at the same time and sell another couple as well. But there were also times when I was scratching around to find the next job.

In consultancy, if there is one thing worse than having too much to do, it is having time on your hands. Given the rather short career expectancy of any consultant who is not well utilised, this situation makes cons very twitchy. I had one colleague, an excellent technical specialist, who was almost always in considerable demand and usually booked out for months or even years at a time. And yet, whenever he was within a couple of months of finishing a job, he started getting nervous about where the next one would come from. One result of this sort of atmosphere is that cons may hoard work and contribute to their own overloading even when there are well qualified colleagues with little to do.

Many cons want nothing more than a nice steady stream of work to get stuck into. Instead, they lurch from famine to feast. In their eyes, at least, this is the fault of the firm's management. Rightly or wrongly, I suspect this is where a lot of the negative vibes about poor management start.

Short termism. Show me a business whose employees do *not* feel that senior management has an overly short-term perspective. This feeling is widespread and, possibly, with good reason.

There are plenty of reasons to criticise consultancies for short termism. Rather than putting long-term effort into genuine innovation, they have shown a great willingness to leap onto every bandwagon that happens to be passing (re-engineering being the prime example). Rather than planning the skills and resource that they need for the long term, they have consistently followed policies of hiring or firing at the least sign of a market uptick or downturn. As a con, you are only ever as good as your last job and your next sale.

Poor internal communication. Every consultant will advise his or her clients that good communication is essential. It ranks alongside the need for senior level commitment as one of the great truisms of management theory.

My own experience as a con, which may not be untypical, was that internal communication in the firm was seriously flawed. For a start, a lot of auditors and consultants *never* spoke to each other if they could avoid it, which made a bit of a nonsense of the idea that we provided a seamless service to our clients. Even within the consultancy, those of us fortunate enough to be located away from Head Office tended to feel that we were on another planet. And communications between parts of the firm in different countries were often haphazard when not downright hostile.

This is not a trivial matter, given the pretensions of consulting firms. If a methodology is developed in one part of the organisation, it is of limited value unless it can be adopted elsewhere. If a particular skill base exists in another country, there is no general benefit from it unless others are aware of its existence. If you are a con trying to sell work to a business in Europe, it will probably help if you are aware of your colleagues' relationship with its parent in the US. We had no systematic mechanisms in place to achieve any of these things.

Poor communication leads to two related problems:

- *Poor use of the available resource.* This was a particular issue for us at the international level. Expertise might exist in the US but the firm in the UK would fail to call it in to assist. The same thing happened between the opposite sides of the English Channel. This was partly a communication problem and partly down to turf wars, which I discuss below. In fairness to my ex-employers, bringing the various bits of the firm into a closer relationship – and sharing expertise and resource – has now become the focus of major management effort on their part.

- *Reinventing the wheel.* If you do not know what someone else has done before, there is a real risk that you may have to reinvent it. Another concept much sold by consultants is that of the 'learning organisation'. Consultancies themselves have every reason to try and learn from best practice outside and inside the firm. More often, though, each part of our organisation seemed to be operating in a vacuum and had no means of learning from the work, or the mistakes, of another. This can give clients a poor deal and is frustrating for cons themselves.

Turf wars. Turf wars – the overzealous defence of your own particular patch – are endemic to consultancies. They are partly about personalities (usually the rivalry between two or more Partners) but also the result of the systematic way in which individuals are judged on their ability to grab as much chargeable work as possible for themselves and their teams.

Clients, one hopes, will rarely be aware of internecine conflict going on behind the scenes. Where it affects them, however, is when a Partner grabs a job that would be much better done by another or fails for selfish reasons to allocate the best available con to the work. In these situations, the quality of the service given to clients may be at risk.

Poor attitude to staff. I observed in an earlier chapter that consultancy is, to a very high degree, a people business. The assets, the know-how, the skills, the experience *are* the cons themselves. One would expect consulting firms to go out of their way to motivate staff, celebrate their achievements and help them to achieve their potential.

It may be so in some firms but attitudes of this kind seemed all too rare in the environment where I worked. At the coal face, the cons felt that they were frequently treated with something approaching contempt. I have already mentioned the time when redundancies in one office were announced at the staff Christmas party. Elsewhere, a Partner to whom I voiced some concerns about the morale of his staff replied that he did not care if they all left the firm tomorrow, as he could always go out and get replacements. As for personal development: not only did the firm prefer to renew its skills by firing and hiring, rather than by training, but the first whiff of recession led to training budgets being cut to shreds.

Leading from the back. Before I upset old friends, I had better say at this point that I worked primarily for a Partner who was immensely supportive and from whom I learned a great deal. He also gave me a startling amount of rope as I tried to develop new initiatives, in many of which I freely admit to having failed. Who am I to criticise Partners?

Having said that, I will now do so. I also witnessed, repeatedly, Partners who were happy to lead from the back. Now, being a Partner is a very senior role. You cannot expect a Partner to get stuck into the nitty gritty of project work. But if a Partner is not going to do the selling, and not going to manage the day-to-day work of the project, and not going to do the analysis, and not going to come up with the recommendations, and not going to front-up when the going gets rough at the presentation . . . what exactly is he there for? Buying the lunch is not a sufficient response.

The obvious answer to the question is that Partners are there to *manage the business*. The symptoms that I am describing, however, indicate the weaknesses that seem to characterise the management of consultancies. When a Partner runs off with the credit for a successful job, and passes the buck when things get sticky, this is not managing the business nor does it do anything for staff morale.

In the absence of real management, *petty bureaucracy* floods in to fill the gap. We seemed to be masters at generating procedures that everyone loved to hate. The timesheet is every con's bête noire but you soon get used to filling one in every couple of weeks. Woe betide, though, the project manager who forgets to apply for a project number at the appropriate time or to get a sign-off on the quality plan.

Quality was one area where Partners had a leading role to play, as they ultimately carried the can through personal liability to clients. But when a Partner has led a project from the back how is she going to judge the quality of the output? On various occasions I submitted a report for the Partner to review (usually, in fairness, about two minutes before the deadline for it to be sent to the client) and got it back with the commas crossed out and replaced with colons and the word 'but' substituted for 'however'. Reducing the Partner to the role of sub-editor is ludicrous and I do not imagine he enjoyed it either.

I can hear teeth being gnashed in the public gallery. Yes, there are some first-rate consultancy Partners. Yes, some top notch cons are rewarded by being promoted to Partner and, despite their new elevation, they may continue to do a brilliant job. But the prosecution rests its case on the evidence presented above and points the finger of blame at senior management. As we have seen, consultancies too often appear unfocused, bad at managing their workloads, too concerned with the short term, poor at internal communication, riven by turf wars, bogged down in petty bureaucracy and led from the back by senior staff who display a deplorable contempt of their juniors. The blame, surely, must lie at the top?

The case for the defence

The defence attorney's case is outrageous in its simplicity. Some may see it as a cop-out. Others may see it as the truth but not necessarily the whole truth. It boils down to this: big consultancies manage their businesses badly because *they are by their nature very hard businesses to run*.

There are several aspects to this, which I discuss below.

The nature of the business. Consultancy is all about change: leading it, responding to it, catalysing it, forcing it. This also means that consultancies themselves have to be capable of changing fast and responding to the market.

I voiced the criticism of short termism, but how can you focus on the long term if client demands are changing so rapidly? Take the pace of change in the computer industry and then think about what it means not simply to keep up with it but to try and be one step ahead. How can consultancies spend six months training someone when they have three clients wanting help yesterday? How can they ignore falling utilisation levels, and allow poorly-utilised staff to hang around, when the business is so highly geared to the level of charge-able work? Our part of the firm used typically to have up to three months of order book. Anything beyond that was, by definition, over the horizon.

Consultancy is a scramble: this is the case for the individual, rushing from client to client, but also for the firm which has constantly to renew its skills and its people in order to keep ahead or just keep up.

Consultancy is also driven by its clients and by the kind of work that they want to buy. My experience as a consultancy manager was that every time we tried to plan ahead and set targets for our business, a new client would appear from a quite unanticipated direction and take us somewhere we never expected to go.

You can set yourself up to help engineering manufacturers stream-line their workflows but, if a big food retailer walks through the door and offers you a year's work redesigning their shops, are you seriously going to refuse? It is not easy to research the potential consultancy market: businesses seldom plan their consulting needs in advance and may not know that they will need help until . . . well, until the day when they need it. If you cannot research the market, it is very hard to plan where the work is going to come from and where your business is going.

The nature of the market. In recent years, the word on the lips of many consultancy Partners has been *globalisation.* Clients, they argue, are becoming global organisations and demand global support and assis-tance. Consultancies, they suggest, must therefore be capable of offer-ing the same kinds of service to the same standard (the word seamless usually comes into the sentence around this point) anywhere in the world. The leader of at least one major consultancy has suggested that there will in the future be no more than four truly international consultancies able to do this – on the assumption, naturally, that his own firm will be among them.

If this is true (and it could be argued that global work for global clients is likely to be the exception, rather than the rule, for many years to come) it ups the ante considerably for the cons. Imagine that you have hundreds or even thousands of consultants scattered around the world and that your reputation depends, with every job that you take, on the quality of their work. How do you set about making sure that the quality is the same in Valparaiso as it is in Vladivostok?

If you are manufacturing sports shoes, no problem. You have a model and a standard. You can inspect every hundredth pair. You can test them after they have been produced and you can watch the production line turning them out. If you are serving hamburgers in the High Street, same answer. Standardise, procedurise, monitor, control.

But consulting is not a business that lends itself to this treatment. At least, not the sort of consulting that I used to do. Each case was different, so was each project and each outcome. Some were doubtless more successful, others less. But there was only one way that the quality of the work could be assured, and that was through the quality of the people doing it. Which brings us to the next set of problems: those with two legs.

The nature of the people. I have had my bitch about Partners. No doubt they would have a few things to say about their staff.

To be a successful consultant, as we saw in the last chapter, you need both technical and personal skills. You need to be able to make sense of a difficult situation, analyse information, spot the key points, determine a course of action and sell it to your client. You also need to manage overlapping relationships with colleagues and clients simultaneously. You need to be able to pick things up very fast and you need the strength of character to stand up under pressure of various kinds. These skills do not make you a hero or a saint, but the sort of people who have them are likely to be individualistic, intelligent, somewhat assertive, probably quite creative and often with a strong risk-taking profile. They also look upon themselves as professionals.

These are not people who are easy to manage.

Traditional bureaucratic models of the organisation assume that work can be standardised and procedures developed to handle it. Consultancy work, very often, is not like this. The models assume that control is exercised from the top, with information passed up and decisions passed down. This is not how you manage consultants. To try and build a corporate identity from a bunch of rampant individualists calls for radically different models.

Why were we apparently incapable of sending out an invoice without a mistake on it? The truth is that none of us were very interested in getting the paperwork right, which is probably why we ended up in consulting in the first place. More worrying, though, is the related thought that a lot of cons are just not very interested in managing the business, preferring to get on with the interesting job of trying to help their clients. If even a few of these cons make it to Partner, is it surprising that the management of consulting firms can seem so weak?

The nature of the management task. Forget big consultancies for a moment. A lot of cons start out as sole traders. An individual with some skills to offer sets up in business on his own. He networks with his former colleagues and business acquaintances; he sells work to clients; he carries out the work and sends the client a bill. After a while, perhaps, he joins forces with a second consultant and they set up a partnership. They may recruit a junior or two and perhaps a part-time secretary, but the partners themselves remain deeply involved in selling, managing and doing the work.

So far, so good. But now think of the firm growing bigger and bigger. With size comes complexity. In most businesses the response is to develop specialised roles: a sales force emerges that is separate from the production team and various support functions are added. At the same time, senior management becomes detached from the nitty-gritty of the work and starts to operate at several removes from the coal face.

In the classic consultancy partnership, however, this process of specialisation and detachment stops halfway. For a start, Partners are personally liable if things go wrong. They are responsible to the client, and clients like to be involved with the man or woman who carries the can. To answer to the client, they need to keep a finger on the pulse of the work and monitor the quality of their staff and the outputs they are generating. This makes detachment difficult.

Specialisation is equally difficult in a business where selling, managing and doing the work are so closely intertwined. Where it occurs it is of a rather peculiar nature: in many firms the Partner is expected to be the main winner of the work, leading to the unusual situation that the higher you rise in the firm the more you tend to become a full-time salesperson. This may or may not suit the character and abilities of the newly promoted Partner. In any event, no Partner is free simply to sell new work. The clients that she wins will still expect her to be involved in the job itself.

In this situation, Partners have two options. They can refuse to get drawn into the detail of the work itself, in which case they are exposed to the risk of quality failures by their staff and will appear to lead from the rear. Or they can attempt still to take a personal involvement in all the projects going on under them, in which case they are liable to be swamped by the workload. Many will fall between these two stools: desperately trying still to run the team as if it were a small practice but never really having the time to give the attention they would wish to each client and each project. Expecting the individual also to plan strategy, communicate a sense of direction, invest in new developments and keep abreast of what is happening elsewhere in the firm may be simply asking too much.

The defence counsel has done his best to make the jury feel sorry for Partners. There is a sound of sniffing in the courtroom. But is it enough? Could consultancies not organise themselves better in order to overcome some of the inherent problems of the business and make the best use of their admittedly awkward staff?

Wait! Who is this rushing up the courthouse steps and demanding to be heard?

The expert witness

Henry Mintzberg, in his book *Structure in Fives: Designing Effective Organisations*[1], analyses how different types of organisation are suited to varying situations.

In the previous section, we touched on what Mintzberg calls the *simple structure* of the small firm, focused on the founder with a small team. The question is what happens as this unit grows. One option is repeatedly to replicate the simple structure. The accountancy-based consultancies grew as a loose coalition of groups, each based around a Partner. However, when a firm of this kind wishes to assemble a larger team, or spread knowledge from one group to another, or develop a consistent approach or standard across the whole business, it runs into major problems. New initiatives tend to get bogged down in internal negotiations. The very features which contribute to the strength of the small firm – flexibility of roles, no distinction between sellers and doers, customer-focus, direct involvement of senior staff with the work – can become a weakness as the size of the firm increases. So what are the alternatives?

In a *machine bureaucracy*, perhaps the most familiar form of organisation, the operating base is controlled from the top via middle management. It functions through formalised procedures, rules, centralised authority and the standardisation of tasks. This mechanistic model may work on the production line but it is inappropriate as a way of organising the work of the autonomous and intelligent individuals that make up a consultancy.

For this situation, Mintzberg identifies a variant that he calls the *professional bureaucracy*. Its key feature is that the work of its employees is coordinated not through the sort of command structures that are found in the machine bureaucracy but by standardising their skills. Typically, this involves external training and qualification of a rigorous nature. Once an employee has acquired these skills, she can work largely autonomously of her colleagues while yet delivering the same

---

[1] Prentice-Hall, 1983. Mintzberg's work is complex and I have plucked only certain elements from it. I hope that I have managed to do so without misrepresenting his thesis but the interpretation is mine.

results. A classic case is healthcare: doctors are trained to a common standard which governs both diagnosis and treatment without the need for line management to intervene. The standardisation of skills is also the way that audit firms operate: it is therefore not surprising that the professional bureaucracy is one of the models adopted for consultancy organisations.

Attractive though this model may sound, it has one major disadvantage: it can only exist in situations where the skill base is stable and can be shared, which makes the professional bureaucracy inflexible and poor at innovation.

Where professionals work together in more innovative ways, Mintzberg identifies the appropriate structure as the *adhocracy*. In this, employees group together in ad-hoc project teams: the organisation is fluid, with little formalisation of tasks and procedures, and the key means of coordination is the 'mutual adjustment' of those working in it rather than the standardisation of skills found in professional bureaucracies. Work units are small and 'managers', particularly project managers, abound: but their role is to liaise and coordinate and work alongside their team, rather than to give orders.

This model is also attractive for consultancies but it, too, has its drawbacks. The adhocracy is fluid in a way that enables it to tackle difficult and innovative tasks, but which can also be destabilising and confusing for those in it. It is marked by political manoeuvring and this can easily turn into conflict. Above all, it is inefficient at delivering straightforward products because it incurs high costs in internal communication and has no mechanism to standardise outputs. It is liable to reinvent the wheel, repeatedly, and is almost certain to have badly unbalanced workloads between different groups within it. As we have already seen, these problems are common in consulting.

Does this mean that the professional bureaucracy is the better model, since it offers the prospect of eliminating many of the problems demonstrated by the prosecution? Tempting though this conclusion may be, it is fundamentally flawed. Mintzberg's evidence suggests that *both* adhocracy and professional bureaucracy are appropriate forms for consultancies. They are suited, however, to different kinds of consulting and different types of project. The standardised roll-out of a computer implementation (such as SAP, currently the source of considerable income for consultancies) is best done by a professional bureaucracy using a standard methodology. Working with a client to develop a new and creative strategy cannot be done in the same way and calls for the cons to operate as an adhocracy.

The professional bureaucracy is the ideal structure for delivering a standardised service at the lowest possible cost, while the adhocracy is inherently much better at delivering creative solutions and adapting to future change. Consultancies using a standard methodology are vulnerable to the market moving on from their particular product: examples come to mind of re-engineering specialists who boomed for a few years and then failed to find another big idea to keep up the momentum.

The essential thing is that there should be consistency between the type of work that a firm sets out to do, the profile of cons that it employs and the organisational form that it adopts. Consultancies that are serious about offering seamless global services have to standardise their products and invest heavily in training if they are to benefit from the efficiencies of a professional bureaucracy. Those that are serious about creativity and innovation need to recruit consultants with a high tolerance of uncertainty and let them work and interact as they see fit, accepting as an inevitable by-product the rather chaotic situation that may result. The thing to avoid is falling between the two stools. Consultancies that like the look of the economics of the professional bureaucracy but fail to invest in the training to support it, or who profess a wish to offer clients a tailored service but expect to provide it with junior staff, are heading for failure.

There is an interesting further thought. If adhocracy brings with it additional costs (communication, wasted resource, reinventing the wheel) as a price that you have to pay for the benefits of innovation, then these services should be priced more highly than those which can be delivered through professional bureaucracy. However, the going rate for consultants delivering methodology-driven services (from re-engineering to SAP implementations) does not appear to be much different from that charged for more creative work, with the exception of the real élite of strategy cons. This suggests either that clients are getting creative work done on the cheap, or that they are paying through the nose for the standardised offering, or possibly both.

A plea on behalf of the victim

The model of the 'efficient' professional bureaucracy is alluring but can only really be applied to situations where it is possible to train staff to apply a standard set of skills. The rise in popularity of methodology-based consulting is precisely because it lends itself to a degree of standardisation, allows the organisation to be run as a professional bureaucracy and thereby removes much of the inefficiency associated with adhocracy.

Unfortunately, many victims (sorry: *clients*) do not want the standard offering but are looking for an approach that is both creative and tailored to them. Figure 10.2 shows that, when choosing cons, clients were overwhelmingly favourable to those who showed a real understanding of their problem. Putting together a tailored approach scored far more highly than having a methodology. Elsewhere in the questionnaire, only 38% of clients (but 79% of consultants) considered a methodology to be an important selling factor for cons; 19% rated it as a definite drawback.

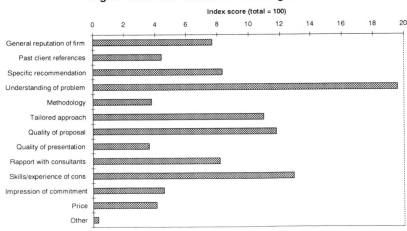

Figure 10.2: Main factors in choosing cons

It concerns me that consultancies seem to be moving away from tailored, client-specific and innovative ways of working and that methodologies and bureaucratisation are seen as the only way to serve the global client. I am not convinced that this is what clients want; and I do not accept that there is no alternative for cons themselves.

A degree of waste and inefficiency may be inherent in adhocracy, but that does not mean that the choice is between running a bureaucracy and running a shambles. I believe that consultancies can provide the customised services that clients want, while avoiding the worst side-effects, if they concentrate on:

• Drawing a clear line between methodology-based and bespoke forms of consulting. Where a firm crosses into both territories, there is no reason why staffing policies, utilisation targets, fee rates or anything else should be common to both parts.

• Abandoning their pursuit of distractions ranging from international liaison committees to inappropriate methodology development teams, allowing the operating Partners to get back to concentrating on their clients and their projects.

• Placing absolute emphasis on the development of the individuals within the operational core of the consultancy.

• Investing in and professionalising their support staff to play a more active role in both resource allocation and marketing.

• Flattening the organisation and encouraging cons to develop as doers, sellers or managers[2] as best suits their talents. I never understood why we had such a hierarchical structure, including seven grades from Partner to Analyst (and a few more below). What matters are the skills, not the grades. Projects should be led by those with strong management skills. Job quality should be judged by those who excel technically. Selling should be done by the best sellers. Those who achieve the most, in any of these three areas, may be rewarded with the rank of Partner. But why expect them

---

[2] In the previous chapter I described doing, selling and managing the work as the three legs of the consultancy stool.

then to turn into something that they are not? And, whether they excel as sellers, managers or doers, Partners must be closely involved with their staff and their work and stop leading from the rear.

Summing up

It is time to bang the gavel and sum up the arguments.

The charge against the cons is a serious one: that they fail to practice the high standards of management that they preach. The prosecution has piled up evidence ('Much of it,' the Judge adds, 'highly circumstantial and subjective in nature . . .') of apparent management failure. The defence has suggested, in response, that many of the supposed weaknesses are simply a reflection of the nature of the business and the market. Furthermore, an expert witness has suggested that communication failures, wasteful politicking and unbalanced resources are the result of organising as an adhocracy, a structure which nonetheless offers considerable advantages in doing some types of work. Even so, must they be considered inevitable?

Poor management or unfortunate side-effects? Guilty or Not Guilty? I leave the reader to decide.

At the start of this chapter, two questions were asked. Firstly, if cons are judged to run their own affairs poorly, does this not undermine their right to advise others? Secondly, does the alleged poor management of consultancies jeopardise the service they give their clients?

On the whole, I think that the answer to the first question is no. Consultancy is not an easy business to run and clients, by and large, seem unaware of the conflicts and contradictions within consulting organisations.

To the second question my answer is that consultancies are in danger of doing their clients a disservice if they decide that the only model is to sell large-scale methodology-driven projects to international businesses. This is appropriate to some situations but by no means to all. Furthermore, I believe that it does consultants themselves few favours by stifling genuine innovation and turning cons into something more like auditors: replaceable resources whose main task is to follow the manual.

If the large consultancies are to deliver genuinely tailored services in the future, and make money at it (and, if they don't, small firms will certainly continue to do so), they need to manage and organise the business appropriately. Unsurprisingly, in a business where people are the only assets worth talking about, it is all about how you manage the cons themselves. If I were to offer three simple messages to consulting Partners they would be:

- Respect your staff.

- Look for ways of releasing their creativity, rather than forcing them into a mould.

- Lead from the front.

Obvious? Of course it is. But if these three rules were followed more often, cons might be less inclined to find themselves guilty of poor management.

CHAPTER 11: THE HOLLOW ORGANISATION – AN ESSAY

THROUGHOUT THIS BOOK, A LEAVENING OF FACT HAS BEEN COMBINED WITH a large dollop of my own views. I admit freely that a good deal of what I have said is subjective. It is based, by and large, on my own experience but I have no real means of knowing how typical or otherwise that might be. I have tried to substantiate and supplement my experience, where possible, from the research carried out for this book. Nonetheless, I cannot claim to have written a scientifically objective work, nor (to be frank) did I ever set out to do so.

In this chapter, I shall abandon any pretence of objectivity. This is, as it is called, an essay: a 'brief composition', as my dictionary describes it, but also a 'test or trial' of some ideas which I believe need to be aired. I offer them as contributions to the ever-continuing debate about management and how it should be practised. They may, and I hope they will, spur further discussion and possibly some academic research beyond what I have been able to attempt. My thoughts are certainly not conclusive and I cannot prove them. The reader has my permission to ignore them, if he or she chooses.

Let me start by returning to the question which I asked at the beginning of Chapter 1: 'Just why do organisations use consultants?' We have looked at this question from several directions. We have thought about the good and the bad reasons for using cons. We have recognised the vital need for change and considered how outside help may facilitate this. We have seen that, according to the research, clients are

motivated by a recognition of this need for change, by a desire to facilitate their internal processes and, above all, by a shortage of time and
skills in their own organisations.

Should we be worried about this? We can all agree that the business
environment is changing constantly, perhaps faster than ever, and that
companies have to be capable of adapting and reinventing themselves
in response. Should we not be concerned that major organisations, far
from beefing up their internal competence in order to do this, are
apparently unable to find the people in their own ranks to develop a
vision of where they want to be or a plan of how to get there? Is it not
a worry that AT&T, a major corporation by any measure, found it
necessary in the first half of the 1990s to spend over a billion dollars
on consultants? That it apparently had so few skills and so little time
that at one stage more than a thousand firms of cons were reportedly
working for it?[1] Is this not just a teeny-weeny bit alarming?

Figure 11.1 shows the response from the research sample to the
suggestion that business is now over-dependent upon consultants.
Only 11% of cons agreed but almost a third of clients felt this to be the
case – a significant minority. Given that it comprises managers who
have made substantial use of consultants, and who might therefore be
supposed to be relaxed about the idea of business relying on cons, it
lends weight to my concerns.

Figure 11.1: 'Business is now over-dependent on consultants'

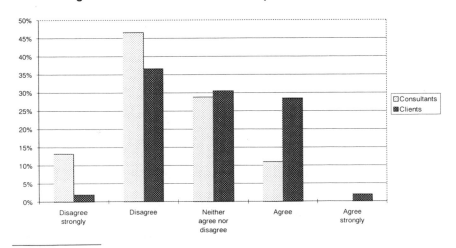

---

[1] Source: the *Economist*, 22 March, 1997.

By questioning whether it is a good thing for clients to depend so heavily on cons, I am flying in the face of everything that consultants have been preaching for years. If there is one message that they have been universally keen to spread, it is that there is no shame in having to bring in consultants. This can be argued in various ways. If consultants are the possessors of unique wisdom enshrined in their methodologies, then it is simply good practice to employ them. If consultants are smarter than the average bear, it shows the good taste and discretion of the CEO when he offers them a blank cheque to help him. If the basic business of improving the operation is tedious and grubby, is it not better left to someone else? Whichever spin you put on it, the argument comes back to the same notion: using consultants is good and healthy.

I cannot get away from an instinctive feeling that this proposition is deeply flawed. For a start, I simply do not accept the idea that cons are on a plane of existence far above anything that managers can aspire to. Secondly, I find it hard to shake the notion that it is management's job to manage, and the role of a leader to lead: what exactly is the CEO there for if he needs someone else to tell him where the business should be heading? Thirdly, and perhaps most fundamentally, I believe that organisations need people – their own people – capable of running and transforming their own operations and need senior management who understand the business well enough to lead this constant renewal from the front.

Before I throw the baby out with the bathwater, let me state also that there is unquestionably a major role for consultancies both in spreading skills between businesses and in supporting their change processes. What worries me is the dependence on consultants which appears to be spreading ever wider, and the fact that this is somehow accepted as normal. In consulting, as in adultery, perhaps it is time to bring back the notion of shame.

It can hardly be coincidence that consultancy clients report major shortages of skills and time in an age where so many have been through the mill of *downsizing*. In the name of efficiency, whole layers of middle management have been removed. Staff roles, planners and technocrats have been systematically axed. Now, much of this was undoubtedly necessary and – in some cases – overdue. Some fine corporations have come out the other end of the process evidently leaner and fitter. I am certainly not going to argue for a return to the bloated corporate headquarters of the 1960s and 1970s. Nonetheless, the question surely has to be asked: has the downsizing and delayering gone too far? To borrow a chapter heading from a recent book, 'You cannot shrink to greatness.'[2]

What the crash diet may have created is not so much the lean organisation as the hollow organisation. It retains its outer skin, often represented by a brand name to which it has been fashionable to attribute a value in hard cash. It has its strategic apex, to use Mintzberg's term[3], and it has a base of operators who live under the constant threat of losing their jobs if they fail to hit short-term targets. In between, it is hollow: it lacks the ability to connect strategy with operations and it lacks management capable of developing an understanding of the business into a real programme for change. To do this, it has to resort to outside assistance.

Am I making this up or is it a reasonable description of the way many organisations are headed? There is a possible further stage, too. A concept which has been doing the rounds and finding some favour with business commentators is that of the *virtual corporation*. We are told that it is unimportant for a business even to have an operating core. Within the shell represented by the brand, virtually all functions can be outsourced. This would truly be a hollow corporation: a strategic apex floating inside the hollow shell, serviced by subcontractors performing all other tasks.

Not long ago, this kind of reasoning led to the suggestion that British Airways might become a virtual airline. What does it matter, the argument went, if BA does not own any aircraft of its own? Or employ any cabin crew? These were suggested to be somehow non-fundamental to the entity that is BA. If you follow this logic, there is no part of the operation that is immune. You end up arguing that BA

---

[2] Dwight L. Gertz and João P. A. Baptista: *Grow to be Great* (The Free Press, 1995).

[3] See Chapter 10.

is just a brand: nothing else *is* BA, therefore there is nothing that cannot be outsourced.

As this thinking started to gather some momentum in the press, I was relieved that BA moved to scotch it and stated that it had no intention of being a virtual airline. In my view, whatever the theoretical argument, a virtual business would be immensely vulnerable. Producing your outputs (goods or services) more efficiently than the competition, bringing them to market more rapidly, delivering them to a higher quality or selling them more energetically are the things that can give you an edge in a competitive marketplace. To leave these competences to someone else is inherently risky. It implies that they are commodities and that you can safely be neither better nor worse at them than your rivals who have equal access to the identical external resource. To shed all in-house expertise, so that there is no longer even the knowledge in the business to challenge the work of your subcontractors, is doubly risky but that is precisely what happens when some companies rush to outsource. It seems, also, to be what some are doing at the managerial level as they abdicate responsibility to consultants.

In my view, the success of a business does not stem from having an attractive brand but from the effective delivery (in every sense) to the market of its goods or services. An ability to manage (not necessarily to own) this sharp-end of the business is therefore fundamental to today's prosperity. And an ability to transform it in order to meet future changes is equally fundamental to tomorrow's survival. The virtual corporation, theoretically attractive though it may be, lacks the ability to do these things without massive external assistance. It has lost control of its destiny.

An old adage has it that 'retail is detail'. Tidying up a display can be enough to persuade customers to inspect the goods on show. Moving a product from one side of the store to another can double its turnover. A shop may have 10,000 lines on its shelves but it takes only one out-of-stock to persuade a customer to try the competitor down the road. Getting the details right makes all the difference.

There is only one problem with this old maxim: why limit it to retailing? In my view, the success of *any* business is critically dependent upon getting the detail right. A success case that business books like to cite is that of Dell Computers, who broke away from established trade channels and started selling PCs direct to the consumer. It was a good idea, and doubtless a bold one at the time. But what really made the business succeed? Was it the big idea, or was it the painstaking implementation of each part of that idea: getting the right training for the telephone operators, installing the best computer system for handling orders, ensuring that credit card details could be handled without delay, providing the right menu of configuration options for your PC, maintaining build quality on every system shipped, working out the best way to deliver it to the customer's door . . . These details are far harder to imitate than the big idea from which they started. Getting the details right is never glamorous and seldom understood by financial analysts and brokers, but every corporation worth its salt not only worries about the details but celebrates those who succeed in putting the jigsaw together.

This does not mean that businesses have to own every element of their design, production and fulfilment processes. In almost all industries, we have grown accustomed to working through partners and contractors of many kinds. There is a big difference, though, between choosing to outsource elements of an organisation's activities and abdicating responsibility for getting the details right.

What worries me deeply is whether senior management in some of our major organisations is losing its grip on the detail of their business. For a start, do they actually know the business? In the past, most directors or CEOs would have come up through the ranks of the corporation. Happily, this is by no means an extinct practice but we have also seen the emergence of a new breed of crown princes, equipped with MBAs from prestigious schools but short on real business experience, reaching Board level at younger and younger ages. Few of them will know the business in depth; some of them may not even know the industry. According to *Business Week*[4], nearly a third of the top 1,000 US companies are now led by newcomers to those corporations.

---

[4] 11 August, 1997.

So what? Who wants a CEO who knows the details when, sensibly, she should be leaving these to her subordinates? But if the subordinates themselves are generalists lacking in-depth experience, and if the level below them has been removed in last year's downsizing, and the next tier is rushing around madly trying to firefight day-to-day problems or keeping its collective head down in the hope of keeping its job, *who* is going to communicate the realities of the business to the CEO or carry through her big ideas into practice? Is this not the situation, with possibly a little exaggeration, in which many corporations now find themselves and in which so many turn to consultants?

It would be easy at this point to lapse into anecdotalism. I could point to the success of someone like John Browne, Chief Executive of BP, who came up from within the business and has transformed it by getting back to fundamentals such as finding new oil reserves. I could contrast this with the experience of Liam Strong, until recently Chief Executive of the troubled UK stores group Sears, into which he came as a non-retailer. He struggled to turn Sears around by selling assets and doing deals but never seemed able to get to grips with the basics of improving the business. Ultimately, he departed in something much less than a blaze of glory.

Interesting though they may be, these stories prove nothing. You could point to plenty of companies which sank into oblivion in the hands of men who had spent their lifetime in the business and were unable to change their ways. You could also cite examples of moribund companies transformed by the injection of new leadership from outside and even by the contribution of cons. The issue cannot be proven by anecdote. Moreover, you cannot sensibly discuss the role of the CEO without entering the subjective world of values. Do we value those who persevere at getting the details right or those who tell a good story? Do we recognise the knowledge of our own staff or only the supposed expertise of the external adviser? Does the City back Chief Executives who invest in building the competence of their own people and take the long haul to organic growth, or is it only impressed by deal-makers who claim to deliver quick fixes by fancy financial footwork?

The process of hollowing-out reflects a casual disregard not only for employees as individuals but, more significantly, for the layers of experience and understanding of the business that they represent. The only possible justification for this is that organisations become bureaucratic and fossilised over time, necessitating a periodic clearing out and opening of the windows to fresh air. No one could argue with this: the issue is in the *how* and the *how far*. If using consultants is an alternative to changing and developing your own people, all I can say is that it is a very expensive way of keeping up to date.

Delayering has left many businesses looking over-stretched. This may add up to 'efficiency' in the short term, but it leaves them without the resource to plan and manage change. How many organisations regard 'spare' resource as an unacceptable luxury but then buy in similar time and skills from consultants at several times the price?

In a recent piece by Mark McCormack[5], he describes an unnamed CEO who strives to have enough talented people in his organisation to stand the loss of up to a dozen senior executives without it becoming a 'mediocre company'. This degree of duplication may seem like a waste of resource and money in the short term but the CEO reports that having these people around makes things happen and leads to them finding new ways of growing the business.

Change – anticipating it, creating it, using it, managing it, responding to it – is right at the top of every senior manager's agenda. Consultancies are in the business of change and, as seen earlier in this book, have their place in helping shift companies from old paradigms to new. Ultimately, though, they cannot do the job for the client. If the client does not have the competence to take over the programme as it develops, or to sustain it in the long term, the work of the cons is almost certain to fail. I do not believe that the hollow corporation is desirable or sustainable.

Jim Autry, in a business book unusual for the humanity that it conveys[6], sums it up thus:

[5] 'Playing the Take-Away Game to Win': *Mastering Management Review*, May, 1997.
[6] James A. Autry: *Confessions of an Accidental Businessman* (Berrett-Koehler, 1996).

'All growth and most good things come from paying attention.
Leadership is largely a matter of paying attention. So is life, for that
matter. This means paying attention, and attending, to the relationships
in our lives, whether with a spouse or child or friend or colleague or
vendor or customer.'

How many top executives turn to the external adviser because they cannot be bothered to pay attention in this way? If they put half the money and energy expended on consultants into developing and motivating their own people, I believe they would stand a far better chance of making the continual improvements needed for future success.

I said at the start of this chapter that it makes no claim to be anything other than subjective. So let me nail my colours to the mast and state some of the things that I believe in:

- I believe that senior management should pay attention. I believe they should know and understand their own business and lead from the front. I believe they should value their own people, their skills and experience, more than many of them seem to.

- I believe that constant change and improvement has to be a way of life for any organisation. I believe that the best way of facing up to (or, preferably, leading) change is through developing the organisation's own abilities and that means its own people.

- I believe that too much value is attributed to the big idea, to the smart talker and to the quick fix. I believe that the key to business success lies in the detail and is rarely visible to Chief Executives, consultants, business academics or the financial community.

- I believe that a business which does not *control* the key processes involved in serving its customers is incapable of protecting its future. I am not against appropriate outsourcing but against the hollowing out which reflects senior management's failure to pay attention to the sharp end of the business.

- I believe that consultants can play a very valuable role alongside management, but that they can never fill the void in the hollow corporation.

So much for what I think. As I already said, the purpose of this essay was to provoke ideas and perhaps suggest some areas where further research and thinking is required. So let me end with a rephrasing of the basic questions which underlie this chapter:

- Is it effective and efficient to use consultants as a substitute for strong internal management competence?

- Have downsizing, delayering and re-engineering hollowed out businesses to the point of damaging their ability to think strategically and act effectively?

To the first of these the answer can only be no. I await with interest an objective answer to the second.

CHAPTER 12: IF YOU REALLY MUST USE CONSULTANTS, GET IT RIGHT

THE OBVIOUS WAY TO STRUCTURE THIS BOOK, FOR PROSPECTIVE CLIENTS OF consultants, would have been to follow the course of a typical project from start to finish. I could have progressed logically, chapter by chapter, from developing the terms of reference via drawing up a contract to signing off the final report. Each chapter could have had a nice little checklist at the end for the reader to tick off as he worked through the approach.

Frankly though, grinding through 300 pages of blow-by-blow instructions and 'how to' checklists is not my idea of a good time. Instead, in the previous chapters I have concentrated on the things that interest me. If I have said virtually nothing about drawing up a contract between client and cons, or about public-sector purchasing rules, or how to write a proposal letter and what point-size to use on a bullet chart, it is because these topics are pretty tedious. If I have wandered off on pet hobbyhorses like the menace of methodologies and the perils of partnerships, it is pure self-indulgence.

Through it all, though, I have tried to maintain a minimum of structure and indeed I *have* followed, albeit with diversions, the process of the project from conception to something approaching completion.

The Vatican's definition (or so I have been told) of the consummation of marriage requires four acts to be performed *and in the right order*[1]. I believe I have gone through enough of the mechanics of each stage to consummate my authorial relationship with the reader, even if I have not covered all the available positions.

Be that as it may, in this final chapter I will attempt to pull things together from the client's point of view and to run through the project process from start to finish. This is a framework, not a prescription. Not every job can be managed or carried out in the same way: a lot will depend on the nature and size of the task, the resources available, the client organisation and so on. The purpose of this chapter is to use an outline project structure to summarise and reiterate some of the key points which have already been made, if not always in the most logical sequence, in earlier chapters. By now, there should be few if any surprises for the reader, which of course is the way every good con likes to work.

Step 1: Define the business issue
Time and time again in this book I have come back to the same message: be clear about your objectives. I make no apology for this as it was a message which also came over loud and clear from the research: in the free comments made by clients and consultants alike, it was far and away the commonest refrain.

Even before defining the objectives for the study, however, you must be absolutely clear in your own mind about the business objectives and what it is that you are trying to change. Is the real issue stagnating sales or failures in customer service? Is it market maturity or changing technology? Is it new opportunities for growth or the need to cut costs? And, whatever the issue, what is it that you want to do about it? Do you need an overview of new markets or a detailed implementation plan to restore profitability? Are you trying to catch up with a rival or shift the whole basis of competition in your industry? Be clear and be specific.

---

[1] The four are: *introductio, penetratio, copulatio* and *ejaculatio*. As I said, the order is important.

Step 2: Identify what you need from outside

A good way of determining what you want consultants for is to think about what you can do with your own people and other resources within your organisation.

As we have seen, there is no point in paying a lot of money for someone else to gather your own data together, unless you really are totally lacking in internal resource (in which case you might wish to think about recruiting another staff member or two). Nor is there much sense in spending a lot of time educating cons in the details of your business, if you can find in-house expertise to do the job.

The research showed that many clients look to consultants simply because they lack the time or the skills in-house. This is a good reason, providing it is true. I suspect that, often, organisations have more skills than they perhaps realise. Do not assume that the outsider is automatically cleverer than your own subordinates. Take a bit of time to *look* for suitable people within the business.

What you really need may not be time or technical skills at all. It may be project management. It may be facilitation of the process: drawing the best out of your own people. It may be a transfer of knowledge from other industries. Whatever it is, the same advice applies as in the previous section: define it clearly and specifically.

In most cases, you should be able to do this on your own and before you start talking to consultants. It may be, however, that you feel it useful to explore some of the issues with one or two potential cons before you are able to determine just what you might ask them to bring to the party. If, for example, you are looking for data from outside your industry, you may wish to explore the kinds of information that cons can provide and what is or is not a realistic expectation. Do this, if you feel it is helpful to you. However, always ensure that:

- You make an explicit distinction between meeting consultants for this purpose and asking them to bid for the work.

- You do not skip over the next steps, as set out below.

Something else that you should consider at the same time is how far you require the consultants to go in order to deliver what you really need. It is easy to commission cons to gather every possible fact about a subject, or analyse every conceivable avenue, or fill in every last bit of shading on the picture. Do you really need this? What are the aspects that really matter? Can 20% of the effort give you the 80% of the answer that is probably quite good enough? You can save yourself a lot of time and money by getting this right.

Step 3: Write down what it is that you want

If you have followed the first two steps, you will now be clear about what it is that your business or organisation needs to achieve and what part in this you require external consultants to play.

The next bit is so easy that you will be inclined not to bother: *write it down* in the form of very concrete and specific deliverables. Vague wish-lists are not good enough and almost certainly mean that you have not done the first steps properly.

I can feel the reader wanting to skip all this and get on with the interesting bit of choosing the consultants. All I can say is: you omit this step at your peril. You may feel that you are absolutely clear in your own mind about what you are trying to achieve. You may feel that there is no point in writing something down when you are not going to send it in that form to anyone. Think again. By the time you have had a few presentations from consultants, or got to the second review meeting of the project, or been presented with a final report, there is nothing more useful than to be able to go right back to the beginning and ask the question: 'Is this what I was after?' By then, so much water will have flowed under the bridge that you will simply not be able to recreate mentally your original ideas and motivation. Get them down on paper now, while you have the chance.

Step 4: Check for commitment

If you are bringing in consultants to work in an area that falls totally under your responsibility, you may feel that you need no one else to be involved. In many cases, however, the work is likely to overlap organisational boundaries and stray into the territory of other managers. Also, it may be that you cannot commission a major piece of work without the approval either of your Director, the Chief

Executive or the whole Board. In this case, you need to share the vision with them before you go any further.

Another important thing that you may need at this stage is outline approval of a budget for the work. Getting some sort of a feel for likely costs is a further reason why you may have had preliminary discussions with cons in Step 2. For now, any figures have to be treated (as they will be given) as simply indicative of the general order of magnitude. Vague though this may be, it is useful to know how many noughts you need to have on your budget application.

Any project, to be successful, must have from the client organisation:

- Full commitment to the work which the cons will be asked to undertake.

- Championing of this work within the business.

In responding to the research, a number of cons cited lack of commitment by clients' senior management as a prime cause of project failure. There really is no point being half-hearted about using consultants: if you are going to use them, get everything and everyone possible behind the project. If the project is your idea, it is likely to be *you* that has to champion the work, and you need also to be confident that you can do this within the constraints of your other responsibilities.

It is a waste of everyone's time for a project to be done without full commitment. It is also time-wasting, and divisive, for a project to run into the sand because of political obstacles placed in its way by other parts of the client organisation. Consultants are unlikely to sort out your political problems for you: if these are the major issue, you will need to address them first, as far as possible, in order to clear the way for the project.

Realistically, not all of your peers may be as enthusiastic as you about the job that you are commissioning consultants to tackle. This is not too important provided that they either cannot, or will not, hinder its progress and that you (or someone of sufficient seniority) are prepared to champion the work. It does not matter overmuch if others are reluctant, provided they are not obstructive. If you have the support of the CEO, and the grudging acceptance of your colleagues, get on with it. You will have to decide for yourself whether or not the vision is sufficiently shared, and your own commitment sufficiently strong, for the process to stand a good chance of succeeding. Now is the time.

Step 5: Draw up a shortlist of cons

When asked about the factors that influenced them in choosing consultants, clients put 'specific recommendation' only in fifth place.

This is probably about where it deserves to be in the overall scheme of things: by the time you come to choose your preferred firm, their understanding of your problem and the calibre of their team and their proposal will count the most. However, in coming up with a first list of prospective consultancies, recommendations can be most valuable.

You may, of course, be 'recommending' cons to yourself based on past projects. You may, equally, think of turning to colleagues who have had experience of cons, or to industry contacts that you have, or to other friends or acquaintances. The only warning I would give is that you restrict your enquiries to projects reasonably close to the one you intend to set up. If it is a market study, the fact that your IT colleagues had a good experience with a certain consultancy is frankly irrelevant. Much more useful may be recommendations from other marketing professionals that you may know through a professional body or institute. This is where 'networking' through such bodies can really have a value.

If you have no such source of recommendations, you may turn to published articles, conference papers and similar sources in the public domain. It is part of the normal work of consultants to seek opportunities such as these to put their wares in front of the public. Do not be over-impressed by their solo appearances on conference platforms or in the trade press, but take note where the cons are backed up by a recent or current client. If the Marketing Director of another business has appeared on a conference platform to talk about what he has achieved in partnership with a certain consultancy, he was probably pretty impressed by the work they had done for him. Do not just assume this, however: track him down and ask him. Similarly for published articles mentioning a certain client. Ask also who else was considered for the consultancy job, and why the particular choice was made. Find out what then went badly with the project as well as what went well. Most managers will be happy enough to discuss this kind of thing for five minutes in response to a reasonable request.

Bottom of the heap, definitely, is trying to find consultants through directories, industry yearbooks, the Internet or their own professional associations. If you do resort to these, you will have to be doubly careful later to check out references and get further information about the firms.

How many cons you want to have on your shortlist is a matter of pragmatics more than principle. If you have done your homework by asking around, three may be enough and five is probably ample. You should certainly be looking to get the shortlist down to this kind of number by the time you reach the proposal stage (Step 6). The smaller the job, the less sensible is it to expect a long list of potential consultants to prepare detailed proposals and (possibly) present them to you formally. At the limit, there are situations where you may only consider a single bidder, but these will usually be where you have direct and recent experience of the firm or there is something genuinely unique in their offering.

In the public sector, all sorts of rules may apply to tenders and shortlists. You will need to know exactly what you can and cannot do; more than that it is pointless for me to say.

Step 6: Getting to proposal stage

This step is harder to prescribe since so much variation creeps in at this point in the process. The variants can be characterised loosely according to their degree of formality. At the informal end of the scale, you may have a brief meeting with interested cons and walk them round your organisation. At the formal end, you may request written statements of qualification and have to provide standardised briefings to all interested parties. In between lie many other flavours of vanilla.

It is by no means unheard of for a project to be agreed, and started, before any formal proposal is written or contract signed. I have heard it suggested that these are often the best projects, but this may well not be a matter of cause and effect. If cons are chosen with little or no formal selection process it is probably because the client already knows them well, and knows precisely what to expect from them. This presages well for the work. Alternatively, it is just possible that the firm's qualifications are so strong, and the rapport with the client at the first meeting is so good, that they can walk straight into the job. Nice work if you can get it.

In most cases, however, a bit more than that is going to be needed. Having drawn up your shortlist of cons, the first thing – obviously enough – is to meet them. This is the start of a process of two-way information flow: the cons need enough from you to enable them to assess and scope the job, while you are already assessing their abilities as well as the personal and cultural fit with your own organisation. You may or may not wish to hand them directly the written requirements that you prepared in Step 3, but you certainly need to communicate what you want from the job. You may or may not want them to meet a selection of your own team or to do a presentation of their general qualifications. Whichever route you adopt, you are trying to gauge a number of factors which include:

• How well the cons understand your business.

• How they pick up and respond to the explanation of your needs, however it is given to them. This is the point where you may start to find yourself being shoe-horned into a standardised methodology.

• The technical skills that the consultants possess, compared to what the project will demand.

• The personal skills of the cons (remembering that those who make the initial response to your call may or may not ultimately be involved in the work) and whether they will be able to work with your team.

• The commitment that they have to you and to client service in general. Do they handle your enquiry effectively? Do they deliver their proposal on time? Points like this can be symptomatic.

Step 7: The proposal

As already noted, there is not always a proposal in the sense of a formal document. Usually, however, even in a single-bidder situation, some kind of written proposal is required and it will also become in many cases the document against which the success of the work will be judged.

Proposals can be a single-page letter or a massive tome of several hundred pages. You may want a continuous text or may prefer bullet points. The format really does not matter and is largely a question of taste. However, whatever the format, you should expect to find:

- A clear statement of the issue to be tackled (not the same thing as reams of waffle about industry background).

- Specific deliverables, as tightly defined as you may require.

- A clear explanation of *who* is going to do *what* by *when* (not to be confused with half a dozen CVs of cons who may or may not appear on the job).

- Probably some indication of *how* the cons will achieve the deliverables, but detailing the approach is in many ways the least important thing at this stage. For now, think in terms of phasing and timescales, not plans.

- An explanation of the consultancy inputs required, fees and expenses.

- *Relevant* experience of the consultants. By relevant I mean that it should be recent, genuinely similar in nature and should have involved one or more of the cons who will work on your project. If the last is not the case, treat the experience as irrelevant unless there is a very clear explanation of how the cons will transfer the skills from elsewhere in the firm.

Step 8: Make your choice

By the time you have met a few consulting firms, and had proposals from say three of them, you may well have come to a conclusion about who you want to work with. On the other hand, there may still be questions in your mind and – if you are in the public sector – you will probably not be allowed to take the decision as casually as this. In any event, a little caution is called for before making what may be a pretty major commitment.

Among the factors that you may need to confirm are:

• Have you met the cons who will actually do the work? If not, I cannot urge you strongly enough to ensure that you do. If the proposal was vague in allocating roles to names, put the consultants on the spot and get it firmed up.

• How good are the cons' references? Very few of my clients ever asked to be allowed to check things out with our previous customers, although we were happy enough to agree to this if requested (what choice did we have?). Not taking up references is to miss an invaluable opportunity to find out what it is really like to work with a particular firm, or specific individuals. It may take a few days but it is surely worth it for any large project.

• Is their skill/knowledge/understanding of your problem more than skin-deep? Question, challenge, probe. Try to see through the bullshit and jargon and find out what is really underneath.

• How will they work together with you or your staff? Are they prepared to run the project as a mixed team or do they really just want to go away and be left alone to produce a result? What inputs will they require from you? What skills can they transfer to your own people?

Again, there are many ways in which this process can be conducted. You may choose the classic route of the 'beauty parade': a formal presentation at which each bidder is invited in turn to present their proposal. You may prefer to keep things more informal. Often, a preferred bidder is selected from the proposals and invited to come for further discussions. Do it as you may choose, but do not forget to cover the ground thoroughly.

When consultancies are bidding for a large project against a complex set of criteria, some kind of marking system may be useful or even essential. Work out in advance the main things that you are looking for and weight them by deciding how many 'points' each factor is worth. When you receive the proposal, or hear the presentation, mark the consultants against each of the factors and then add up the points to get a final score.

Two final comments on this. Firstly, beware of the pitfall of inviting too many consultancies to give you a formal presentation. The large-scale beauty parade can be numbingly boring and by the time you reach the last firm you will probably have forgotten the first one. Secondly, whatever scoring system you adopt, personal 'fit' between you and your consulting partners is vitally important. A firm may be technically flawless but, if you do not feel that you can work comfortably with them or that they can get the best from your own people, you have every reason to reject their proposal.

Step 9: Think about implementation

I like the suggestion, made by a respondent to the research, that you should think before you start a project about how it will be implemented. Hopefully, if you followed the first three steps properly, you will already have done some of this. Now that you have had the proposals, seen what the cons can offer and possibly changed your own ideas about the project, it is time to revisit this question.

Get out the piece of paper on which you wrote down in Stage 3 what it was that you wanted. Ask yourself the question: is the consultancy intervention, as now defined, going to deliver this? Do not duck this. If the answer is no, it is still possible to start again or call the whole thing off. If the answer is that you now wish to change what you wrote down, think very carefully before doing so. What has changed? Were you being unrealistic or are you now fudging things? Has someone talked you out of a requirement which actually was perfectly reasonable?

Whether or not things have changed, think about the implementation. Assuming the project delivers everything expected of it, what then? Who will be responsible for the next stages? Will they have acquired everything that they need to take things forward? Do you need to start making other plans, for recruitment, training or whatever? Think ahead.

Step 10: Confirm the plan

In Step 7 I suggested that you need not be too concerned with *how* the consultants intend to produce the required deliverables. My view is that, if you get the right cons, with the right references, who understand your situation and have a good personal fit with you and your organisation, producing a sensible approach and plan is unlikely to be a problem.

Before you start the work, though, you will need to firm this up. Even if there was a reasonably detailed plan in the proposal, some confirmation of dates and milestones will be needed. I had one client, a US-based firm, which was insistent that it wanted us to visit all of its European subsidiaries in August. We suggested that this was unlikely to be realistic but they were quite adamant so it went in the proposal. Of course, when it came to actually starting work, they found that most of the key managers were going to be absent at that time and the whole start-up had to be slipped by a month.

If the plan was previously drawn only at a high level, this is the time to refine it and make sure that everything is included. The cons should identify the key deliverables at each stage and set milestones for when they should be completed. Make it clear that you attach great importance to these. If they depend on data or other inputs from your own firm, get a detailed list of what has to be produced if the cons are to deliver their side of the bargain. Set the milestones firmly by putting dates in everyone's diary for key review meetings. Try telling the cons that you have to book *now* the room for their final presentation. That should concentrate minds.

At the same time you will need to plan for the involvement of those members of your own staff who are to work alongside the consultants. Their roles should be defined (see Step 11 for further consideration of what these might be) and their time involvement planned in some detail. You should also discuss suitable candidates with the cons and arrange for them to meet.

Finally, you will need to confirm to the cons your acceptance of their proposal. This may precede the planning stage or follow it, depending upon the complexity of the task (for a simple job, the planning may not be a big issue and can be done at the first project meeting once things are up and running). Once again, there is a range of ways in which this can be done. Many of our proposals were accepted informally, with a handshake or a telephone call, but it is good practice at least to send a letter of confirmation.

The formal approach is to have a contract, signed by both parties. Some may insist on this but it is far from essential in most cases. What you need to remember, though, is that in the absence of a separate contract the work will be governed by the proposal and any subsequent correspondence. If you have raised important points after the proposal stage, either get them from the cons in writing or put them in your letter of confirmation as the basis for your acceptance. Add the plan to the back of this letter and, in effect, you have your contract.

If you do want to go to the lengths of having a separate formal contract, try to make sure that it focuses on points that are really going to make a difference rather than on the minutiae of project definition. A suggestion that I liked in a recent article[2] is that you not only specify the individual cons who are to work on the job, and their respective time inputs, but that you add a clause allowing you to remove anyone from the project team and retain a right of veto over the replacement. This reinforces how much depends on the individuals who will work for you.

Step 11: Mobilise your own resources
Another recommendation which came out strongly from the research is to involve your own staff, in a substantial way, alongside the consultants. This is something which you have already planned if you did Steps 8 and 10 properly, but now is the time to make it happen.

---

[2] Ronald B. Lieber and Joyce E. Davis: 'Controlling your consultants' *Fortune*, 14 October, 1996.

There are various roles that you or your people can play in working with the cons. Some of them are:

- Facilitator: client staff can act as guides and facilitators for the cons, pointing them to the right people and helping them find their way around your organisation.

- Expert witness: you, or other experienced staff, may be the 'voice of experience' on the team, acting as a sounding board for new ideas and testing them against practice in your business or industry. This can be a useful pragmatic check as long as it is not a drag on innovation.

- Data gatherer: client staff can be used to do much of the spade-work, finding the information requested by the consultants.

- Quality controller: this role speaks for itself, and may be critical in challenging and probing the work of the cons.

- Full team member: there may be discreet pieces of the work which are given to client staff to perform, just as they might be given to a specialist consultant to provide. This is teamwork at its fullest stage of development.

Whatever role is to be played, it must be taken seriously and provided for properly. It is simply not sufficient to expect busy managers to work alongside the cons 'in their spare time' if you want more than a superficial involvement. Taking a substantial role in the work, which is strongly recommended, may mean one or several people working full-time under the consultants' project manager.

This last point is also fundamental. It is your job to manage the cons. It is the cons' job to manage the work. This means that, if your people are working on the project, they should be fully integrated into the management structure of the consulting team. For the purposes of the work they answer to the lead consultant.

Step 12: Make time and keep in touch
It is difficult to say much about the progress of the work itself, as this will be so specific to you and your requirements. Moreover, if I have

concentrated on the steps leading up to the start of the work itself, it is because I agree with one consultant who completed the research questionnaire with the following simple advice to clients: 'Spend a lot of time up-front on the objectives, plan and deliverables.' If you do that, the rest should follow.

Despite many differences, what is common to all jobs is the need for the client's project manager to make enough time for the cons and to keep in touch. In planning the project you should have put in your diary some dates for key review meetings. These may be at the end of each main stage of the work, or on a more or less regular monthly or other basis, and they act as important drivers for the work. However, they are not sufficient: if you are responsible for the consultancy involvement, even if you have staff closely involved with the work, you really need to keep your finger on its pulse at all times. To touch base with the cons once a week, even if only by telephone, should be a minimum.

Making time also means making yourself available when they want to bounce ideas off you or check their understanding of the situation. This role *may* be left to one or more of your staff if they have been put in the role of 'expert witness'. If not, you need to be prepared to play it yourself. Consultants do not generally work well in a void.

Step 13: Review, challenge, understand
I discussed at some length in previous chapters the need to get behind the jargon and inside the analysis which the cons may produce. Do not believe something just because they say it. Do not assume that they have based their findings on detailed analysis unless you know exactly where the results have come from. In short, challenge and question their work at all times.

This may well be one of the roles played by your own people on the project team, in which case you may wish to probe *them* to make sure they have done the job properly! If you are the ultimate arbiter of the work of the consultants, it is *you* who must be satisfied and you will have only yourself to blame if you do not come out of the process with what you wanted.

If the project has been planned in stages, it is particularly important that you are happy with each phase before the team presses on to the next: in most cases, the work in subsequent phases will depend upon the conclusions of earlier stages. If you are asked to sign off assumptions, make sure you realise their implications. If you are asked to approve preliminary deliverables, check them out carefully and do not assume you can always come back to them later.

This questioning and probing is important for quality control but it is more than that. By fully understanding what the cons are putting forward, you will tend to develop your own commitment to it. It becomes less *their* view and progressively more your own. There is a danger in a major project that your own people on the consulting team will start to identify increasingly with the cons and become, in your organisation's view, more 'them' than 'us'. Conversely, consultants sometimes have a tendency to 'go native' when left for lengthy stretches on a single client's projects. This kind of emotional commitment is natural enough and valuable provided it does not go too far. You *want* your consultants to be committed to your needs. You also want to build up in your own organisation the kind of emotional commitment to the project which is the best guarantee of implementation.

Step 14: When things have to be changed
I have tended to avoid the word *partnership* in discussing the relationship of client and con. The word is loaded with scope for misinterpretation and it has been abused too often to be used ingenuously[3]. Something of a partnership spirit should nonetheless prevail between clients and cons. At the end of the day, getting a top-class result can probably not be achieved by either party on its own: they have to work together.

This cooperation is right and fitting but must never be allowed to deflect you as client from your insistence on getting the deliverables specified in the project proposal or contract. At key points in the process (milestone meetings, interim deliverables, sign-offs), refer

---

[3] English readers with a liking for irony may like to know that the German for partnership is *Partnerschaft*.

back to these documents and get out the piece of paper on which you originally wrote down what you wanted from the project. These are your benchmarks for judging the overall success of the job as it unfolds.

Chapter 8 set out some of the things that you can do when projects drift away from what they are supposed to achieve. Doing nothing should not be an option. The fundamental choice is between taking action to get the project back on track (changing the team, changing the plan, changing the consultants) and taking action to change the objectives and deliverables that were originally set. You should not do the last, ever, without very careful thought and without once more reading what you originally set down as your requirements. Why were these things important to you then, and what (if anything) has intervened to change this? If and only if there is a good answer to this last question should you change the terms of reference for the project. When this happens, get it down on paper again (typically in the form of an exchange of letters with the cons, confirming the agreed modifications). Then go back to Steps 9 and 10 and replan the remainder of the work.

Step 15: Heading to completion
As the project nears its end, the best advice is simply to keep your mind on the job.

Things can start slipping at this stage, for various reasons. The cons may be keen to sell on the next piece of work and may start losing interest in this one. Alternatively, knowing that they will shortly have to redeploy their staff, they may begin pulling some of the team off the job and getting them involved with other proposals or projects. In this situation, you have every right to demand that the team stay together until the work is done. Another problem is that the time and fees budget may be running low, which will mean that the cons come under pressure from their own management to get the job wound up as quickly as possible. Finally, there is a risk that the team, particularly if they are struggling to do the job properly, may clutch at the first solution that comes to hand and go for it without properly weighing up the alternatives.

If you have followed the previous steps you should be able to nip any of these problems in the bud. If you have your own people working closely alongside the cons, they should spot any slippage in quality of work and any loss of focus by the team. If you set down your requirements properly, and agreed a plan to achieve them, it should by now be second nature to check progress against the agreed deliverables. If you have been involved and available, you will have the kind of relationship with the consultants' project manager that will enable you to deal with issues as they arise and there can be no excuse for the cons now suggesting that you as client have not done what you promised.

It also follows that, if you have done these things, the consultants should automatically adhere to the golden rule: *no surprises*. If the project is approaching completion and you do not really know what its findings or recommendations are going to be, there is something wrong. Call for a pause; get involved again; find out what the cons have been doing and where it is leading.

This is a time to concentrate on the task and on getting results. It is also the time when you should revisit your previous plans for implementation and ask yourself what has to happen next. This assumes that the current project has a deliverable in the form of a recommendation or plan, rather than being an implementation project in its own right.

If the cons were supposed to transfer skills to your team, in order to facilitate implementation, check that it has happened. This may be the moment, also, to go back to Step 1 and start thinking about implementation as the next project. In suggesting this, I do not imply that the cons will automatically get their follow-on sale: remember that Step 1 was all about defining what had to be done without making any commitment to who was going to do it. You should not allow one piece of work simply to slide into the next without going through the first steps afresh.

Step 16: Winding up
Sometimes a project may come to a very clear close: a large-scale final presentation, the handing over of a report, perhaps even an opening

party for a new operation. More commonly, though, consulting jobs end with a whimper and not a bang. The team runs down and starts to drift away. A few letters go to and fro between client and con, tidying up those minor questions which may have been left hanging. A reduced consultancy presence sticks around after the implementation has gone live, dealing with 'snagging' and other final details. In the end they disappear and no-one even notices.

In many ways this is the best kind of ending. If the job has become almost irrelevant, it is hopefully because it has achieved what it set out to do. The client has put the recommendations into practice. The output from the work has enabled the next stage to kick off smoothly. The implementation is well in hand, using the client's own resources. There are many variants but if they mean that the client has outgrown the original project then that is as it should be.

There is one thing, though, that I think is a worthwhile idea even though in six years I have to admit I was never asked to do it: a formal post-project review. Did things go to plan? If not, why not? How could the project have been run better? Was its management appropriate? Did the client fulfil its side of the bargain? This exercise can be done by clients and cons individually but to run through it jointly has to be the best approach.

As the authors of an article from which I have already quoted[4] in Chapter 6 say in their conclusion: 'None of us can afford not to search for better ways.'

---

[4] Shapiro, Eccles and Soske: *Sloan Management Review*, 1993, vol. 34 no. 4.

EPILOGUE: LEAVE THE MONEY ON THE TABLE

FINISHED ALREADY? NEVER MIND, IT HAPPENS TO LOTS OF PEOPLE.

The growth in consultancy is an extraordinary phenomenon but also a frustrating one to write about. Every consultant and every client is different and, in a business that is all about people and their skills, this makes every generalisation dangerous. Even when you come up with what seem pretty firm rules there is bound to be an exception lying in wait for you. The single message that came out loudest from my research was the importance of getting the project objectives properly defined in advance. It is vital, fundamental and quite obvious once it is mentioned. And yet, one respondent (a con) urged clients not always to tie consultants to tight objectives: 'torching the spec', he suggested, can give the best outcomes. I do not doubt that he spoke from experience – and who am I to argue?

Another obvious truth is that the rise in consultancy has been driven by the ever-increasing pace of change. But are we even sure about this? Michel de Montaigne, writing at the end of the sixteenth century, was struck by the way that the whole world seemed to be constantly turned upside down. As he put it: *La constance mesme n'est autre chose qu'un branle plus languissant.*[1] On one occasion, presenting to a prospective client in France, I thought I was being terribly clever when

---

[1] 'Stability itself is but a more leisurely see-sawing' (*Essais*: 'Du Repentir' – my translation).

261

I used this quotation on a presentation slide. I got rather a funny look when we reached that point but it was only afterwards that I found out that *'branle'*, which in Old French meant a rocking or oscillation, is modern slang for masturbation. Woe betide the clever consultant.

I have looked at consulting from various angles in this book and would like to think that, if nothing else, I have asked a few pertinent questions. And yet, I feel no nearer to answering the really big ones: are consultants truly adding value to businesses, despite what Lord Weinstock had to say about them, and what does this tell us about the state of our corporations and other organisations? I hate to fall back on lame cliché, but: *it all depends.*

So it does, too, at the micro-level of the individual project and the individual con. Those who have been there and done the job will no doubt have had other experiences, some similar and some perhaps quite different. My account may not embrace all facets of the business but I have tried to be honest about consulting as I have experienced it. I *was* that prostitute of the business world.

Those new to consulting, or hesitating on the brink of a consultancy career, should realise too that their experience is unlikely to match my own. We all invent our own lives and careers as we go along. If you are convinced that you can do better than I did, then get on with it and do not let me put you off. Just remember, always, to add value to the client. If you achieve that you will deserve to succeed.

As for clients and prospective clients of consultants, I hope I have given you some useful advice but I never promised miracles. If you were hoping for a big bang and feel that all you got was a quick flash, console yourself with the thought that you have only been *conned* out of the price of this book, which is pretty trivial compared to spending half a million on the wrong job or the wrong cons. I said in the Introduction that you need to be as professional as the consultants who work for you. I have tried to help you ask the right questions and to give you a few cards to hold up your sleeve when dealing with them. The rest is up to you.

The end of a project comes when the client no longer needs the con. And this is it.

APPENDIX: RESEARCH QUESTIONNAIRE AND FINDINGS

The Research

To support this book, research was undertaken into the views of both consultants and their clients.

The approach taken was to send a postal questionnaire in March 1997 to approximately 370 alumni of the London Business School, respecting the rules of the LBS Alumni Association of which the author is a member. The sample was evenly divided between cons and senior managers in a wide range of industries who I hoped might have had experience of consultants. The complete text of the questionnaire can be found at the end of this *Appendix*.

From the mailing, 96 completed replies were received. This represents a response rate of over 25%, a figure which astonished me and seems to indicate the strength of interest in the topic.

The replies were also almost equally split between consultants and clients. Once allowance is made for some individuals who have experienced both roles (and responded accordingly by completing both parts of the questionnaire), the total numbers of valid replies was 54 for consultants and 57 for clients.

Within the consulting category, a balance was achieved between large firms and small practitioners:

- 61 % were from major consultancies

- 39 % represented smaller firms or sole practitioners

Within the client category, there was a wide spread of industry sectors:

- 30% were from general manufacturing or primary industries;

- 18% were from suppliers of fast-moving consumer goods (FMCG)

- 14% were from the financial sector

- 12% represented IT, telecoms or media companies

- 12% were transport or distribution-related

- 6% were in retailing

- 8% were from other areas, including healthcare and the public sector

In one important respect, however, the sample is acknowledged to be skewed. No attempt was made to achieve a wide international balance of respondents and all were, in fact, from the UK. It is clearly possible, and indeed quite likely, that different responses might be forthcoming from other countries.

One other health warning is appropriate. The questionnaire asked for respondents' views, based on their experience. Their *behaviour* may or may not be in line with their expressed opinions. In other words, there may be an element of 'do as I say, not as I do'.

Some of the results have been included elsewhere in this book; for convenience, however, the responses to all the questions are given below.

The Findings
Respondent profile. Both clients and cons provided details of their experience. The sample of consultants can be analysed according to their length of service, as shown below[1]:

---

[1] All the charts which follow are numbered in accordance with the questionnaire. "Question A1" denotes question 1 in Part A of the questionnaire; "Question B/C1" designates question 1 in both Part B (for consultants) and Part C (for clients).

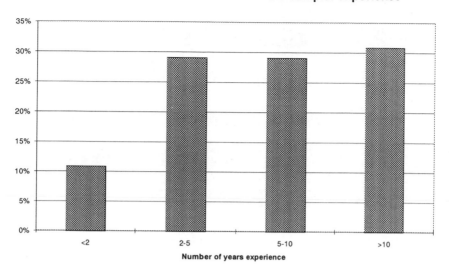

Clients can be analysed according to the number of projects in which they have been involved and the value of these:

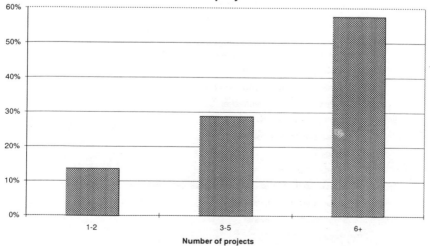

Question A3: Clients in the sample – value of projects undertaken

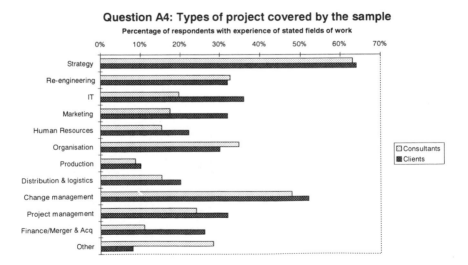

The above shows a wide range of project sizes. A number of clients indicated that they had been involved in six or more projects all of at least £500,000 in value.

The following chart compares the types of work of which both groups had experience:

Question A4: Types of project covered by the sample

Percentage of respondents with experience of stated fields of work

As can be seen, strategy assignments were the most frequently encountered, for both consultants and clients, followed by change management. The sample of consultants appeared to be rather light in the areas of information technology and marketing, as well as financial assignments. Among the 'other' category were cited various forms of cost reduction or performance improvement, procurement, innovation and 'learning'.

General views. All participants were asked for their reactions to a series of general propositions about consultancy. They were asked to indicate whether they 'agreed strongly', 'agreed', 'neither agreed nor disagreed', 'disagreed' or 'disagreed strongly'. The replies are shown below.

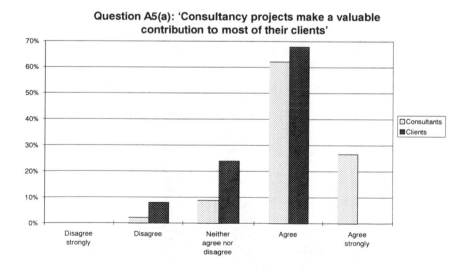

The answers to question 5(a) show that nearly 90% of consultants were, unsurprisingly, in agreement with the proposition. Clients also gave it strong endorsement: 68% agreed.

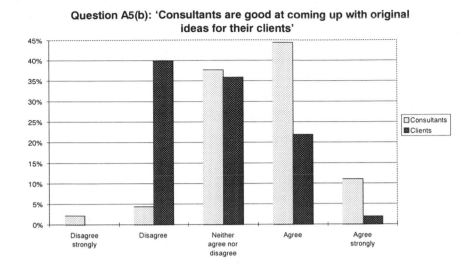

Question A5(b): 'Consultants are good at coming up with original ideas for their clients'

Here there was far less agreement. While 55% of consultants felt that they were indeed good at coming up with new ideas, only 24% of clients took this view compared to 40% who disagreed.

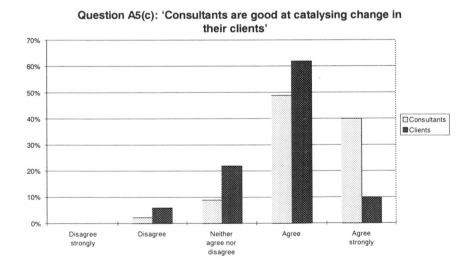

Question A5(c): 'Consultants are good at catalysing change in their clients'

Catalysing change is clearly something that both consultants and their clients see as a strength of the profession.

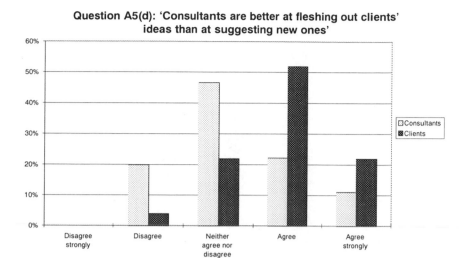

Question A5(d): 'Consultants are better at fleshing out clients' ideas than at suggesting new ones'

74% of clients agreed, or agreed strongly, that cons do indeed borrow the client's watch to tell the time! A third of the consultants shared this view, although the largest number sat on the fence.

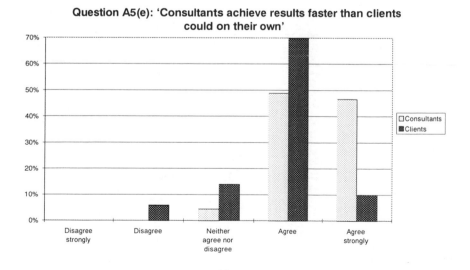

Question A5(e): 'Consultants achieve results faster than clients could on their own'

Little controversy here: getting the job done quicker is another classic expectation of consultants.

Question A5(f): 'Consultants are good value for money'

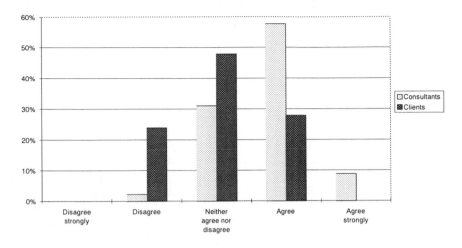

A close call from the clients! A quarter of them actively disagreed with the idea that cons are good value for money. Cons, not surprisingly, saw it differently.

Question A5(g): Most consultancy results, however good in themselves, cannot be implemented

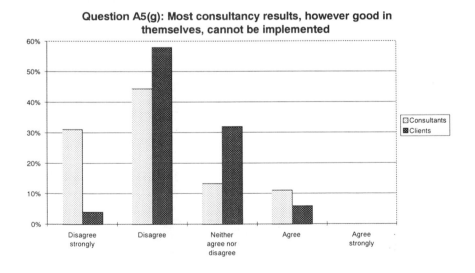

While a failure to deliver results that can be implemented is something for which cons are often blamed anecdotally, few respondents (although more cons than clients) saw this as a general problem.

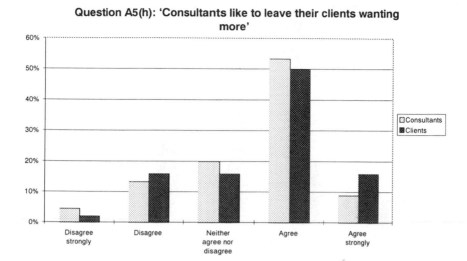

Question A5(h): 'Consultants like to leave their clients wanting more'

Two thirds of both clients and cons agreed that this is indeed the case.

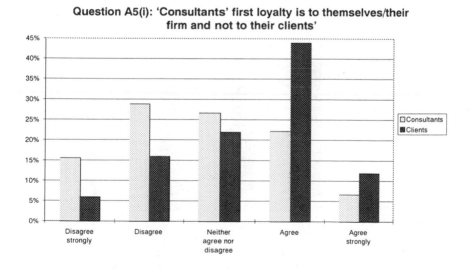

Question A5(i): 'Consultants' first loyalty is to themselves/their firm and not to their clients'

A difference of opinion is apparent above. A majority of clients agreed or agreed strongly. Nearly a third of consultants took the same view but the larger part disagreed, many of them strongly.

Question A5(j): 'Consultants are good at managing everyone's business except their own'

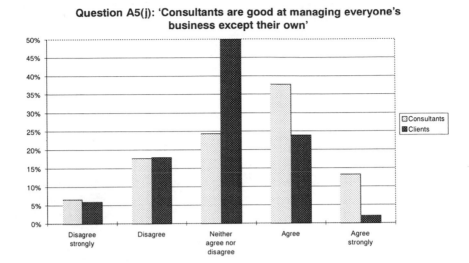

Over half of the cons in the sample agreed that they run their own businesses poorly. Clients were divided, with half undecided.

Question A5(k): 'Business is now over-dependent on consultants'

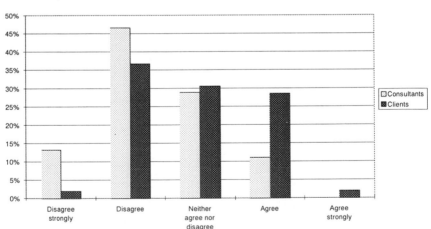

Among cons, over half disagreed. As far as clients were concerned, another close call: 31% in agreement, 39% against. The significant minority that agreed is large enough to be of concern, especially as buyers of consultancy services may be more favourably disposed towards cons than 'outsiders' would be.

Detailed questions. Parts B and C of the questionnaire investigated various more detailed aspects of the respondents' experience. Part B was for cons and Part C for their clients. Many of the questions, however, were identical and the results are compared below.

Question B/C 1: Why do clients call in consultants?

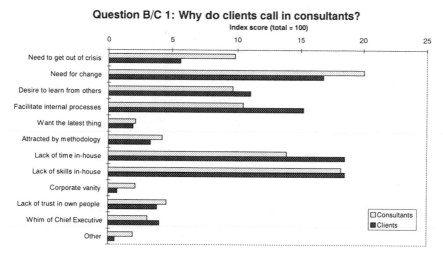

On the basic question of why clients use cons, although the results for clients and cons are similar, there is nonetheless an interesting difference. Cons are more likely to think that they are being called in because of a perceived need for change or even to get the client out of a crisis. Clients, although recognising change as a key driver, are more likely to see the need for consulting as a matter of not having sufficient time themselves. They also attribute more importance to facilitating their own internal processes. Both sides agree that lack of skills is another major factor.

Question B/C2: How successful were projects overall?

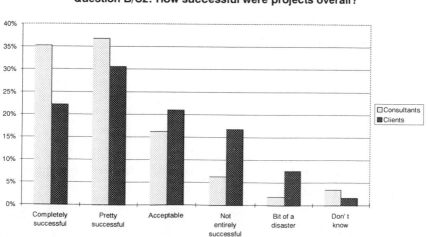

The preceding graph speaks for itself and shows clearly the difference in perception between clients and cons. Bearing in mind that clients are 'implicated' in the work that they commission, neither they nor cons can be described as strictly neutral witnesses. The same comments apply to the following:

Question B/C3: How successful was project implementation?

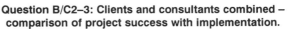

Question B/C2–3: Clients and consultants combined – comparison of project success with implementation.

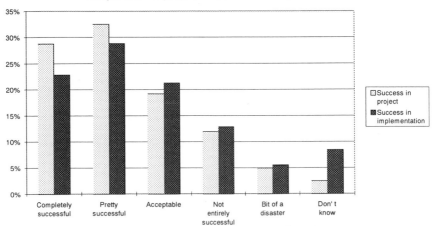

Although implementation gets a slightly lower success rating than the project itself, the difference is relatively marginal.

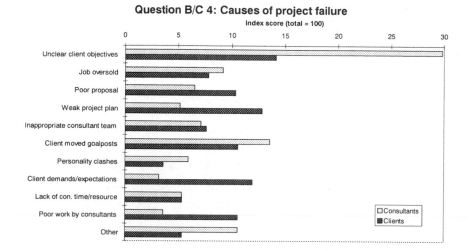

Question B/C 4: Causes of project failure

Index score (total = 100)

Interesting differences emerge here between clients and cons. Consultants overwhelmingly identify lack of clarity in objectives as the main cause of project failure, followed by the client moving the goalposts. For clients themselves, although unclear objectives are still at the top of the list, poor proposals, weak plans and poor work by the cons are almost equally important. Expecting too much from the project is also identified as a cause of failure. Under 'other' the most common suggestion was lack of real commitment on the part of the client, with mentions too for political obstacles and unwillingness to change.

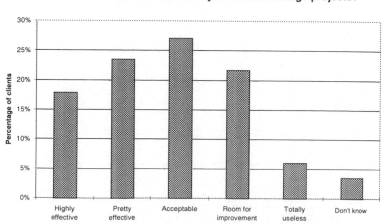

Question B5: How effectively do clients manage projects?

Only consultants were asked this question. The verdict is reasonably favourable to clients although hardly overwhelming, with 28% of clients being said to show room for improvement – or worse!

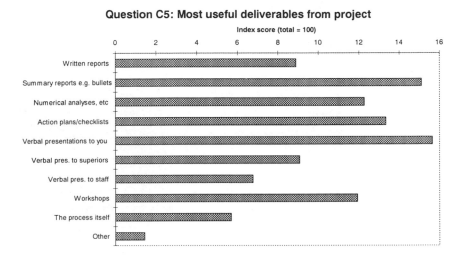

Question C5: Most useful deliverables from project

A question for clients alone, which showed that a number of types of output ranked similarly. Overall, verbal presentations to the client were the most popular, followed by bullet charts and other summaries, action plans, numerical analyses and workshops.

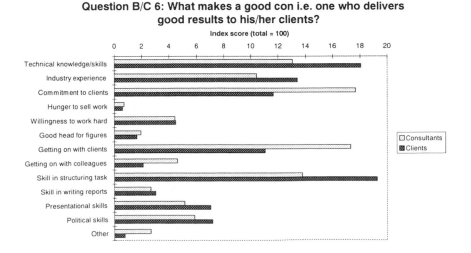

Question B/C 6: What makes a good con i.e. one who delivers good results to his/her clients?

Again, interesting differences in the perceptions of clients and cons. Clients' choices are very task-oriented, favouring skill in structuring the job, technical knowledge and industry experience. Cons themselves give a higher rating to getting on with their clients. However, this was beaten to first place by the importance of commitment shown towards clients. Clients are less impressed by this than cons seem to think.

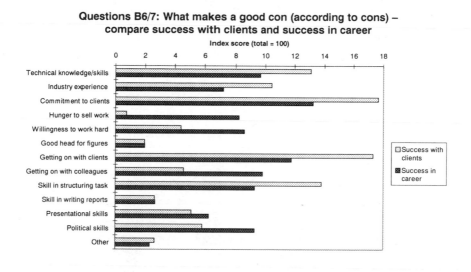

Questions B6/7: What makes a good con (according to cons) – compare success with clients and success in career

Index score (total = 100)

Having assessed what makes for success with clients, consultants were asked the same question again with reference to success within their own firms. The balance shifted significantly, as the above chart shows. Although the top two factors retain their positions, they shrink in importance as other factors come into play: getting on with your colleagues, working hard, being hungry for sales and showing political skills. In their free comments, several cons suggested that the route to the top was by brown-nosing Partners.

The next three charts are concerned with methodologies and how these are perceived by clients and cons:

Question B8: Importance of methodologies to cons

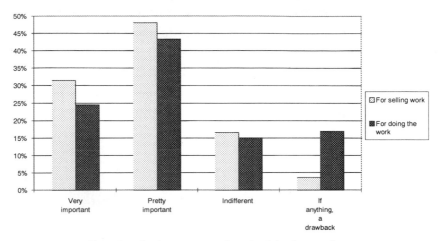

Question C7: Importance of methodologies to clients

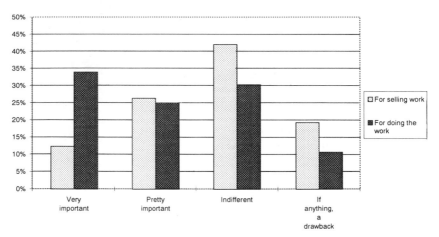

Question B8/C7: Importance of methodologies for doing the work – comparison of clients and consultants

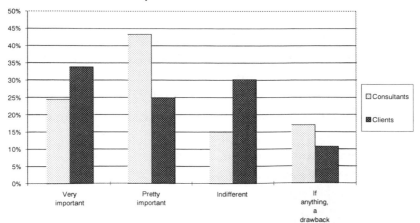

Consultants generally rated methodologies highly: almost 80% saw them as important or pretty important for selling work and over two-thirds gave the same rating to the place of methodologies in doing the work. A significant minority (17%), however, considered them to be a positive drawback in doing the work. Among clients, opinions were quite sharply divided. At the time of choosing consultants 38% were impressed by methodologies but the majority were either indifferent or downright negative. When it came to doing the work, rather more were in favour but there were still 41% either opposed or indifferent. This range of views may reflect different requirements for different types of work, or simply varying experiences with consultants.

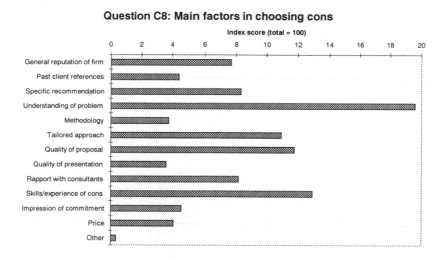

Question C8: Main factors in choosing cons

How do clients choose their consultants? Overwhelmingly, Question C8 shows that the most important factor is the cons' understanding of the problem, followed by their skills and experience, the quality of the proposal and the tailoring of their approach to the individual client. Clients claim to be unimpressed by the methodologies to which cons attach such importance for selling work, and by the commitment which cons see as fundamental for success. If these answers are true (and, in any survey of this kind, perception may not be quite the same thing as reality) they show once again that clients are highly focused on task-related issues and pay far less attention to human issues like whether or not they get on with the cons.

Question B9: Consultancy as a career – recommendation of cons

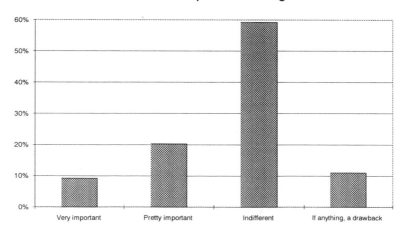

Suggested length of career as a consultant

Very few cons like to see it as a long-term career. Ten years appears to be the limit, for most of them. However, referring back to Question A1, over 30% of the respondents had been consultants for more than this time. Perhaps they just never managed to get out!

Question C9: Importance of a big name firm

There is little apparent solace above for the large consultancies. Most clients claim to be indifferent to whether or not they use a prestigious firm. It would be legitimate to question, however, whether this is reflected in their buying behaviour. The research does not give an answer to this.

Question C10: How likely are you to use consultants again?

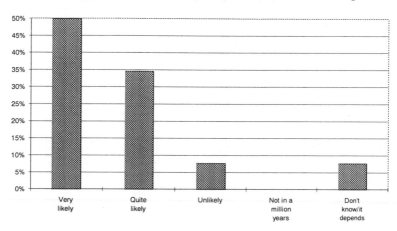

Finally, a pretty ringing endorsement from clients. Whatever the travails of working with consultants, however unpopular they may be in some quarters, most of this sample of managers with significant experience of working with cons consider it very likely that they will use them again. Consultants must be doing something right.

Unprompted suggestions. At the end of the questionnaire, respondents were asked to give up to three pieces of advice for both clients and cons. These, by their nature, cannot be analysed in the same way. However, many of the comments were sufficiently similar to be grouped into 'themes'. The most popular themes were as follows (within each category, those with most mentions come first, and so on):

Advice from consultants to new consultants:

- Listen to the client/admit your weaknesses/be humble

- Build a network of contacts, within the firm and externally

- Get broad experience/learn as much as you can

- Develop a specialism or niche role

Advice from clients to consultants:

- Listen to the client/admit your weaknesses/be humble

- Give practical advice/keep it simple

- Show innovation and creativity and avoid the 'standard solution'

- Focus on deliverables

- Work as a team with the client

Advice from clients to other clients:

- Have clear objectives and required deliverables

- Be involved a lot with your cons and work as a team

- Get your own staff working on the job, alongside the cons

- Have a proper plan

Advice from consultants to clients:

- Have clear objectives and required deliverables

- Be involved a lot with your cons and work as a team

- Select carefully the individual consultants for the job (not just the firm)

- Manage your consultants

The Questionnaire

The text of the questionnaire is reproduced below, in full.

CONSULTANCY QUESTIONNAIRE

«Ref»

All respondents please answer **Part A.**

If you are/have been a consultant, please answer **Part B.**

If you are/have been a "client", please answer **Part C.**

If you have been both, you may answer both or choose whichever you prefer!

**All responses will be treated in confidence and no details of individual replies
will be published or disclosed.
If you would like a copy of the summary results, please tick:** ☐
Address to send summary to (or fax number)

....

....

MANY THANKS FOR YOUR RESPONSE

PART A: General

Name:
Current job title: Employer:
(if applicable) Previous Employment as Consultant:

1. If you are or have been a consultant:
   Number of years consulting experience (please tick one)
   - ☐ < 2 years
   - ☐ 2 < 5 years
   - ☐ 5 < 10 years
   - ☐ 10+ years

2. If you are or have been a 'client' of consultants:
   Roughly how many projects have you been directly involved in? (please tick)
   - ☐ 1 or 2
   - ☐ 3 to 5
   - ☐ 6 or more

   Rough value per project (tick any of which you have experience)
   - ☐ <£20,000
   - ☐ £20–50,000
   - ☐ £50–100,000
   - ☐ £100–500,000
   - ☐ >£500,000

3. Would you be happy to discuss your experience in more detail, if requested,
   by phone or in person? (Y/N)   ☐
   If yes, contact phone number: ....

4. What is your main area of expertise as a consultant, or what kind of consultants have you worked with as their client? Tick any of the following that apply:

Business strategy ☐   Re-engineering ☐
Information technology ☐   Marketing ☐
Human resources ☐   Organisation ☐
Production ☐   Distribution/logistics ☐
Change management ☐   Project management ☐
Finance/M&A ☐   Other.................... ☐

5. Do you agree or disagree with each of the following general statements about consultancy? Tick the box which best describes your views:

	Agree strongly	Agree	Neither agree nor disagree	Disagree	Disagree strongly
a. Consultancy projects make a valuable contribution to most of their clients	☐	☐	☐	☐	☐
b. Consultants are good at coming up with original ideas for their clients	☐	☐	☐	☐	☐
c. Consultants are good at catalysing change in their clients	☐	☐	☐	☐	☐
d. Consultants are better at fleshing out clients' ideas than at suggesting new ones	☐	☐	☐	☐	☐
e. Consultants achieve results faster than clients could on their own	☐	☐	☐	☐	☐
f. Consultants are good value for money	☐	☐	☐	☐	☐
g. Most consultancy results, however good in themselves, cannot be implemented	☐	☐	☐	☐	☐
h. Consultants like to leave their clients wanting more	☐	☐	☐	☐	☐
i. Consultants' first loyalty is to themselves/their firm and not to their clients	☐	☐	☐	☐	☐
j. Consultants are good at managing everyone's business except their own	☐	☐	☐	☐	☐
k. Business is now over-dependent on consultants	☐	☐	☐	☐	☐

PART B: For Consultants

1. What, based on your experience, are the main reasons clients call in consultants? Rank as many of the following as you consider important, by writing '1' against the most important factor, '2' against the second most important, etc.

Need to get out of a crisis	☐	Recognition of need for change	☐
Desire to learn from others	☐	Wish to facilitate internal processes	☐
Want the latest thing	☐	Attracted by a methodology	☐
Lack of time in-house	☐	Lack of skills in-house	☐
Corporate vanity	☐	Lack of trust in own people	☐
Whim of senior executive	☐	Other	☐

2. Thinking back over the projects that you have undertaken, how successful were they overall? Show below what approximate percentage of them achieved the objectives set for them. For instance, if you think 50% were a complete success, write '50' on the first line.

Success in achieving objectives

Completely successful	.......%
Pretty successful	.......%
Acceptable	.......%
Not entirely successful	.......%
A bit of a disaster	.......%
Don't know	.......% COLUMN TOTAL = 100%!

3. Now score them again in terms of your clients' success in implementing your recommendations.

Success in implementation

Completely successful	.......%
Pretty successful	.......%
Acceptable	.......%
Not entirely successful	.......%
A bit of a disaster	.......%
Don't know/not applicable	.......% COLUMN TOTAL = 100%!

4. When a project failed to go as planned, what were the most important causes? Rank as many as you wish, starting from '1' for the most important.

Client not clear about objectives	☐	Job was oversold to client	☐
Poorly conceived proposal	☐	Weakness of project plan	☐
Inappropriate consultant team	☐	Client moved goalposts	☐
Personality clashes with client	☐	Unreasonable demands by client	☐
Lack of consulting time/resource	☐	Poor work by consultants	☐
Other	☐	Not applicable	☐

5. Do you feel that your clients got the best out of you? How effectively have they managed the projects on which you have worked? Show approximate percentages for the following categories:

Clients' effectiveness at managing consultants

Highly effective	.......%
Pretty effective	.......%
Acceptable	.......%
Room for improvement	.......%
Totally useless	.......%
Don't know	.......% COLUMN TOTAL = 100%!

Further comments may be given in your response to question 11.

6. What are the most important characteristics or skills that enable a consultant to deliver good results for his or her clients? Rank as many as you wish, starting from '1' for the most important.

Technical knowledge/skills	☐	Industry experience	☐
Commitment to clients	☐	Hunger to sell work	☐
Willingness to work hard/long hours	☐	Good head for figures	☐
Ability to get on with clients	☐	Ability to get on with colleagues	☐
Skill at structuring difficult tasks	☐	Skill at writing reports	☐
Presentational skills	☐	Political skills	☐
Other...................	☐		

7. Now score them again in terms of how they contribute to a consultant's success within his or her own firm. Rank as many as you wish, starting from '1' for the most important.

Technical knowledge/skills	☐	Industry experience	☐
Commitment to clients	☐	Hunger to sell work	☐
Willingness to work hard/long hours	☐	Good head for figures	☐
Ability to get on with clients	☐	Ability to get on with colleagues	☐
Skill at structuring difficult tasks	☐	Skill at writing reports	☐
Presentational skills	☐	Political skills	☐
Other...................	☐		

8. How important do you think it is to have a 'methodology' to meet you clients' needs? Tick one in each column.

	For selling work	For doing work
Very important	☐	☐
Pretty important	☐	☐
Indifferent	☐	☐
If anything, a drawback!	☐	☐

9. Is consultancy a long-term or short-term career option? If you were to advise a new entrant to the profession, how long would you suggest he/she should stay in it? Tick one:

No more than 5 years	☐
5–10 years	☐
Over 10 years but not for life!	☐
Whole career	☐

10. What advice would you give the new CONSULTANT to help him/her succeed in the profession? Suggest up to three ideas:

....
....
....

11. What advice would you give CLIENTS to help them get a better result from their consultants? Suggest up to three ideas:

....
....
....

PART C: For Clients of Consultants

1. What were the main reasons you/your firm called in consultants? Rank as many of the following as you consider important, by writing '1' against the most important factor, '2' against the second most important, etc.

Need to get out of a crisis ☐	Recognition of need for change	☐
Desire to learn from others ☐	Wish to facilitate internal processes	☐
Wanted the latest thing ☐	Attracted by a methodology	☐
Lack of time in-house ☐	Lack of skills in-house	☐
Corporate vanity ☐	Lack of trust in own people	☐
Whim of senior executive ☐	Other	☐

2. Thinking back over the projects that you were responsible for or involved in, how successful were they overall? Show below what approximate percentage of them achieved the objectives set for them. For instance, if you think 50% were a complete success, write '50' on the first line. If you have only had experience of a single project, write '100' on the line which best describes the outcome.

	Success in achieving objectives	
Completely successful	.......%	
Pretty successful	.......%	
Acceptable	.......%	
Not entirely successful	.......%	
A bit of a disaster	.......%	
Don't know	.......%	COLUMN TOTAL = 100%!

3. Now score them again in terms of your success in implementing the consultants' recommendations

	Success in implementation	
Completely successful	.......%	
Pretty successful	.......%	
Acceptable	.......%	
Not entirely successful	.......%	
A bit of a disaster	.......%	
Don't know/not applicable	.......%	COLUMN TOTAL = 100%!

4. If a project failed to go as planned, what were the most important causes? Rank as many as you wish, starting from '1' for the most important.

Your objectives were not clear ☐	Job was oversold to you	☐
Poorly conceived proposal ☐	Weakness of project plan	☐
Inappropriate consultant team ☐	You/your firm moved goalposts	☐
Personality clashes with consultants ☐	You expected too much	☐
Lack of consulting time/resource ☐	Poor work by consultants	☐
Other .... ☐	Not applicable	☐

5. What outputs or deliverables from the projects did you find most useful? Rank as many of the following as you wish, starting from '1' for the most useful

Written reports ☐	Summary reports (eg bullet charts)	☐
Numerical analyses, tables, graphs ☐	Action plans/checklists	☐
Verbal presentations to you ☐	Verbal presentations to superiors	☐
Verbal presentations to staff ☐	Workshops	☐

No 'outputs' as such. Most useful thing was the consultancy process itself ☐

Other .... ☐

6. What are the most important characteristics or skills that enable a consultant to deliver good
results for his or her clients? Rank as many as you wish, starting from '1' for the most
important.

Technical knowledge/skills ☐   Industry experience ☐
Commitment to clients ☐   Hunger to sell work ☐
Willingness to work hard/long hours ☐   Good head for figures ☐
Ability to get on with clients ☐   Ability to get on with colleagues ☐
Skill at structuring difficult tasks ☐   Skill at writing reports ☐
Presentational skills ☐   Political skills ☐
Other .... ☐

7. How important is it to you as client for a consultancy to have a 'methodology'? Tick one in each
column:

	For selling work to you	For doing work
Very important	☐	☐
Pretty important	☐	☐
Indifferent	☐	☐
If anything, a drawback!	☐	☐

8. If you have been involved in selecting consultants, which factors were most influential in your choice?
Rank as many as you wish, starting from '1' for the most important.

General reputation of firm ☐   Past client references ☐
Specific recommendation ☐   Understanding of your problems ☐
Methodology ☐   Approach tailored to your needs ☐
Quality of proposal ☐   Quality of presentation ☐
Rapport with consultants ☐   Skills/experience of proposed team ☐
Impression of commitment ☐   Price ☐
Other................... ☐

9. How important is it to you in choosing a consultancy that the firm has a well-established name (e.g.
a 'Big Six' firm or a famous strategy boutique)? Tick one.

Very important ☐
Pretty important ☐
Indifferent ☐
If anything, a drawback! ☐

10. Based on your previous experience, how likely are you to use consultants again?

Very likely ☐
Quite likely ☐
Unlikely ☐
Not in a million years ☐
Don't know/it all depends ☐

11. What advice would you give CONSULTANTS to help them succeed in meeting clients' needs?
Suggest up to three ideas:

....
....
....

12. What advice would you give CLIENTS to help them get a better result from their consultants? Suggest
up to three ideas:

....
....
....

INDEX

cons = consultants
c after number = chart
n after number = note